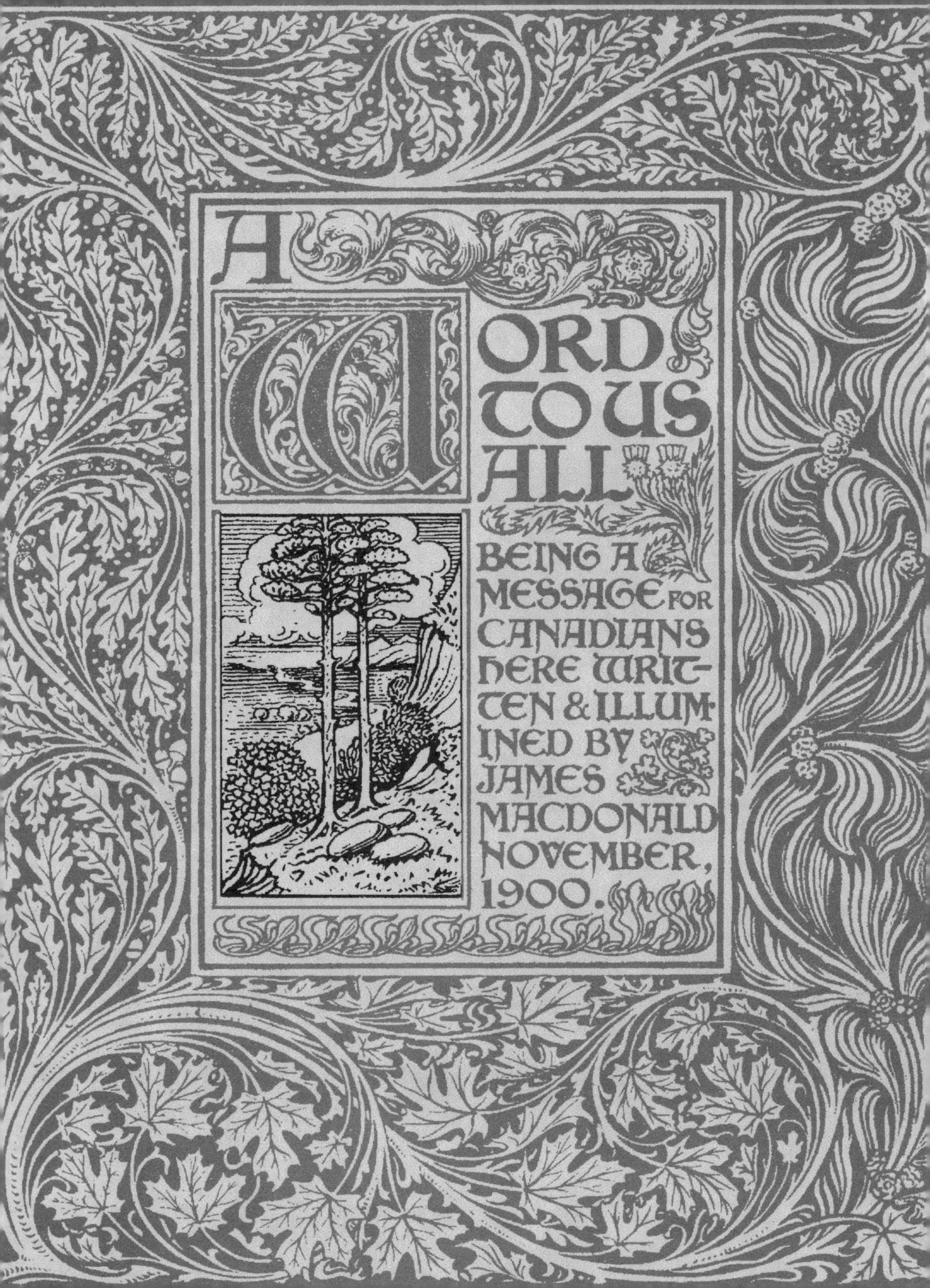
A WORD TO US ALL
BEING A MESSAGE FOR CANADIANS HERE WRITTEN & ILLUMINED BY JAMES MACDONALD NOVEMBER, 1900.

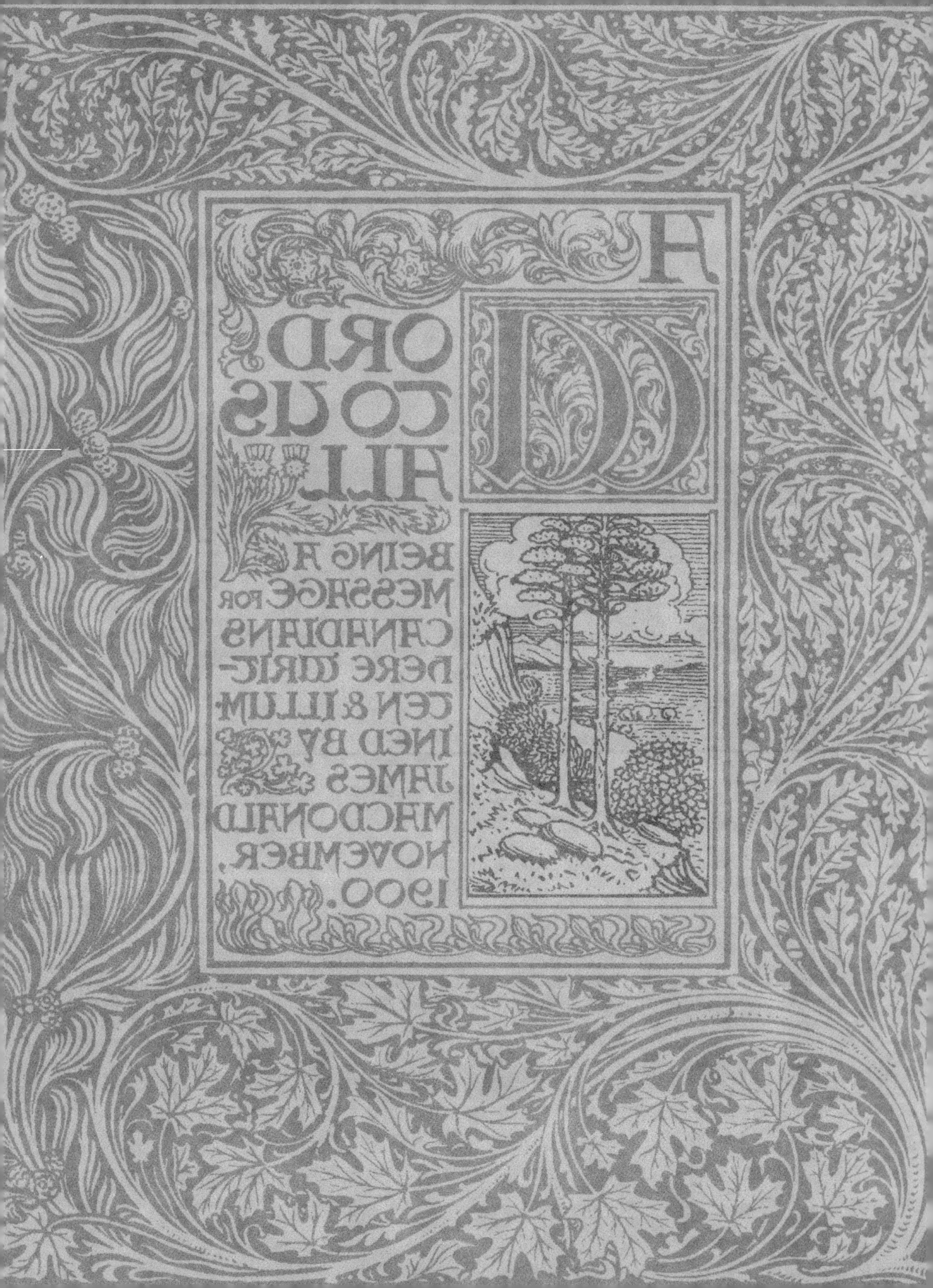
A WORD TO US ALL
BEING A MESSAGE FOR CANADIANS HERE WRIT-TEN & ILLUM-INED BY JAMES MACDONALD
NOVEMBER, 1900.

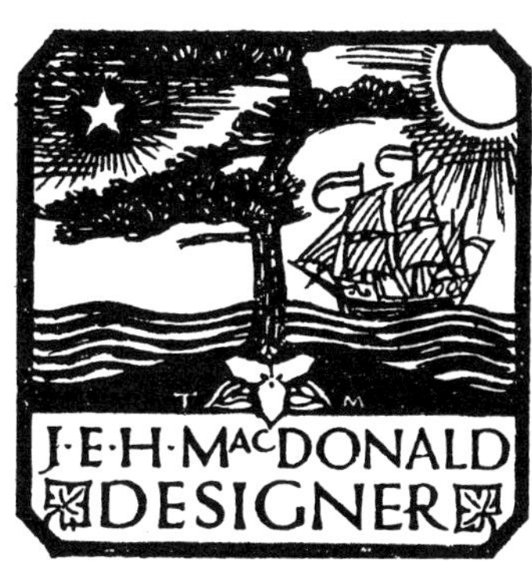
J·E·H·MACDONALD
DESIGNER

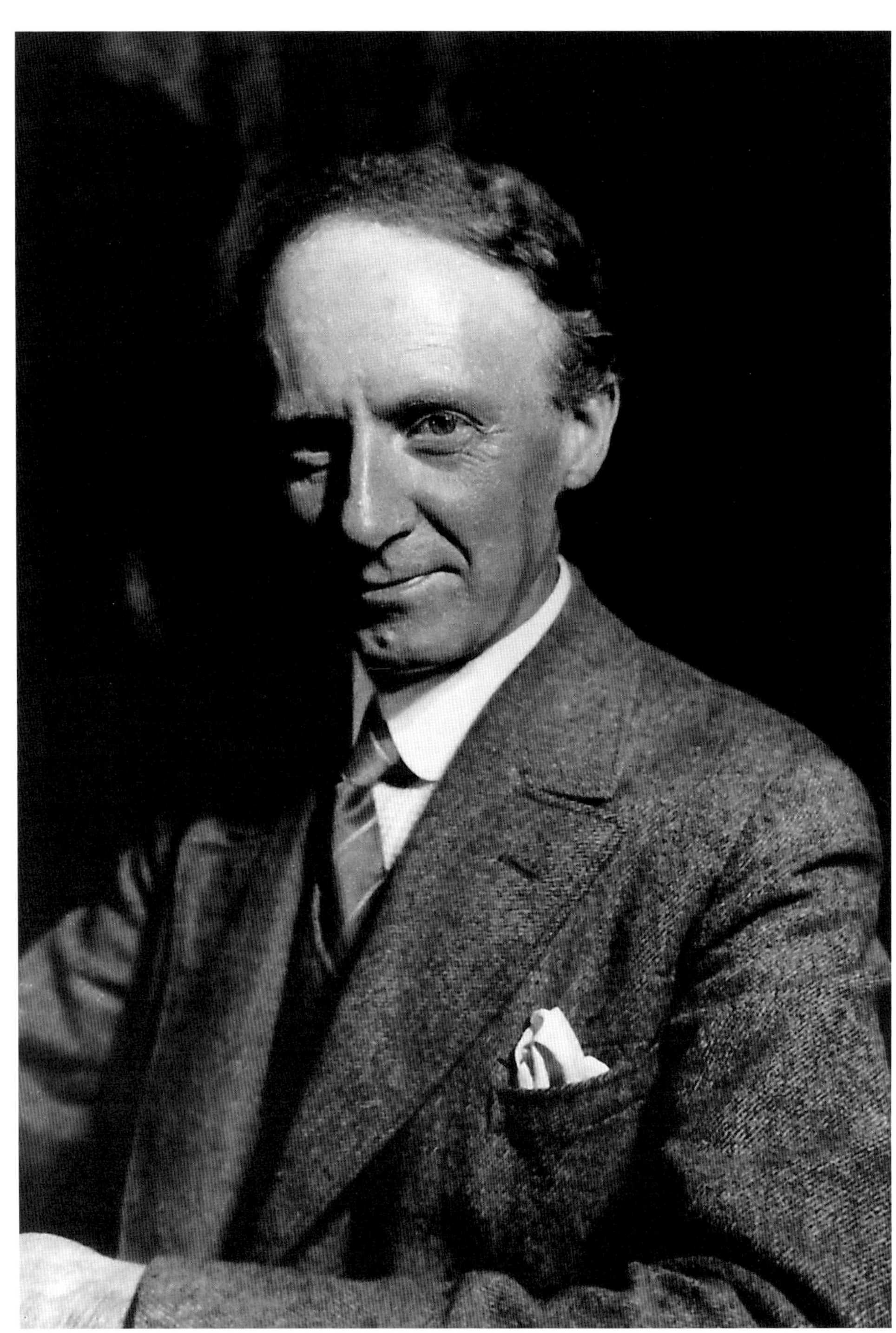

J.E.H. MacDONALD
Designer

An Anthology of
Graphic Design, Illustration and Lettering

Robert Stacey
with research by
Hunter Bishop

Archives of Canadian Art
an imprint of
Carleton University Press

Printed and bound in Canada

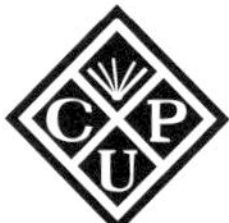

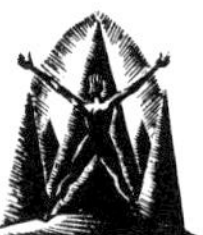

Canadian Cataloguing in Publication Data

Stacey, Robert, 1949-
J.E.H. MacDonald, designer : an anthology of graphic design, illustration and lettering

Includes bibliographical references.

ISBN 0-88629-304-9

1. MacDonald, J.E.H. (James Edward Hervey), 1873-1932. I. Archives of Canadian Art. II. Title.

NC143.M314S83 1996 741.6'092 C96-900490-7

Published by: Archives of Canadian Art
An imprint of Carleton University Press

Copy Editing: Margaret Keith, Jennie Strickland
Design: Glenn McArthur, Toronto
Photography: Thomas E. Moore Photography Inc.; Robert Stacey; the various institutions in possession of original MacDonald artworks; or as otherwise credited in the captions
Printer: Ampersand Printing, Guelph
Binder: Martin's Bookbinding, Etobicoke

Front cover: J.E.H. MacDonald, *Victory Year, 1919* (poster and catalogue cover); *Canada and the Call, 1914* (exhibition poster); *The Lamps,* (detail) December 1911 (hand-lettered magazine title); *The Red Canoe*, 1931 (Christmas card); Thoreau MacDonald, letterhead logo design for J.E.H. MacDonald, c. 1922-24.

Front and back flyleaf: reproduced from *A Word to Us All*, 1900 (present whereabouts of original artwork unknown).

Frontispiece: photograph of J.E.H. MacDonald by M.O. Hammond, 1927; M.O. Hammond Papers, Archives of Ontario.

Dedication page: from front cover, Alan Sullivan, *I Believe That* ... (Toronto, 1912).

Initial letters, vignettes and tailpieces: all by J.E.H. MacDonald, from various published and unpublished sources, mostly dating from the period 1910s-20s.

Back dust-jacket: J.E.H. MacDonald and Joan MacDonald, Thornhill, Ontario, c. 1910s-20s, photographer unknown (Thoreau MacDonald?), Hunter Bishop Papers; sunflower design (magazine endpiece), 1920s.

Carleton University Press gratefully acknowledges the support extended to its publishing program by the Canada Council and the financial assistance of the Ontario Arts Council. The Press would also like to thank the Department of Canadian Heritage, Government of Canada, and the Government of Ontario through the Ministry of Culture, Tourism and Recreation, for their assistance.

CONTENTS

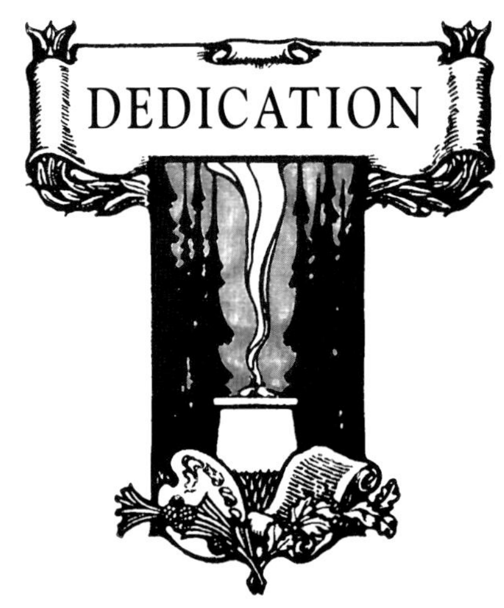

This book is dedicated to the memories
of J.E.H. MacDonald
Thoreau MacDonald
and Hunter Bishop.

ABBREVIATIONS

AAM: Art Association of Montreal
AGO: Art Gallery of Ontario
AGT: Art Gallery of Toronto
ALC: Arts and Letters Club, Toronto
AMT: Art Museum of Toronto (renamed Art Gallery of Toronto, 1920)
AO: Archives of Ontario, Toronto
BIIA: British Institute of Industrial Art, London
CGR: Canadian Government Railway, Moncton, New Brunswick
CNE: Canadian National Exhibition, Toronto
CNR: Canadian National Railway, Montreal
CNS: Canadian Northern Steamships, Montreal
COSAD: Central Ontario School of Art and Design, Toronto
CPR: Canadian Pacific Railway, Montreal
CSAA: Canadian Society of Applied Art
CSGA: Canadian Society of Graphic Arts
CSPWC: Canadian Society of Painters in Water Colours
CTA: City of Toronto Archives
DLBSC: Dovercourt Land, Building & Savings Co., Toronto
DM: Design Museum, Butler's Wharf, London, England
EPTRL: E.P. Taylor Reference Library, Art Gallery of Ontario
FTc: Fred Turner collection, Toronto
GAC: Graphic Arts Club
Grip P. & P.: Grip Printing and Publishing Ltd., Toronto
G7: Group of Seven
HA-Cc: Hugh Anson-Cartwright collection, Toronto
HBP: Hunter Bishop Papers, Toronto
HH: Hart House, University of Toronto
JM: J.E.H. MacDonald
JEHMf: J.E.H. MacDonald *fonds*, National Archives of Canada, Ottawa
LKc: Leon Katz collection, Toronto
McMCAC: McMichael Canadian Collection, Kleinburg, Ontario
McMCC, MP: McMichael Canadian Art Collection, MacDonald Papers
M&S: McClelland & Stewart Ltd., Toronto
MSc: Dr. J. Murray Speirs collection, Pickering, Ontario
MTRL: Metropolitan Toronto Reference Library
NDc: Nancy Dillow collection, Willowdale, Ontario
NGC: National Gallery of Canada, Ottawa
NTC: National Trust Co., Toronto
OAA: Ontario Association of Architects, Toronto
OC: Osborne Collection, Toronto Public Library
OCA: Ontario College of Art, Toronto
OSA: Ontario Society of Artists
RAIC: Royal Architectural Institute of Canada
RCA: Royal Canadian Academy of Arts
RHc: Richard Howard collection, Toronto
RL: MacLennan-Redpath Library, McGill University, Montreal
ROM: Royal Ontario Museum, Toronto
RSc: Robert Stacey collection, Toronto
SCP-E: Society of Canadian Painter-Etchers
SCS: The Shaw Correspondence School, Toronto
SNL: Sheridan Nurseries Ltd., Toronto
TAL: Toronto Art League (formerly, Toronto Art Students' League)
TASL: Toronto Art Students' League (became Toronto Art League, 1898)
TFRBL: Thomas Fisher Rare Book Library, University of Toronto
TGH: Toronto General Hospital
TM: Thoreau MacDonald
TMP: Thoreau MacDonald Papers, E.R. Hunter Collection, Thomas Fisher Rare Book Library
TPL: Toronto Public Library
U. of T.: University of Toronto
UTA: University of Toronto Archives
VAG: Vancouver Art Gallery
VSAD: Victoria School of Art and Design, Halifax
WCC: William Colgate Collection, MacLennan-Redpath Library
WCP: William Colgate Papers, Archives of Ontario

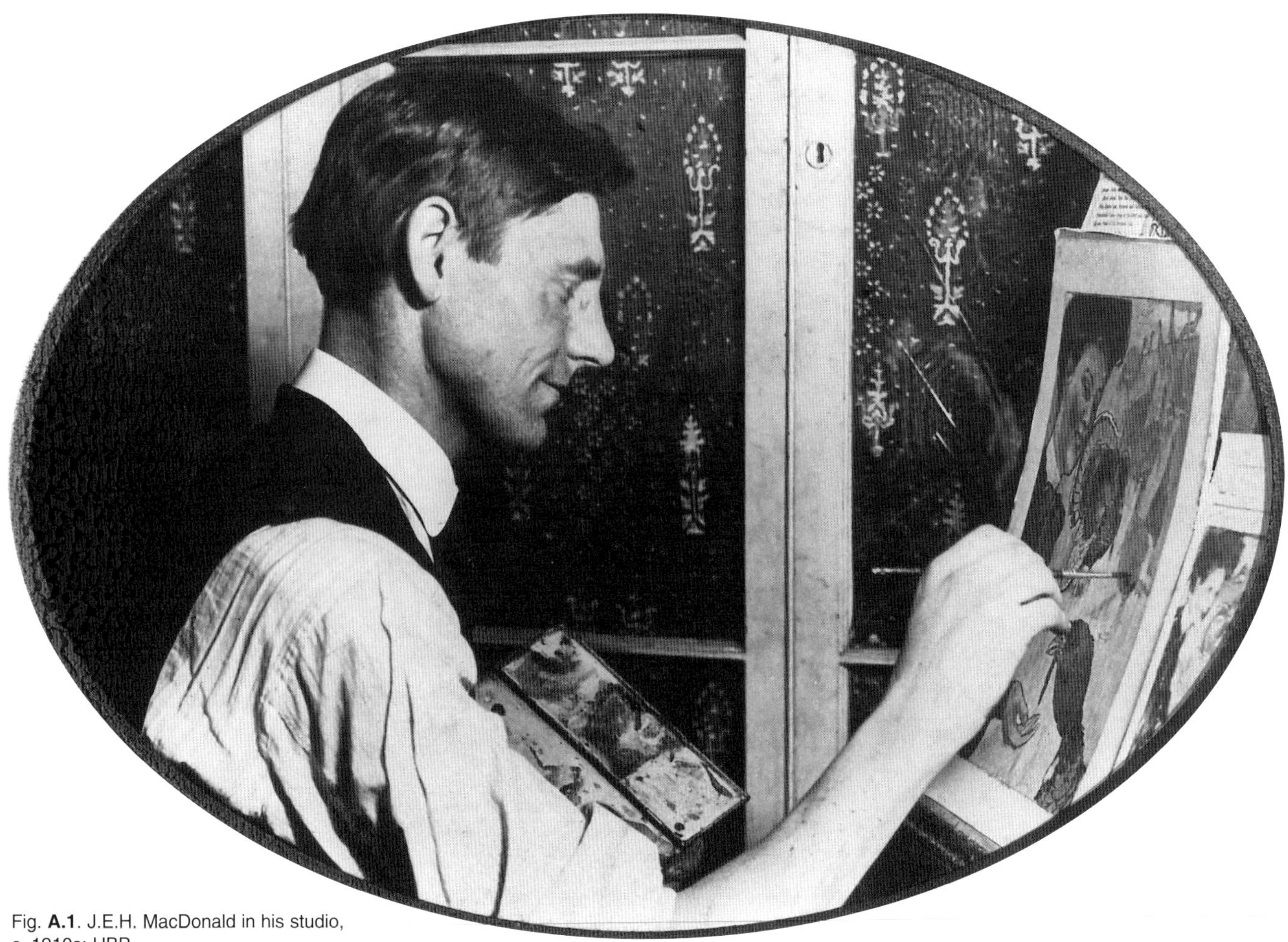

Fig. **A.1**. J.E.H. MacDonald in his studio, c. 1910s; HBP.

FOREWORD

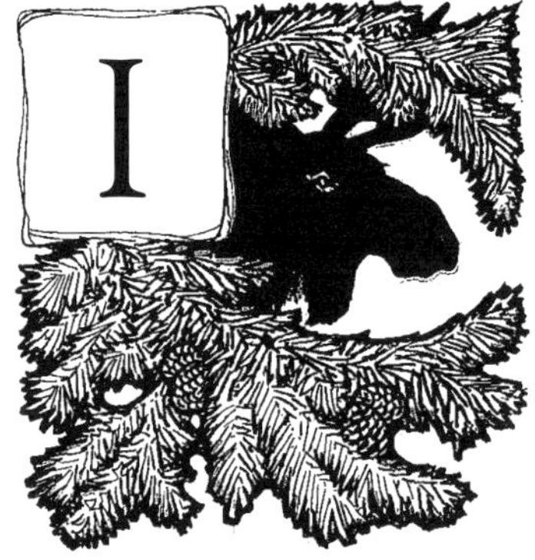

It is perhaps inevitable that the design work of J.E.H. MacDonald has always been overshadowed by his painting, but it should not be ignored. Not only was graphic design of central importance to his career, but in other countries, where the role of graphic design in visual culture is more clearly recognized than in Canada, his stature as a designer would have long been acknowledged in monographs and exhibitions.

In fact, the career of J.E.H. MacDonald is inseparable from the development of the graphic design industry in Toronto from the 1890s to the 1930s. MacDonald's graphic design background was typical of many of his colleagues in the Toronto Art Students' League and later the Group of Seven; he began as a lithographic apprentice and then worked for Grip Printing and Publishing in Toronto, and at Carlton Studio in London, then again at Grip Ltd. when it was the seedbed of this country's most important national art movement. The Group is justly famous for being the first generation of Canadian artists to see Canada without European pictorial baggage, but it was also among the first to benefit from the growing printing and publishing industries in Toronto. The increasing need for illustration and design gave MacDonald and his friends a livelihood, a stimulus to develop their skills, and the support and fellowship of one another.

They also benefited from the introduction of photographic reproduction technologies in the closing years of the nineteenth century. The resulting opportunities to draw and paint images for direct reproduction, without reinterpretation by engravers or lithographers, gave artists unprecedented creative freedom to develop their own styles, resulting in a "golden age" of book and magazine illustration. The pattern of development of visual production in Canada can be seen as the reverse of the European situation, where a dominant fine-art culture preceded graphic design; the first visual art credited with being uniquely Canadian grew out of the critical mass of creative skills required by the needs of industry.

MacDonald was not uncomfortable with this close relationship of art, printing-trade skills and commerce. He reflected the dominant influences in Canadian design of the period: the stylistic features and ideals of the Arts and Crafts movement and the professional practices of the United States (links with New York were strong, and several Toronto designers were attracted there by greater opportunities than could be found at home). William Morris's revival of interest in fine printing and book design, marrying craftsmanship with high standards of typography and decorative illustration, was massively influential in North America and had a lasting impact on MacDonald, who interpreted Arts and Crafts decorative principles with Canadian motifs. However, like the Americans, he and his colleagues embraced new methods of working and were not uncritical acolytes.

They re-exported back to Britain an elegant yet functional interpretation of their own, more suited to the needs of mass visual culture, and with it the modern concept of the design studio. Carlton Studio, founded by MacDonald's colleagues from the Toronto Art Students' League and Grip, introduced what Carlton's Canadian-born business manager, William Wallace, termed "an intelligent harmony of various specialisations," thus replacing the individual artisan with a more systematic division of labour and becoming, in the process, very successful commercially. It is interesting that, now, the introduction of digital technology is reversing the trend toward specialization caused by the first industrial revolution, re-uniting disparate crafts such as typesetting, illustration and layout in the designer's hands.

The significance of the ease with which MacDonald and many other major Canadian artists moved between the worlds of fine and commercial art is not generally understood. The bias of traditional art history and the scantiness of the records have not helped. MacDonald was at home in the continuous spectrum of visual production found in industrial societies, a place widely inhabited but still unevenly mapped. Graphic design and fine art must be seen as integral aspects of social, economic and political processes at the heart of our culture.

Therefore there is a real need for publishing documents in the area of Canadian design history. Since the second half of the 1980s, the cultural importance of design has been explored by a flood of publishing in Europe, the United States and Japan. This led not only to the recognition of design as a subject for serious study, but also to a radical reframing of the scope and quality of design discourse in general, to the benefit of design practice. The sharp increase in design publishing did not apply to Canada, however, where there is very little available of any scholarly merit, and design has a low profile (being regarded as an activity which takes place elsewhere). Books such as *J.E.H. MacDonald: Designer* should be encouraged, as they will help to correct this misconception, raise general awareness of design as part of Canadian visual culture, and grant students access to their heritage.

Dr. Michael Large, Coordinator,
Graphic Design Program, Sheridan College, Oakville, Ontario

PREFACE

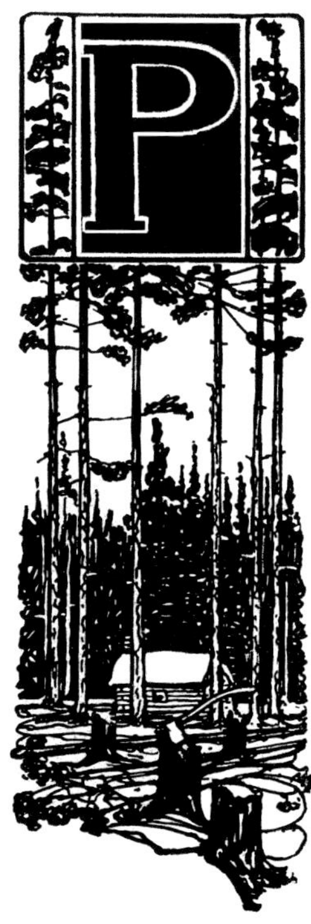

Published seventy-five years after the formation of the Group of Seven in 1920, and on the eve of the 125th anniversary of the birth of J.E.H. MacDonald (fig. **A.1**) near Durham, England in 1872 (but also on the centenary of the death of his hero, William Morris, in 1896), this book is a pictorial celebration of an astonishingly diverse artist's first but too-often forgotten callings: graphic design, illustration, lettering, applied art in both its narrowest and widest interpretations. Of necessity, in these pages we cannot begin to do justice to MacDonald's myriad contributions to all the other popular and public media and formats in which he worked, such as mural decoration, mosaics and other forms of "art for architecture," nor to his writing and lectures on typography and the decorative arts, nor again to his teaching career, which was largely confined to the interrelated subjects of lettering, book illustration, and "commercial design."

The selection of images showcased here is an introductory sampling of some of the best of the productions by which MacDonald made his living for the better part of his four-decade working life. To stay within prescribed limits of length and cost, we have had to concentrate on material intended for some type of reproduction, whether in the form of a printed advertisement, brochure, poster, broadside, greeting-card, or book or magazine illustration. Another category is that of the "one-off" which, however, contains most of the elements of reprographic work, such as illuminated presentation addresses, corporate and institutional emblems, trademarks and word-marks, heraldic devices and coats-of-arms, outdoor signs and plaques, and designs for coinage (unfortunately never struck).

The objective here is to present, without preliminary ado, as wide-ranging a visual overview of MacDonald-the-designer as possible. The present volume does not pretend or propose to offer a thorough-going history or critique of his production in all the applied-art fields in which he practised. It will be followed by a comprehensive, chronological account of his activities as an exponent of the "Design Idea" and the "Decorative Ideal." This longer study looks closely at the late-nineteenth-century milieu from which MacDonald emerged — the rich background of engraving and lithography houses, artists' and art students' sketching clubs and life classes, and the arts-and-crafts exhibition societies then in the unwitting process of hatching a modern material culture and a national consciousness. It then traces MacDonald's progress as a working designer/illustrator, in parallel with his career as a painter, first at the Toronto Lithographing Co. and Grip Printing & Publishing Ltd., and later, in the new century, at London's Carlton Studio, and once more at Grip Ltd., where he met and became friends with the artists with whom he would go on to form the Group of Seven in 1920. It concludes with chapters on his latter years as a freelance designer, and as a teacher of commercial art and design, first with the Shaw Correspondence School and at then at the Ontario College of Art.

Throughout this companion volume, MacDonald's unique manner of "Canadianizing" the theories, beliefs and motifs of John Ruskin, William Morris, Walter Crane and Lewis F. Day — the four pillars of the British Arts and Crafts movement — will be examined and analysed. Part Two of *J.E.H. MacDonald: Designer* also contains a full bibliography of primary and secondary sources, including a listing of MacDonald's own published and unpublished writings, and of collections in which manuscript material by and about him is to be found. The present Selected References lists only the essential titles, and is intended for a general readership.

It is hoped that this book will be but the first in a series of studies and showcases of the work of other distinguished Canadian designers, illustrators, photographers, and craftspeople. To date, these artworkers, whom Ruskin and Morris saw as the true builders of society, have been neglected not only by the art academy and the art gallery system, but by commerce and industry, even though their (and so our) prosperity increasingly depends on the timely application of the amenities of Design. As it is unlikely that public sources of funding will be available in future to support this crucial line of scholarship, the sectors that materially benefit from the daily labours of these unsung *makers* will have to step into the breach.

A further damning indictment of the state of art-historical scholarship in this country, compared to the other disciplines and other nations, is the fact that, to date, not one member of the Group of Seven — still Canada's most widely recognized artists — has been the subject of a published *catalogue raisonné*. As the Group's spiritual leader, MacDonald, surely, deserves to be the first to receive such a tribute to his genius with brush and palette-knife. He would, however, have agreed on the rightness of his contributions as a Designer (*his* capitalization, by the way) being celebrated in advance of this comprehensive tally of his canvases, sketches, and works on paper.

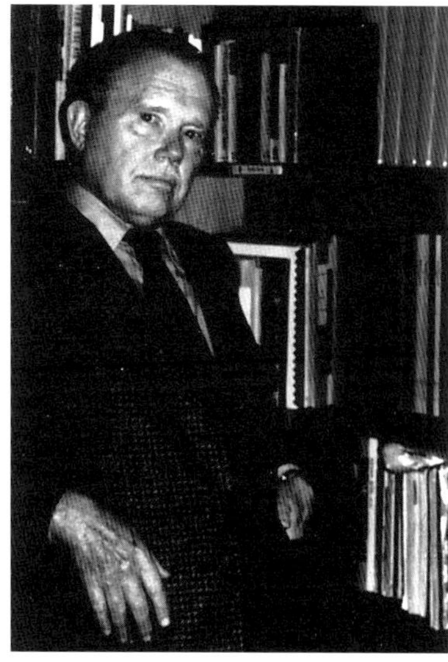
Fig. **A.2**. Hunter Bishop (1918-1985) in the library of the Arts and Letters Club, Toronto; ALC.

The initiator of *J.E.H. MacDonald: Designer* was the late Hunter Bishop (1918-1985) (fig. **A.2**), a passionate devotee of the work not only of J.E.H. (or, as he preferred, JM) but of his equally gifted son, Thoreau MacDonald (1905-1989). It was through his active membership in and service to the Arts and Letters Club of Toronto, which he joined in 1953, that Hunter became aware of the elder MacDonald's innumerable benefactions to his fellow members, in the form not only of exhibitions of his work (including his first one-man show, held at the ALC in 1911), but of insignia, letterheads, mastheads, bookplates, humorous coats-of-arms and heraldic devices, illuminated presentation addresses and annual lists of Club executives, illustrations, articles and poems for the house organ, *The Lamps*, sets, backdrops and banners for pageants, festive events and theatrical productions, and on and on.

After years of collecting and documenting such materials (in many cases rescuing unique copies from oblivion or the waste-basket), Hunter purposed to produce a book devoted to the little-known "other" art of his hero. This volume would disclose for the first time the full range of MacDonald's activities in the fields of graphic design, illustration and lettering, and place this hitherto invisible body of work within the context of a quiet but most un-ordinary life. First, however, he published *J.E.H. MacDonald: Sketchbook 1915-1922* with Penumbra Press in 1979. (Penumbra followed this in 1980 with *Thoreau MacDonald: Notebooks*, edited by John Flood.)

As Hunter found, and as I was to find after him, the project of reconstructing MacDonald's career in the applied arts was often an exercise in frustration. It could never have been attempted with any pretense to comprehensiveness had he not foreseen the necessity of interviewing JM's few surviving contemporaries, younger colleagues, and surviving students before it was too late.

Hunter made an initial stab at his planned profile of MacDonald as a man-of-all-arts in the form of a slide-lecture entitled "Portrait of a President," which he gave at the Arts and Letters Club in March 1981. By way of prologue, I have included an edited version of this text, preceded by two brief tributes to his father by Thoreau MacDonald. All three texts – transcribed "as-is," with minimal emendation – serve nicely to introduce, on a fond, personal note, "Jim" the man as well as JM the complete artist. And as it was Hunter's intention to feature a special supplementary "chapter" of his book that would be devoted exclusively to MacDonald's many contributions to the ALC, his comments on "MacDonald (and the Club)," the second half of "Portrait of a President," are excerpted as a conclusion to this appendix, headed "Designs for the Arts and Letters Club."

It was, I believe, in connection with the exhibition I co-curated in 1978 for the Art Gallery of Ontario, *100 Years of the Canadian Poster*, and the book that came out of it, *The Canadian Poster Book,* published in 1979 by Methuen of Canada (in both of which MacDonald was prominently represented), that I first made Hunter's acquaintance. Having discovered that we were both working on the same case, though often sleuthing on separate trails and turning up different, sometimes conflicting clues, we decided to pool our efforts. For several years thereafter, I had the pleasure and privilege of exchanging references and discoveries with him. Hunter in turn was generous in supplying me with data about another Arts and Letters Club artist whom I began seriously researching in the mid-1970s, C.W. Jefferys, as well as sharing his MacDonald *trouvés.* I was impressed by the fact that the few scraps of new evidence and information that I was able to provide in exchange, he carefully ascribed to my finding. (Would that this creditational carefulness were the practice of all who call themselves scholars – and gentlemen!)

I was Hunter's guest on several occasions at the Club, where he introduced me to fellow members (some of whom had known MacDonald), and proudly guided me through the archives and library he had done so much to pull together and put in order. During the course of his endeavours, he had become aware of just how rich and untapped a source were the bulging, elephant folio-sized ALC scrapbooks, which are incrementally crammed with evidence of MacDonald's intense involvement with all aspects of Club life. Also at the 14 Elm Street headquarters of the beloved institution MacDonald likened to a "church, a home, and a studio," I met Hunter's assistant and eventual successor as archivist, Raymond Peringer, who proved a valuable resource on his own. However, most of my communication with the man I came to think of as HB (an allusion to the senior and junior MacDonalds' habit of modestly signing their drawings, designs and contributions to *The Canadian Forum* with their initials) was by letter or telephone.

The last time I saw Hunter was in 1984, at the Art Gallery of Ontario, after we both had taken in the landmark exhibition *The Magnetic North*, in which JM's wilderness canvases stood up to the formidable European and American competition with understated but unmistakable power. On this occasion, explaining his difficulties in getting about, Hunter asked if I would consider collaborating with him on "The Book," an offer I was honoured to accept. Unfortunately, I had many prior commitments to deal with in the interim, so HB kept plugging away on his own until his death. I can only wish that circumstances had permitted me to fulfill this obligation sooner, but the harsh realities of the contemporary artworld and publishing militate more and more against independent scholarship and authorship, rendering it increasingly difficult to carry to fruition labours of love such as that which Hunter so confidently began in the 1970s.

Working in the late 1980s and early 1990s, I was at the disadvantage of not being able to consult living witnesses of the glory days of the Group of Seven, other than A.J. Casson, C.A.G. ("Chuck") Matthews, Thoreau MacDonald, Franklin Arbuckle, Eric Aldwinckle, Leslie Trevor, Clair Stewart and a few others, most of whose memories were clouded by time and the mythology factor that has made it so difficult to gain a clear picture of what it was that actually happened when the outlandish idea that there could be such a creature as a home-grown Canadian culture suddenly crystalised over lunch at the Arts and Letters Club (fig. **A.3**). Now, with the actual or threatened closure of (or imposition of restricted access and user fees on) publicly funded libraries and archives, the difficulties in conducting research into our printed, built and visual heritage are being compounded, despite all the promises of universal access to the global image-bank held out by the Internet.

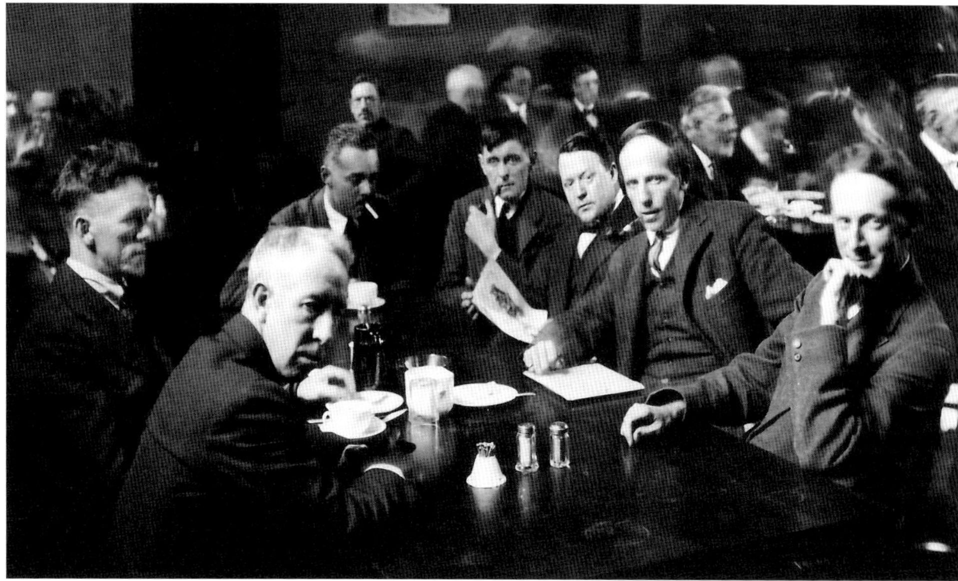

Fig. **A.3**. The newly formed Group of Seven seated around a table at the Arts and Letters Club, Toronto, 1920 ; photo by Arthur Goss. L. to r.: F.H. Varley, A.Y. Jackson, Lawren Harris, Barker Fairley (non-member), Frank Johnston, Arthur Lismer, J.E.H. MacDonald (absent: Frank Carmichael); behind Harris: F.H. Brigden, behind Lismer: G.A. Reid.

From our discussions and correspondence, I gleaned that Hunter's ideas about what he wanted to achieve had been clarified with the appearance in 1973 of *Thoreau MacDonald: A Catalogue of Design and Illustration*, by Margaret E. Edison, with catalogue entries by Richard Landon. This well-illustrated book, handsomely designed for the University of Toronto Press by Will Rueter under the supervision of Allan Fleming, presented a workable model for the first volume of what Hunter was provisionally to entitle *J.E.H. MacDonald: Designer*, after the wording on the letterhead logo devised for JM by TM. "Edison," as this indispensable tool is referred to in the antiquarian book trade, is broken down into the following categories: "Artist and Writer" (i.e., Thoreau MacDonald's own self-illustrated publications), "Illustration and Catalogues," "Books containing Designs or Lettering," "Designs for and in Periodicals," "Joint Work of J.E.H. MacDonald and Thoreau MacDonald," and "Ephemera," after which came two appendices, "Exhibits" and "References in Print," and an index.

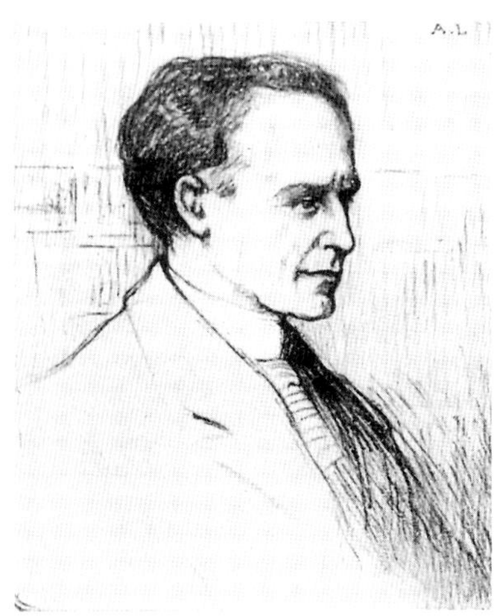

Fig. **A.4**. Arthur Lismer, *J.E.H. MacDonald*, 1911, graphite; reproduced in *The Lamps* (Dec. 1911).

Despite his desire to replicate its format, dimensions and overall appearance as closely as possible, Hunter gradually came to realize that the mode of organization of the Thoreau MacDonald catalogue was not altogether appropriate for his own book (or rather, as he came to see them, books), owing to the different nature of the older artist's labours. For one thing, TM almost invariably worked in black-and-white, whereas JM's designs are frequently rich in colour. Although the son, who considerably outlived his father, was much more prolific, as a designer if not as a painter, his production is more easily grouped into categories, as he did not range as widely either in medium or in application, nor did he tend to mix genres and style the way JM did.

Aside from his privately printed Woodchuck Press booklets, the majority of TM's designs were for one publisher — Ryerson Press — or for specific purposes and occasions. Much of his work consisted of commissions from government agencies, public institutions, or private individuals, only once in a while from a corporation or business. JM being by nature more sociable — "clubbable," to use the Johnsonian term — than the shy and reclusive TM, he frequently put his pen or brush to use for social as well as for commercial purposes, such as ALC functions and benefits for fellow artists, or simply for his own enjoyment and the amusement of his friends, in the same way that his contemporary Arthur Lismer was an inveterate sketcher of drawings, cartoons and caricatures of both colleagues and foes (fig. **A.4**). These results defy easy classification by type — hence the decision to append a separate section consisting exclusively of MacDonald's design work for the Club.

A much more flexible mode of presentation, then, would be required to do justice to the scope, diversity and special qualities of MacDonald's ventures into graphic design, illustration, lettering and other forms of applied and decorative art. The problems entailed in bringing order and coherence to this vast — and mostly uncatalogued, undated, and often unlocated — body of material were daunting. In wrestling with these quandaries, Hunter came up with a number of possible solutions. Here is one of the outlines that he drew up for "The Book":

1. Title	"No Ordinary Life. A Tribute to J.E.H. MacDonald"
2. Endpapers	The four pages which make up "A Word To us All"
3. Dedication	"To Thoreau MacDonald"
4. Foreword	(Explanation of scope of book's contents, etc.)
5. Introduction	By A.J. Casson *or* Charles Comfort
6. Chapter One	Before 1900
7. Chapter Two	1900-1909
8. Chapter Three	1910-1919

9. Chapter Four 1920-1929
10. Chapter Five 1930 and After
11. Appendices
    a) Residences, Studios, Travels
    b) Lectures, Talks
    c) Published Writings
    d) Published Poems
    e) Memberships, Posts Held, Awards
    f) Exhibitions, Catalogues, Reviews
    g) Notebooks, Notes, Miscellaneous Information
    h) Books and articles *about* J.E.H.M.
12. Index

The proposed title of this portrait, "No Ordinary Life" (which I have retained here as a biographical prologue), is a reference to the "Journal of an Ordinary Life" that MacDonald began to keep in September 1896 — the same year in which the budding artist started to carry a small sketchbook with him to record his daily impressions. As Hunter parenthetically noted in his foreword to the "Draft Notes by Year" that he compiled over the course of his researches, "how revealing of his life and work this lost item would now be!"

Alas, Hunter never seems to have gotten around to soliciting an introduction from either A.J. Casson (1898-1992) or Charles Comfort (1900-1994), although he did write to the latter — yet another ALC member — in April 1976 to tell him of his long-held admiration for "that multi-faceted man J.E.H. MacDonald. I have a growing conviction," he continued, "that no-one really appreciates the scope and magnitude of his output in a number of artistic areas. This is partly because some of this output (other than paintings) is 'lost' in the Club archives. As there has never been a complete compilation of MacDonald's work I have therefore begun to record all information to be found with a view to producing a comprehensive book in the form of a tribute."[1]

However, this process of investigation, carried out over the next decade, produced so much biographical data, and so many hitherto unrecorded examples of MacDonald's "Non-Painting Output," that Hunter's proposed method of organization could not accommodate either the quantity or the variety of information and images between two covers. His notes indicate that he himself abandoned the single-volume idea somewhere in the lengthy process of assembling the material. For instance, research in the J.E.H. MacDonald *fonds* in the National Archives of Canada, which Thoreau had donated (after first promising them to the Art Gallery of Ontario), revealed a staggering amount of unpublished manuscript material — lectures, talks, essays, correspondence, random notes, *obiter dicta*, and poetry. Hence the need for a separate, annotated selection of MacDonald's writings on art, design, decorative art, architecture, and art education, as a follow-up and adjunct to the present pictorial survey, and as a complement to the above-mentioned biographical-critical account of his career as a designer and "artist-for-hire."

A note here on the order and grouping of the following visual anthology seems called for. The contemplated decade-by-decade, rather than categorical, arrangement of illustration, lettering and graphic design unfortunately proved unworkable when put to the test. Many of MacDonald's assignments are undated or, at best, only tentatively dateable. Nor did his style change sufficiently over the years to permit definitive attributions to specific years on stylistic grounds alone. The chronological method would also prevent the collecting together of an entire body of work in any given genre or application — book design and illustration, for instance, or inscriptional work, fields in which he laboured over several decades. Better, it seemed to me, to group according to *type* rather than to period, but, as indicated above, listing and illustrating the items within each category as chronologically as possible.

Because MacDonald approached every task, no matter how trivial, with an equal amount of commitment and skill, it seemed contrary to his Morrisean design philosophy to rank these sections in order according to "importance." Instead, they are broken down into six main groupings, as per the Table of Contents, with an additional "Miscellaneous" category in the colour plates section). The appendix, entitled "Designs for the Arts and Letters Club," brings up the rear as a sort of summation to which the strictly chronological (as opposed to categorical) principle can safely and beneficially be applied.

Hunter's voluminous notes suggest that he had intended to include MacDonald's work as a printmaker, and also his contributions to the frequently collaborative art of mural decoration. However, since he devised his plan, publications have appeared that render such treatments redundant or premature. For instance, MacDonald's few experiments with burin, copper plate and sulphuric acid (fig. **A.5**) are included in Rosemarie Tovell's 1996 National Gallery exhibition and catalogue on the Etching Revival in Canada. At any rate, the few prints he produced are more closely related to his fine-art output than to his applied-art graphic work, being essential landscapes-in-miniature, intended for duplication in extremely restricted editions. They belong, therefore, in a

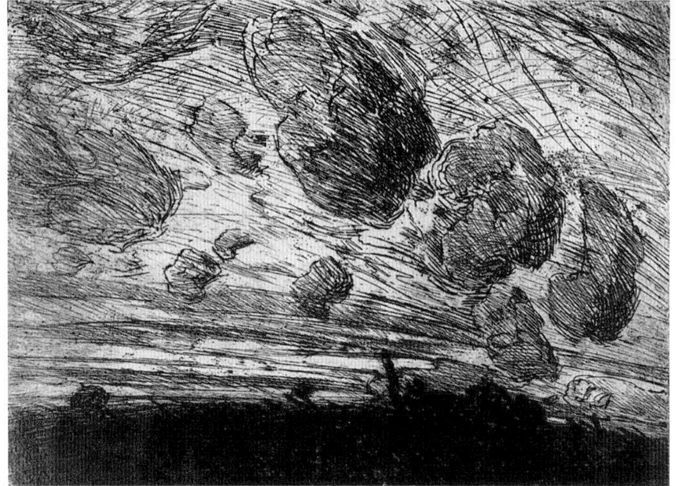

Fig. **A.5**. *Evening Sky*, c. 1913, etching on paper (12.0 x 16.5 cm); AGO.

subsection of the fully illustrated *catalogue raisonné* that I hope someday to be able to undertake.

Similarly, his involvement in mural decoration has received separate attention elsewhere: concerning the wall panels he painted in tandem with Tom Thomson, Arthur Lismer and A.Y. Jackson for the Georgian Bay cottage of Dr. James MacCallum in 1915-1916 (fig. **A.6**), see Dennis Reid's exhibition catalogue *The MacCallum Bequest and Mr. and Mrs. H.R. Jackman Gift* (NGC, 1969), and Pierre B. Landry's 1990 NGC monograph, *The MacCallum-Jackson Cottage Mural Paintings*. Those in search of information about the ambitious mural scheme MacDonald supervised at St. Anne's Anglican Church, Toronto in 1923 (see figs. **B.27-30**) should consult JM's article on the subject, published in the May-June 1925 issue of the *Journal* of the Royal Architectural Institute of Canada, and Catharine Mastin's 1988 York University M.A. thesis on the subject. There is also an extensive periodical literature on the building, its Byzantine-inspired decoration, and the campaigns to preserve and restore the fabric of the church and its interior, which can be consulted at the libraries of the Art Gallery of Ontario, the National Gallery of Canada, the McMichael Canadian Art Collection, the Metropolitan Toronto Library, and other repositories.[2]

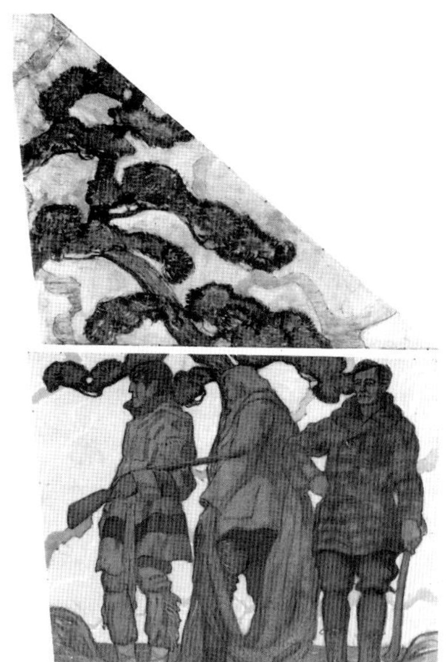

Fig. **A.6**. *Inhabitants of Go-Home Bay, Times Present*, 1915-16, oil on beaverboard; NGC, gift of Mr. and Mrs. H.R. Jackman, 1967. *Note*: the "modern" woodsman on the right is Tom Thomson.

JM's two other major architectural projects, the *art-moderne* foyer-decoration scheme for the Claridge Apartment Building, and the pediment, entrance and lobby mosaics of the "skyscraper-gothic" Concourse Building, Toronto (figs. **A.7-8**), are documented, respectively, in the building trades journal *Construction*, in March and May of 1929.

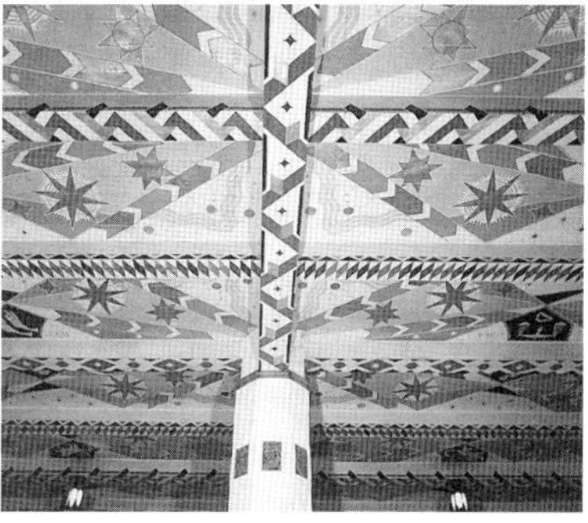

Fig. **A.7**. Foyer beams and ceiling, the Claridge Apartments, Toronto, designed by JM in 1928, painted by Carl Schaefer, 1929; photo by Bill Shelden; HBP.

Finally, for a recent overview of MacDonald as an all-round artist, the reader is advised to consult Bruce Whiteman's readable and well-illustrated monograph, published by Quarry Press in 1995.

With MacDonald's tendency to mix modes and media, it has not always been easy to decide which category is most appropriate for a particular item, as many could fit as conveniently in one as in another, especially when the illustrative content is as prominent as the typographical or lettered, and *vice versa*. In certain cases, it would have made as much sense to create thematic or generic categories to encompass disparate objects which themselves are more or less unique in JM's oeuvre (for instance, his "war work" in aid of the Allied cause from 1914 to the "victory year" of 1919, which includes posters, illustrations, satirical cartoons, and commemorative plaques, in addition to his service on war-memorial advisory boards and design-competitions juries). However, this temptation was resisted as being inconsistent and potentially confusing.

I should remark here that in some instances the only evidence for a particular artwork or publication that I have had to go by is a notation in Hunter's meticulous hand (often with no location, media or dimensions being cited, perhaps because he carried so much information in his head), or a faint and blurry photocopy or yellowing stat. Certain items for whose existence he found reference but which eluded his assiduous sleuthing have defeated my own subsequent detection, with the compensating factor that things not known to Hunter and myself back in the early 1980s have recently come to light. As well, a number of pieces that Hunter registered in the 1970s have since disappeared or changed ownership, leaving no trace of their present whereabouts. Luckily, such cases are not as plentiful as must have been the case when Hunter began his mission of rescuing MacDonald-the-Designer from undeserved obscurity. This publication will inevitably flush out items missed by both of us, and return to view things once known that disappeared over the years. Moreover, they should assist in the attribution or re-attribution to MacDonald of illustrations, illuminated presentation addresses, lettering, etc., that were previously uncredited or assigned to others.

Although Hunter was prevented by ill health from carrying out his authorial objective, he assembled, under circumstances that would have defeated many a physically stronger man, a remarkable archive of material that in itself constitutes a fine tribute to its subject — and, by extension, to its original compiler.

NOTES

1. Hunter Bishop to Charles Comfort, April 1976; carbon copy, HBP.

2. Ann Hemingway's 1988 University of Alberta MA thesis, "J.E.H. MacDonald: The Relations of his Fine and Applied Art and his Poetry," also briefly discusses the mural schemes.

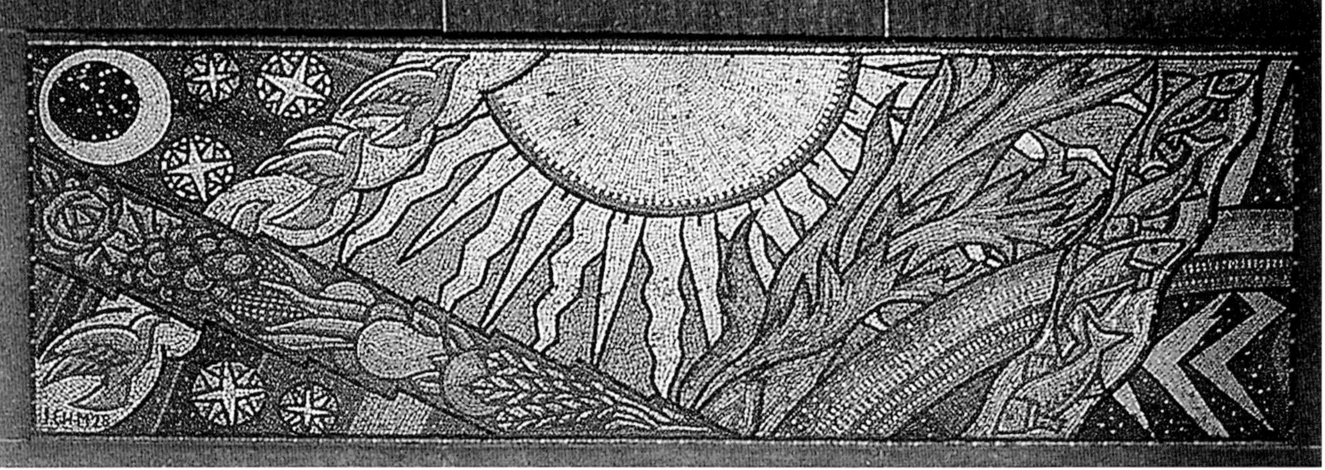

Fig. **A.8**. Mosaic-work frieze above the doorway of the Concourse Building, Adelaide St. W., Toronto, designed by JM, 1928, executed 1929; photo by Bill Shelden; HBP.

ACKNOWLEDGEMENTS

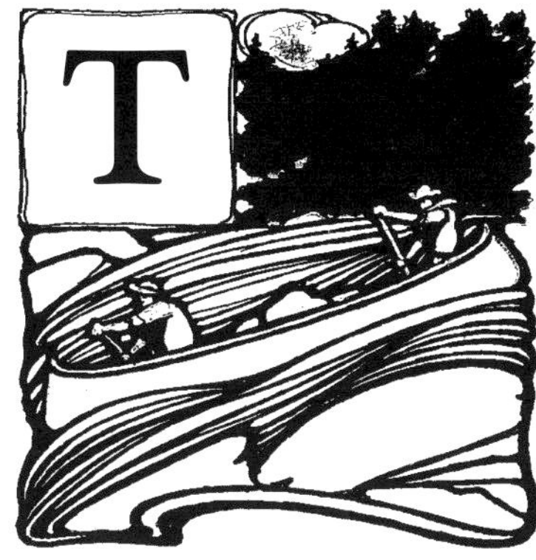

This book is the product of my own work and Hunter Bishop's, but it could not have been completed without the assistance, information, encouragement (and sometimes gentle goading) of a large number of individuals, whom I shall take the rude but space-saving expedient of thanking in alphabetical order: Robert Aaron, Patricia Ainslie, Art Alder, the late Eric Aldwinckle, Franklin Arbuckle, Wynn and Bill Bensen, Stan Bevington, Megan Bice, Jim Burant, Jack A. Carr, Ken Chamberlain, Marc Choko, the late Angela E. Davis, Nancy Dillow, Brian Donnolly, M.J. ("Budd") Feheley, Douglas Fetherling, the late Allan Fleming, John Flood, Robert Fulford, George Gilmour, Ann Goddard, Michael Green, Rachel Grover, Helen Hadden, Charles C. Hill, Alan Horne, Richard Howard, Elizabeth Hulse, E.R. Hunter, Lynda Jessup, Jean Johnson, Jan Kammermans, Leon Katz, Margaret Keith, Gemey Kelly, Neil Kernaghan, Colleen and Robert Koolen, Marie Korey, David Kotin, Richard Landon, David Latham, Michael Large, Kenneth Lochhead, Carol Lowrey, Margaret McBurney, the late Thoreau MacDonald, Karen Mackenzie, Margaret Maloney, David Martin, Katharine Martyn, Mary-Ann Maruska, Catharine Mastin, Peter Matthewman, the late C.A.G. Matthews, Gerda Moray, Joan Murray, Will Novosedlik, John O'Brian, Kate O'Rourke, Stephen Otto, the late Sybille Pantazzi, Nancy and Michael Parke-Taylor, Raymond Peringer, Larry Pfaff, Dennis Reid, Elizabeth Robson, Pat Rogal, Will Rueter, Barbara Rusch, John Sabean, the late Carl Schaefer, Fred and Bev Schaeffer, Douglas E. Schoenherr, Jill Sheffrin, David P. Silcox, Tom Smart, Joyce Sowby, Randall Speller, Dr. J. Murray Speirs, Lorna Spencer, Greg Spurgeon, Clair Stewart, Alan Suddon, Michael Tooby, Rosemarie Tovell, the late Leslie Trevor, Margaret Van Every, Christopher Varley, Murray Waddington, E. Wentworth Walker, Bruce Whiteman, Mary F. Williamson, Virginia Wright, and Jennings Young; and all those additional persons who helped Hunter Bishop in his own researches.

Thanks are owed, too, to the many antiquarian book- and print-dealers who have kept a keen eye out for MacDonaldiana on my behalf, among them Martin Ahvenus, Hugh Anson-Cartwright, Janet Fetherling, Asher Joram, Mike McBurnie, Stephen McCanse, Hugh Macmillan, David Mason, Marvin

Post and Nancy Buckingham, John Rush, Jerry Sherlock, Stephen Temple, and Fred Turner. Hugh Anson-Cartwright helped to make this book a reality at a difficult time in its production.

I am likewise grateful to the staffs of the various institutions I have consulted, including: the Art Gallery of Ontario and its E.P. Taylor Reference Library; the Canadiana Collection, North York Public Library; the Library of the Design Museum, Butler's Wharf, London; the Lorne Pierce Collection, Queen's University Archives; the Library, McMichael Canadian Art Collection, Kleinburg; the McLennan-Redpath Library, McGill University, Montreal; the Metropolitan Toronto Reference Library; the National Archives of Canada; the National Gallery of Canada; the National Library of Canada; the Osborne Collection of Early Children's Books, the Toronto Public Library; the St. Brides' Foundation Printing Library, London; the Thomas Fisher Rare Book Library, University of Toronto; the University of Toronto Archives; the University of Toronto Library; and the Robertson Davies Library, Massey College.

Much of my preliminary work on this book was undertaken at the National Gallery of Canada's Canadian Centre for the Visual Arts, where I was Research Fellow in Historical Canadian Art in 1991-92. My thanks to Gyde Shepherd, the founding Assistant Director of the CCVA, Murray Waddington, Librarian, Peter Trepanier, Head of Special Collections, and their staffs, for their cooperation and support. I am also grateful to the Ontario Arts Council for the Works-in-Progress and Design Arts grants that tided me over for at least part of this protracted trek.

I owe a debt of gratitude to the designer of this book, Glenn McArthur, who has heeded my suggestions and offered creative ideas of his own in coming up with a concept that does justice to MacDonald's own vision of lucid graphic expression.

Finally, to Helen Bishop and her son, John Porter, both the publisher, John Flood, and I wish to express our profound gratitude for their generosity and patience. In turn, the estate of Hunter Bishop wishes to thank the Canadian Hemophilia Society for its generous contribution to the fulfilment of a life-long dream. We can only wish that Hunter, who laid the groundwork and from whose assiduous researches this project stems, were here to share it with us.

— Robert Stacey, Toronto

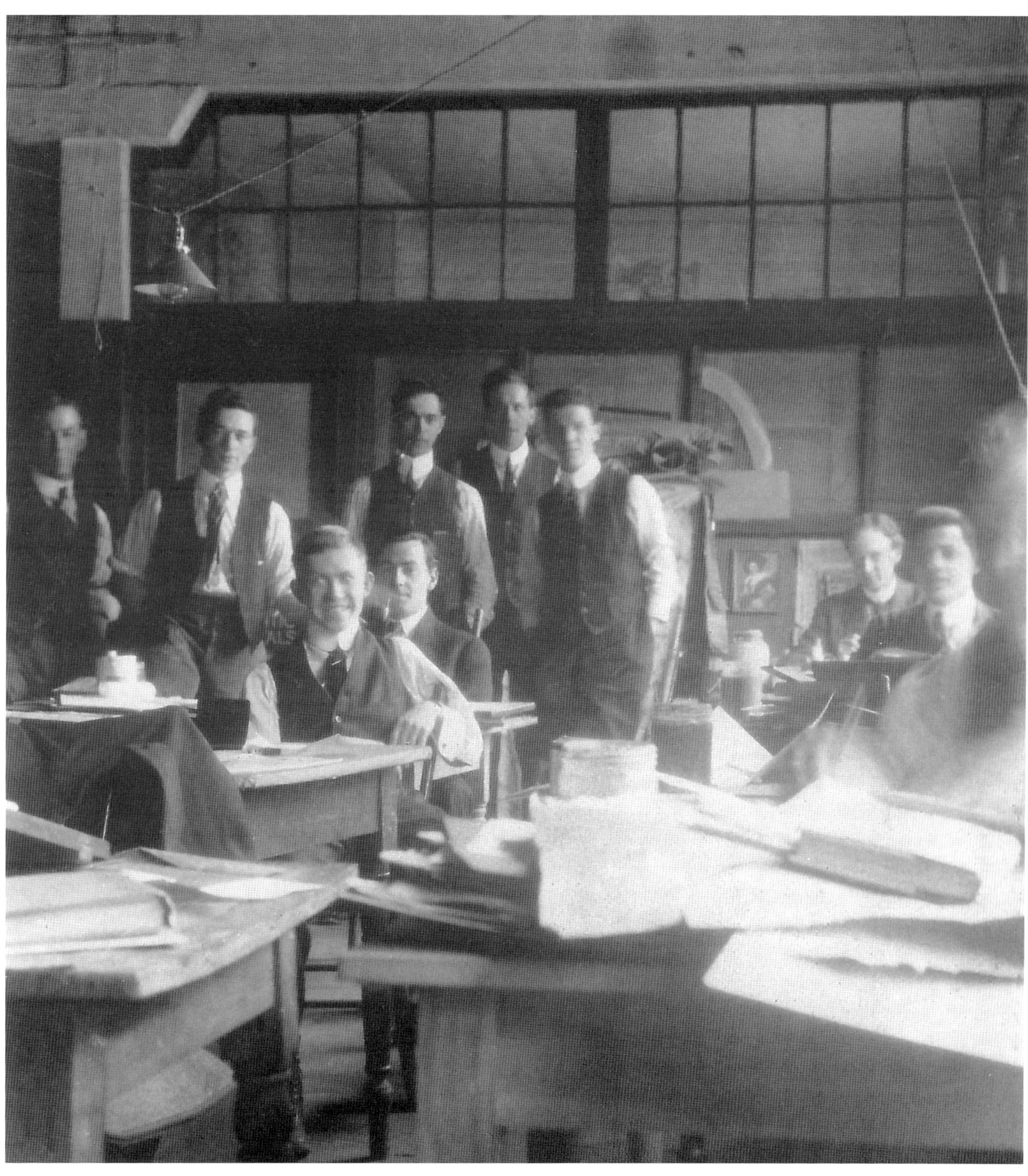

Fig. **A.9**. The art room, Grip Ltd., Toronto, c. January 1911; Library, McMCCAC. L. to r.: Arthur Rossell (?), Stanley Kemp (?), Rowley Murphy (?), Tom Thomson, W.S. Broadhead (standing), Arthur Lismer, Frederick Varley, JM, unknown, unknown.

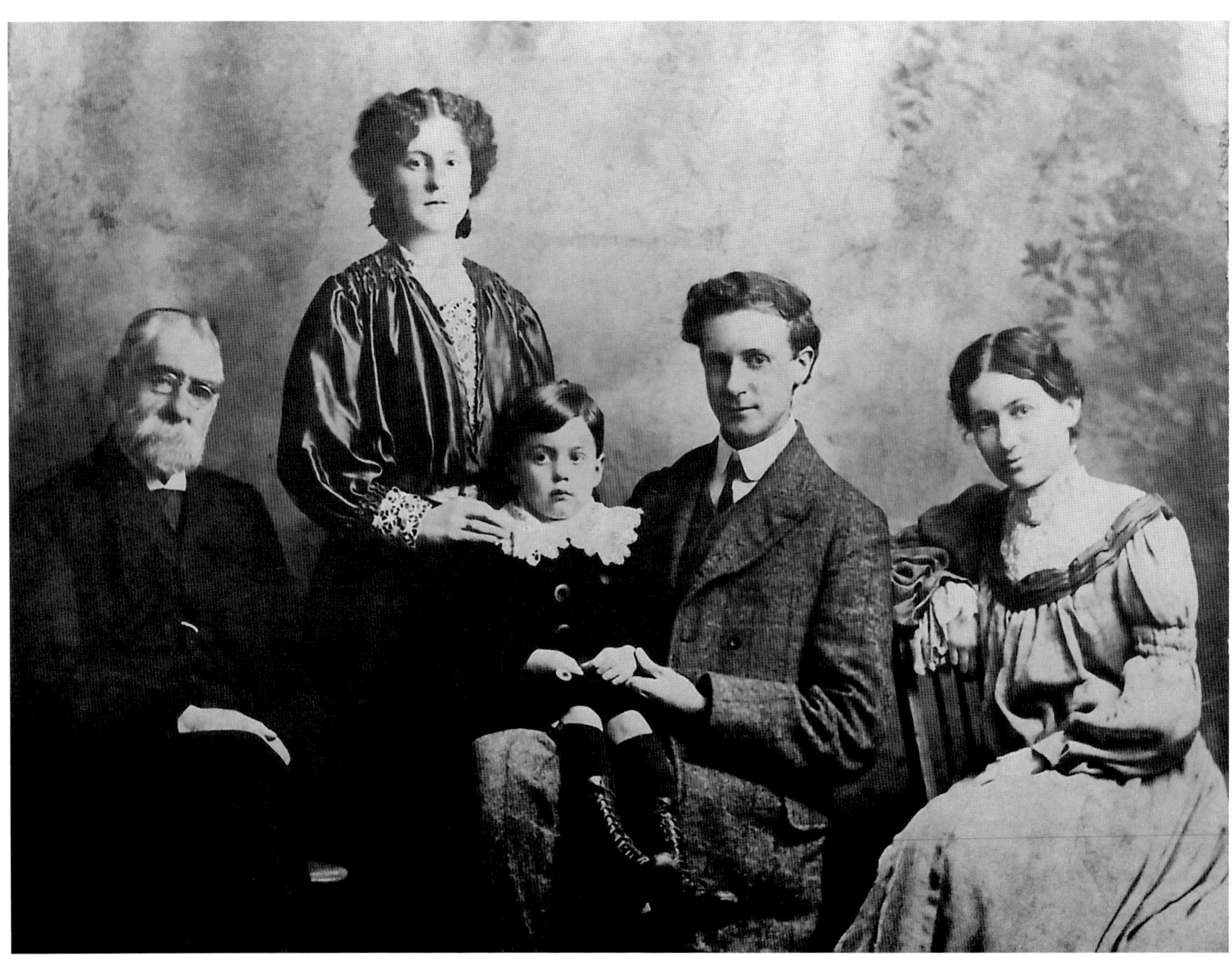

Fig. **B.1**. Left to right: J.E.H. MacDonald's father-in-law, Bertha MacDonald (sister), Thoreau MacDonald (son), JM, and Joan MacDonald (*née* Lavis) (wife), London, 1905; AO.

"NO ORDINARY LIFE"

Thoreau MacDonald and Hunter Bishop on J.E.H. MacDonald

Notes about J.E.H. MacD.

Thoreau MacDonald

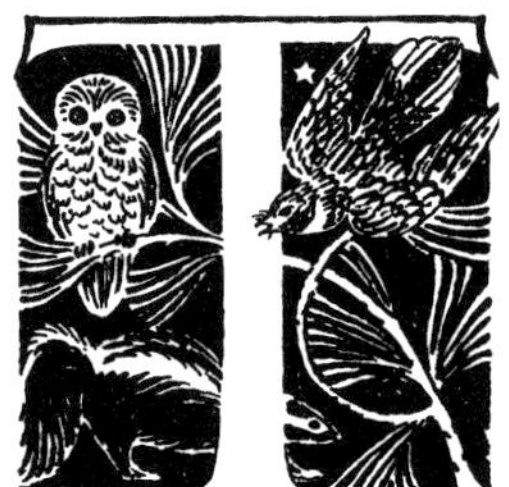

These notes are set down to try and give some idea of J. M. and in the hope that others who knew him less will not try to enlarge too much on his life and work, nor try to attach meanings to it which probably he never intended.

When I was about 5 years old [fig. **B.1**]. I remember Sunday walks when my father would make small oil and water color sketches in the country around High Park and the Humber Valley. In those days that district was a great stretch of open pine, oak and birch woods with only an occasional house. I remember in winter trying to persuade my father to paint near some hill suitable for sleigh-riding or in summer to stop by some small stream where I might make dams. The sketches he made were hardly larger than postcards yet they are carefully designed and hold together well. From them he made some of his rather labored and sombre, yet true and strong early pictures such as "March Evening" [fig. **B.2**]. He painted many dark sunsets and moonlit landscapes in those days from pencil notes made on his way to work.

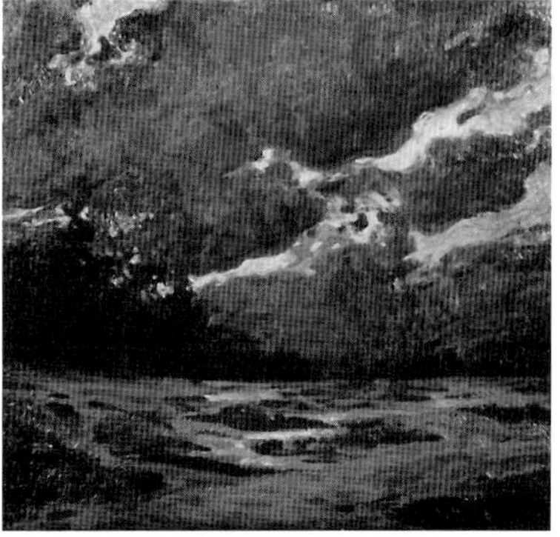

Fig. **B.2**. *A March Evening*, 1911, oil on canvas; private collection.

M. was working at Grip Ltd., an old time Commercial Art and Photo Engraving firm [fig. **B.3**] and he often told me the doings of some of the younger men there by which they relieved the tedium of retouching patent leather books, Bowmanville Organs and "Red Hot Huron" Furnaces. These recreation periods seem to have been mostly boxing and wrestling matches, playing horse or monkey with much stamping, kicking and swinging on the steam pipes.

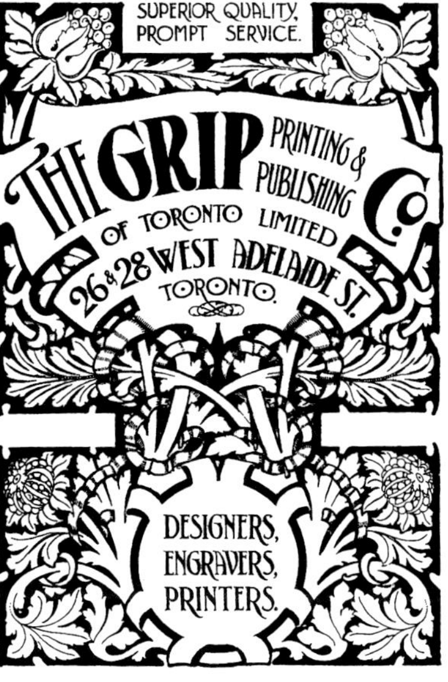

Fig. **B.3**. A.A. Martin, press advertisement for Grip Printing & Publishing of Toronto Ltd., c. 1896; Archives, OCA.

On weekends the boys amused themselves by carrying big chunks of rock on long walks and making sketches on the side. In the evening they might meet to make compositions and criticize each other's work, with strong-man stunts thrown in. A story I often asked for told how one of the boys offered to fast for a week if the others would make it worth his while. A collection was taken up and if I remember rightly $4.00 raised. The fast was carried through in spite of buns and doughnuts hung on strings over the hero's desk.

This was the nursery of much of Canada's art. There was no talk there of

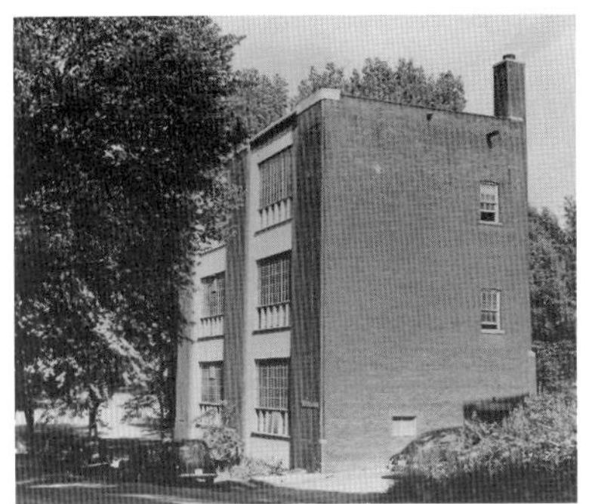

Fig. **B.4**. The Studio Building, Severn St., Toronto, c. 1950; photo by Charles McFadden; HBP.

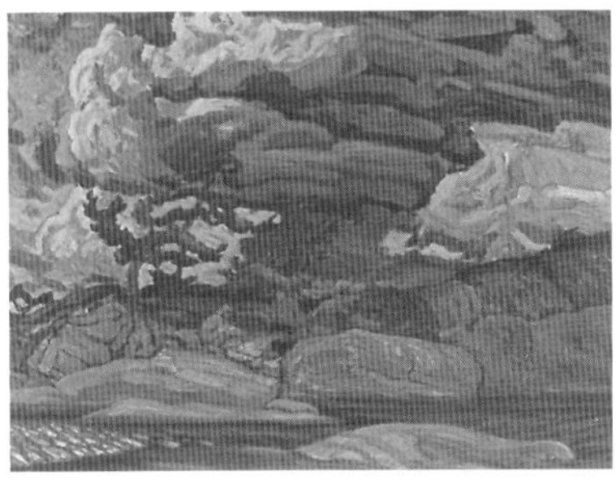

Fig. **B.5**. *The Elements*, 1916, oil on board; AGO.

"awareness", "idioms" and all the rest of the jargon now common, even though there was so much discussion of art that at times the boss had to complain and informed his staff that "he wasn't operating an art school."

In speaking of the beginnings of Canadian art, an art truly Canadian in spirit and subject, M. often mentioned the work done by men like R[obert]. Holmes, C.W. Jefferys, F.H. Brigden and others. They were some of the first nationalists, and he thought a country's art must be strongly national before it can approach what is called universality.

About 1911 M. met Lawren Harris who persuaded and encouraged him to leave Grip Co. and take up painting in earnest. This he did but still spent much time in free-lance commercial work. So began a long struggle with financial troubles and I remember the family excitement and rejoicing when a picture was sold, which was very seldom.

About 1913 Harris and Dr. [James] MacCallum put up the Studio Bldg [fig. **B.4**] and M. had a studio there, no. 6 where A.Y. J[ackson]. is now. Dr. M., at that time a great helper of Canadian Art, had already taken my father up to his island and I was allowed to go too. This was the first of many trips to Georgian Bay mostly made in the Fall.

At first M. made what I think were his poorest sketches there but on our later trips they suddenly became dark and powerful and from them he made "The Wild Ducks" and "Elements". This last [fig. **B.5**] is a rich and strong design with all the wild force of a fall gale, and I think it one of his best though it's not much appreciated being too strong for most of the aesthetes.

In 1912 [i.e., 1913?] we moved to Thornhill to the house where I now write and my father went on sketching in the nearby fields with E[ugène]. L. Beaupré. Here also his sketches at first were pale and weak, not comparable to his later work around High Park. But as I said they suddenly changed about 1915 & 16 becoming richer and stronger until the "Tangled Garden" [fig. **B.6**] burst on the gentle Gallery-goers like a bomb and left the so called art critics shell-shocked and raving. The original Garden was and is on the west side of our house and shows the old horse stable in the background. It seemed true and realistic enough to me though I took little interest in pictures then.

There's no need to tell here the controversy that raged around this and other pictures. Enough to say that the critics were not the profound and meaningless writers of esoteric outpourings that we have today. There was never any doubt of their meaning and such phrases as "Hut Mush", "Frightful Daubs" and "Drunkard's Stomach" filled their art notes....

It's hard to say what caused the change in M's work at this time but it was very marked. He was perhaps stimulated by his association with Jackson and Harris.

Tom Thomson also was now at the height of his powers. About this time [1917] I remember being out in that same Tangled Garden eating some black currents when my father came out much distressed to say T. T. had been drowned in Canoe Lake. Tom had been very kind to me, letting me eat at his shack behind the Studio Bldg., showing me how to make axe handles and giving me other backwoods information. I never looked at his paintings in those days and my clearest memory of Tom shows him mashing potatoes with a whisky bottle and throwing a handful of tea into the pot with a great flourish. He often came to help M. on commercial work, sometimes working all night at our house.

Now the war overshadowed everything and M. felt much oppressed by it as well as various financial worries. In Nov. 1917 we had to rent our home at Thornhill and moved to a small and rotten rickety house at York Mills, directly opposite Pratt's grist mill.

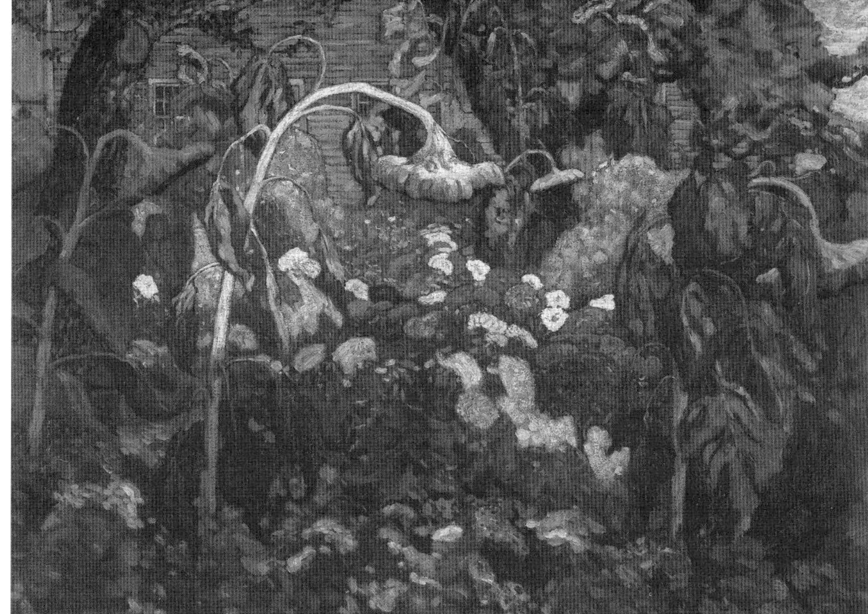

Fig. **B.6**. *The Tangled Garden*, 1916, oil on board; NGC.

The night after moving while all was still in disorder my father had a complete collapse and was unable to get up for many months.

That winter while lying ill he amused himself writing verse. He was encouraged by Barker Fairley (later a sort of lay member of the Group of 7), who published many of them in a small University paper called the *Rebel*. The poem called "The Constant Mill" had its origin there in the mill opposite. Most of the things M. wrote sprang from some local scene or village events. They had roots in reality and I think this is the strength of much of M.'s work. He thought of the artist as an interpreter rather than a creator and certainly much "creative art" is empty stuff. The creative supermen overestimate their powers.

During the summer of 1918 M. slowly recovered and by fall he was able to accompany Lawren Harris, Dr. MacCallum and Frank Johnston on their first trip to Algoma. He wrote an account of one of these trips for the A. & L.C. magazine [i.e., *The Lamps*]. The work he did on this and other visits to Algoma were true products of the northern forests, rich and strong. There's no aenemic simplification there but miles of bush, rivers, rolling ridges and heavy skies. Later he painted many large pictures of that country, notably "The Solemn Land" and "Autumn in Algoma" [fig. **B.7**], perhaps the best thing he ever made.

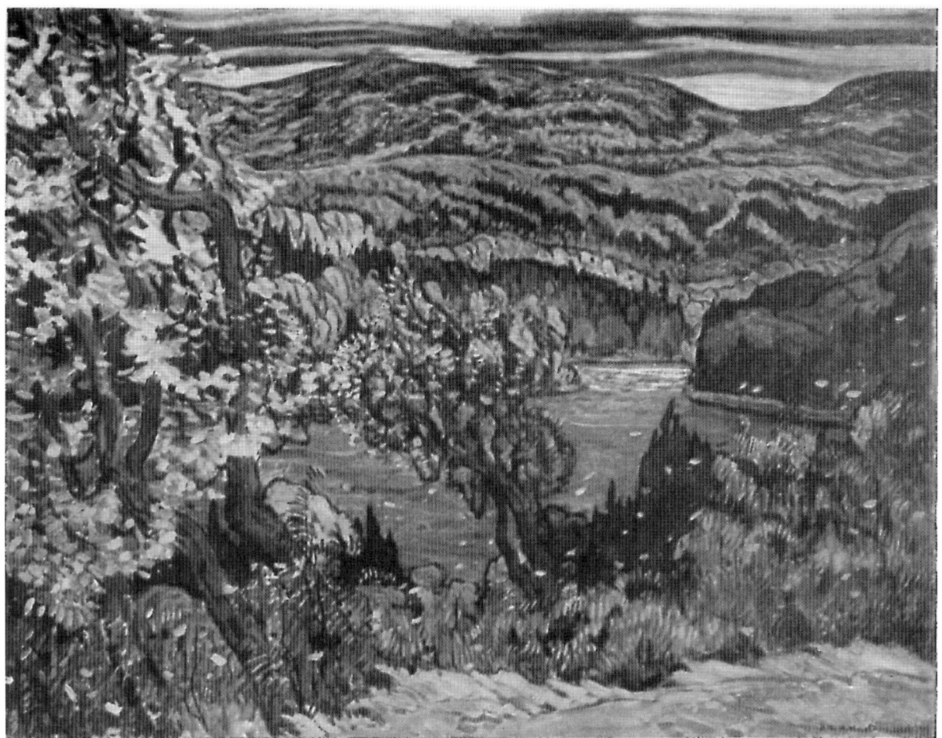

Fig. **B.7**. *Autumn in Algoma*, 1921, oil on canvas; NGC.

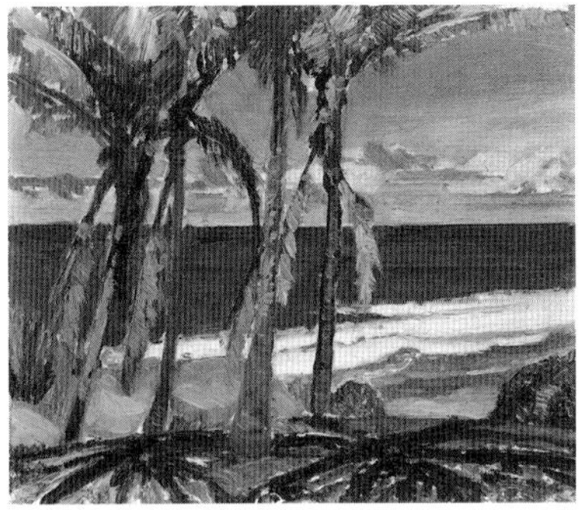

Fig. **B.8**. *Palms — Barbados*, 1932, oil on board; AGO.

About this time he started to teach lettering and design at the Ont[ario]. Coll[ege]. of Art. I don't know that he was a good teacher but certainly he was a conscientious and respected one.

The next few years were uneventful except for a trip to Nova Scotia in '22. His sketches there were not notable except for a few. He seemed mostly interested in the people and boats and made careful notes and measured drawings of dories and other craft, also detailed descriptions of Indian basket and canoe making. This was a habit of his and he had many notebooks full of conversations with local folks, their ways of making things, topography and natural history. In this he rather resembled a man he much admired, H. D. Thoreau, and a line from this writer reminds me of my father — "The Universal Soul has an interest in the stacking of hay and the foddering of cattle."

In 1924 he made the first of seven visits to the Rockies and if there's any after-existence I expect his spirit will be roaming there among the marmots and rock-rabbits still. His enthusiasm for the mountains was unlimited and for weeks after each trip he spoke of little else. As usual, he read everything he could find about them. He was a great admirer of John Muir and his notebooks have some likeness to Muir's writings. Everything interested him, the prairie crops, the cursing of some packers, or the conversation of visiting scientists. He overheard this between two mountain guides, "Well, Charlie, taking round any scenery bums this year?" He was pleased by the coincidence of geological similarity between

Durham, where he was born, and Lake McArthur, according to geologists the only places where this formation occurs.

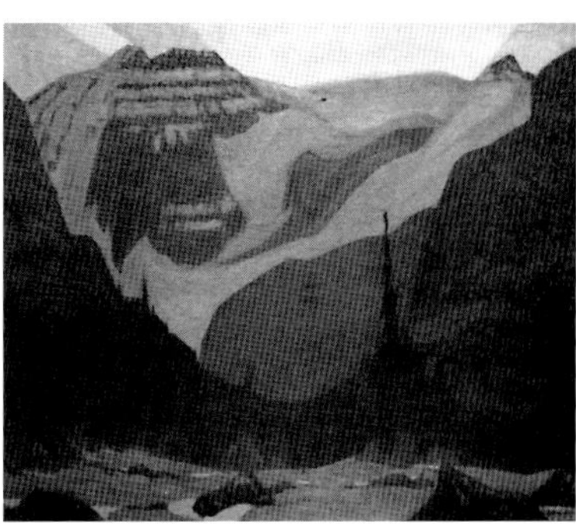

Fig. **B.9**. *Early Morning, Rocky Mountains*, 1932, oil on canvas; private collection.

M's mountain sketches are uneven but he did much of his best work there, especially in dark and stormy weather. These have the same power and richness of his Algoma paintings.

It's this force and richness I like in M's best work; no simplified poverty but plenty of everything and all well knit together by a strong design. He seldom indulged in that modern simplification which is often a way of avoiding work and only results in dead and meaningless areas of painted canvas.

As time went on, the Group of 7 began to show signs of disintegration. They had become known and respected abroad and the critics at home, fearing to be left behind the times, began to change their tune.

But the Group itself perhaps was slowing down. Its followers had merely diluted it. Harris seemed to be trying to translate H. P. B[lavatsky]'s "Secret Doctrine" into landscape painting and M's own work often lacked its old power. He now felt out of step with the other members, though he defended them loyally against outsiders, including the writer of these notes.

In 1932 he had a recurrence of his old illness of '17 and had to take a trip south [i.e., to Barbados]. He did first rate work there [fig. **B.8**] and enjoyed himself as usual, drawing and measuring boats and talking to the negro fishermen. On his return in the spring he cleared a space in the woodshed at Thornhill and among the tools and cordwood he painted the three fine mountain pictures "Goat Range", "Mountain Morning" [fig. **B.9**] and "Mountain Solitude".

In November he was again taken ill at his office and died November 26th, 1932.

I have heard some talk of his philosophy as expressed in his work but I don't think he ever tried to put philosophy into paint. He tried to present what he saw and felt as strongly and directly as possible and let philosophy look out for itself. He had a great interest in the creation in general and didn't attempt to theorize much on its cause or purpose. Some of his ideas are presented in his verses, however. He attended no church but sometimes he said he belonged to the "Universal Brotherhood."

I should have said that he had practically no art training and often regretted it but it's doubtful if it would have greatly helped him. As time goes on it will be seen that there was never a truer Canadian patriot.

Sdg. T.M. Jan./37

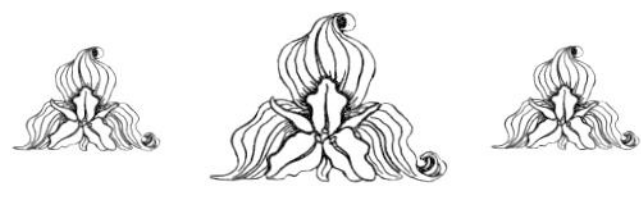

J.E.H. MacDonald, 1873-1932[2]

Thoreau MacDonald

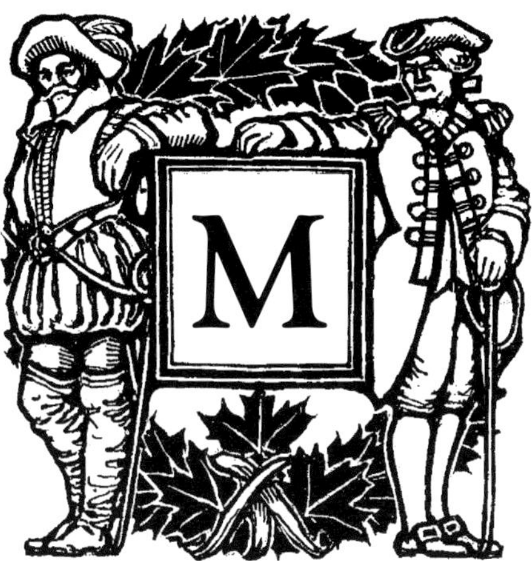

acDonald was one of the pioneers of true Canadian art, a nationalist in the best sense, and one of the founders of the old Group of Seven. He had no formal art training except some night classes in Hamilton and later in Toronto. There he was apprenticed to commercial art and might perhaps have had a worse school. All his life he was a spare-time painter and such noble pictures as *The Solemn Land* and *Autumn in Algoma* were made in the intervals of lettering and other commercial design. His last years were spent in teaching.

Much of his best work was done outdoors on small 8" x 10" panels [fig. **B.10**], often made under difficulties, cold and snow, wind and rain, mosquitoes and blackflies. On sketching trips he tried to make two a day and this he thought the finest pleasure in life for his idea of Heaven was painting in wild country. He had a gift for understanding and summarizing the landscape, for expressing graphically the character of granite or limestone, spruce and pine, poplar or hardwoods, muskeg or farm fields, all the well loved variations of Canadian land and seasons.

But MacDonald's painting trips were comparatively few and he usually had to make the most of things near home. He went several times to Algonquin Park, to Mattawa and the Laurentians twice, to Georgian Bay several times, twice to Algoma (the high point of his work), often to Haliburton and Victoria Counties, twice to Nova Scotia and seven times to the Rockies. After once seeing the mountains he always felt the pull of those great rock masses. He was rather frail in health and never equalled some of his friends in wilderness travel but he was not nearly so helpless in the woods as is sometimes said. He was unexpectedly practical and capable at manual work and for all his limitations as a woodsman he understood the wild country and recorded it as well as any.

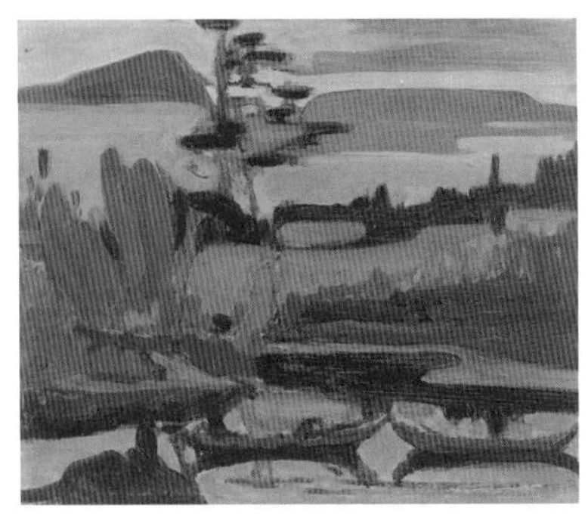

Fig. **B.10**. Sketch for *Mist Fantasy, Sand River, Algoma*, 1920, oil on board; NGC.

He was always on the watch to learn and liked to talk with such specialists as geologists, farmers, botanists, surveyors, section hands, lumbermen. His notes are full of information and observation, much of it technical, some more poetic: "The moonlight behind the dim grandeur of the mountains. They showed the power of a suggested form, the simplicity of mass and impressiveness of a tonality with few values." Another, on the train near Trout Creek, "Fine clouded sky with a glimpse of moon, the points of spruce against blue-gray distance and luminous sky. A broad quiet landscape, some old gray farm buildings near, green-gray fields, dim distance of endless woods."

Here and there are even a few lines of attempted verse that often give a little picture of woods or fields.

> "... far in tumbled trees
> The yarded moose stalking his moody way
> Along the snowpaths of his prisoned day."

———

> "The dark barn broods, loft and wide
> Over the crops within, and by its side
> The banded silo leans, and cattle shove
> To feel beneath the strawstack's hollowed cove."

———

> "... deep graven words of love and loss
> on broken tablet borne
> Cast down by time to lie with those they mourn."

Remembering MacDonald's character after more than twenty years [i.e., in 1957], it seems to me the outstanding qualities are justice and honesty. He never tried to make any account of things more interesting than reality, never tried to put himself in a favorable light, never made statements he was not sure of nor departed from known facts. They were interesting and poetic enough. This truth and accuracy show in his work, illuminated by insight and love for the subject. For all the strong design in his work he took few liberties, didn't seem to add or eliminate much. His pictures are true to the place and time.

In spite of some limitations of time and ability, one of MacDonald's favourite quotations can be truly applied to his own work. "With the breath of the four seasons in one's breast one will be able to create on paper. The five colours (well applied) enlighten the world."

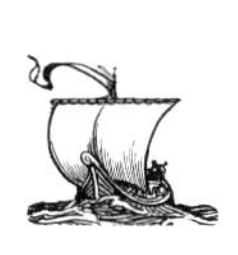 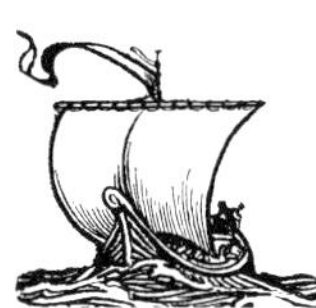 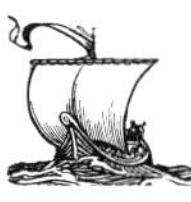

Portrait of a President[3]

A Talk on J.E.H. MacDonald and the Arts and Letters Club

Hunter Bishop

(General)

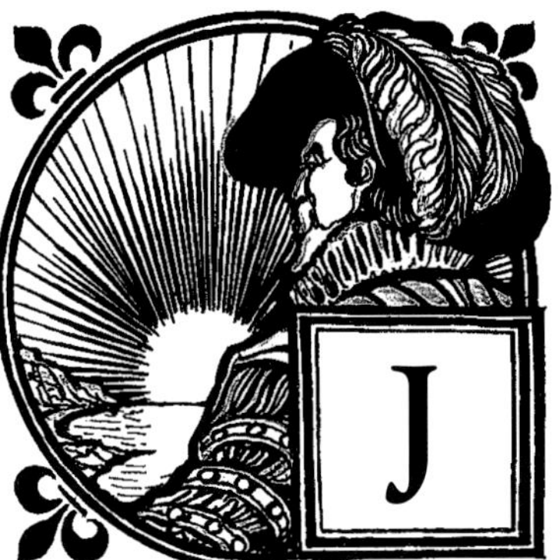

ames Edward Hervey MacDonald. People tend to think of him only as a painter — after all, he *was* senior member of the Group of Seven and he *did* leave between six and eight hundred sketches and about 150 larger canvases. But he was a great deal more. He was a poet who, during the first one-third of this century, had some eighty of his poems published. A writer, he had more than thirty of his articles printed. A lecturer, who gave dozens of talks on the arts. A contributing editor for several periodicals.

There were two overlapping fields to which he devoted his working life — that of the visual arts, and that of teaching. In addition to his paintings and drawings he was a designer, illustrator, calligrapher, decorator, and a graphics specialist who taught commercial and applied art including lettering, lay-out, heraldry, and typography.

His *teaching* career began earlier than is realized; about 1909 he became supervisor of the Art Department of Shaw's Correspondence Schools. He wrote and illustrated the lessons, and set and marked the examinations [fig. **B.11**]. This continued for some fifteen years. As for his long association with the [Ontario] College of Art [fig. **B.12**], many believe that it began when he was appointed an instructor in decorative and commercial design in 1921. But he had been a member of the three-man board of examiners in the college years 1912-13, 17-18 and 19-20. He had run the College's summer school at York Mills in 1914 and again in 1916. And in 1917 the College had appointed MacDonald as one of five instructors to run a summer course for school teachers who taught art; these courses were sponsored by the Department of Education. He was a staff member of the College for about twelve years, during which time he moved from instructor to department head to principal.

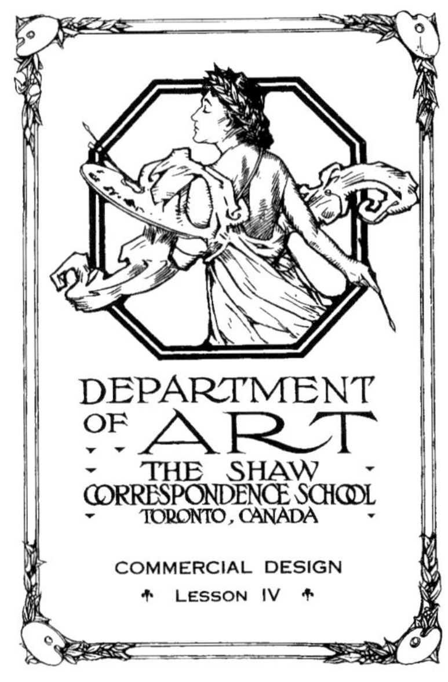

Fig. **B.11**. Front cover, *Department of Art, The Shaw Correspondence School...: Commercial Design* course (Toronto: Shaw Correspondence School, 1913); FTc. *Note*: illustration and lettering by JM.

When one considers the scope of MacDonald's ability and output it is impressive to realize that he had no formal art training, other than evening and

Saturday classes. In 1889 his family moved to Toronto; he was sixteen years old and in the same year became an apprentice at the Toronto Lithographing Company [fig. **B.13**]. Six years later he moved to Grip Printing and Pub. Co. Between 1904 and 1907 he was a designer at the Carlton Studio in London, England [fig. **B.14**]; he then returned to Grip Ltd. as supervisor of the design department [fig. **B.15**]. His first paintings were exhibited in the Ontario Society of Artists show of 1909. At the close of 1911 he was persuaded to freelance; the next few years were stringent indeed, for his paintings were not selling. He sustained his family only by accepting a crushing number of commercial commissions.

In 1909 he became a member of the OSA and in 1912 an associate of the Royal Canadian Academy. He served on a great many committees, and several important art juries. He won a number of competitions, awards for everything from a mural to the design of Canadian coins. For some twenty years he made sketching trips — from Nova Scotia to the Rockies and, on his last trip, Barbados.

He greatly enjoyed the company of artists. He was a member of the Toronto Art League, the Little Billee Sketch Club, the Mahlstick Club, the Graphic Arts Club and, for twenty-one years, this club [i.e., the Arts and Letters Club of Toronto].

MacDonald was a shy and modest man with an engaging sense of humour. His remaining early students recall the man with the greatest affection and admiration. His fellow artists respected his immense ability and his unswerving devotion to the cause of a truly Canadian art. Franz Johnston, who worked with him at Grip Ltd., succinctly summarized one aspect of his character with the remark "He was a gentle man — with a spine of steel."

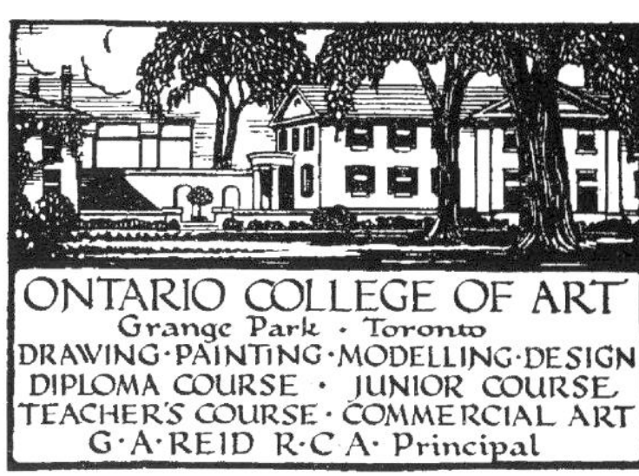

Fig. **B.12**. Press advertisement for OCA, 1925. *Note*: illustration and lettering by JM.

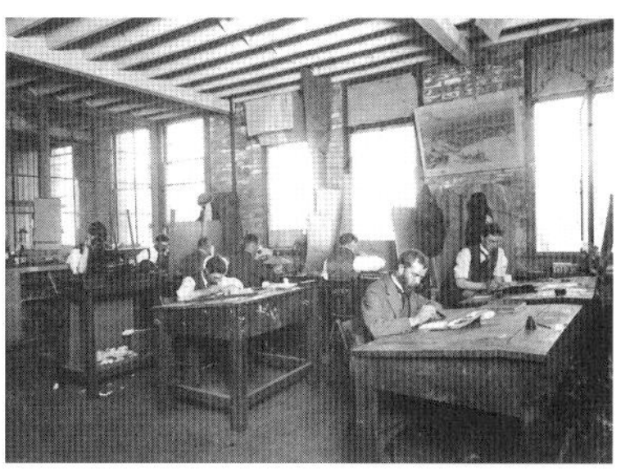

Fig. **B.13**. The art room, Toronto Lithographing Co., 1890s; CTA, Bagshaw Collection. R. foreground: J.D. Kelly (1862-1958) (?); extreme l.: mechanical toning machine.

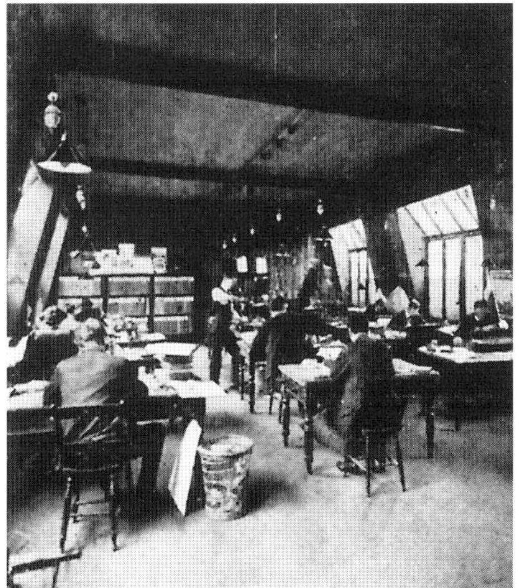

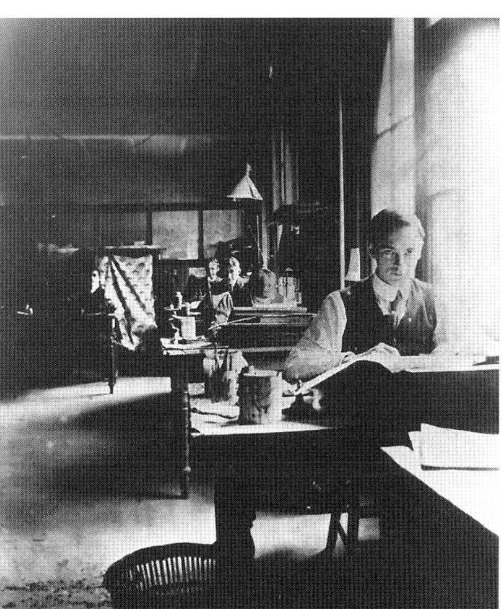

Fig. **B.14**. "Large Central Studio," Carlton Studio, 180 Fleet St., London, press advertisement, 1906; DM.

Fig. **B.15**. The art room, Grip Ltd., Toronto, 1911; WCP. L. to r.: Harold James, JM, ? O'Leary, ? Shea, Stanley Kemp.

(General: Illustrations)

[...]

First let me introduce to you the man himself. In January 1914 MacDonald changed his studio, moving into the newly opened Studio Building on Severn St. Here he shows his usual unease about looking at a camera [fig. **B.16**].

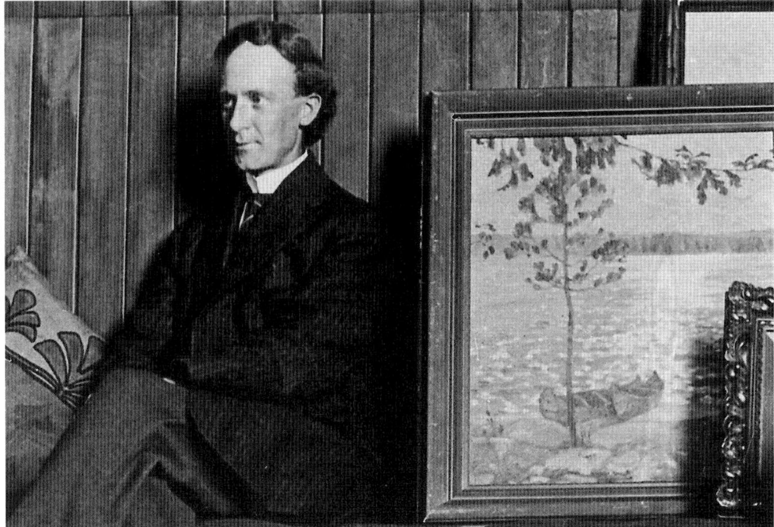

Fig. **B.16**. JM at the Studio Building, Toronto, c. 1914; photo by A.Y. Jackson; HBP.

This lovely drawing [fig. **B.17**] is entitled *Fish Shanties at Bronte* . In 1899 MacDonald and his bride went to Bronte [on Lake Ontario west of Oakville] on their honeymoon. His son Thoreau thinks the drawing was done at that time. It is very similar to illustrations then being used in the T[oronto] A[rt] L[eague] calendars.

This invoice [fig. **B.18**] is very much in early MacDonald style. Gone are the drooping floral tendrils on previous invoices [fig. **B.19**], to be replaced by the strong clear lines which depict the engravers' tools.

In 1911 the entire Lawrence Park area was sub-divided into residential lots. An impressive booklet, with MacDonald illustrations on each page, was produced [fig. **B.20**]. An example of many such booklets he did.

This work was used as the frontispiece of the 1914 R.C.A. catalogue for the *Exhibition of Pictures Given by Canadian Artists for the Patriotic Fund* [fig. **B.21**]. Curiously, the identification on the left side — "Canada and the Call, 1914" — is not present on the original painting now in the possession of the [Ontario] College of Art [see **II:3**].

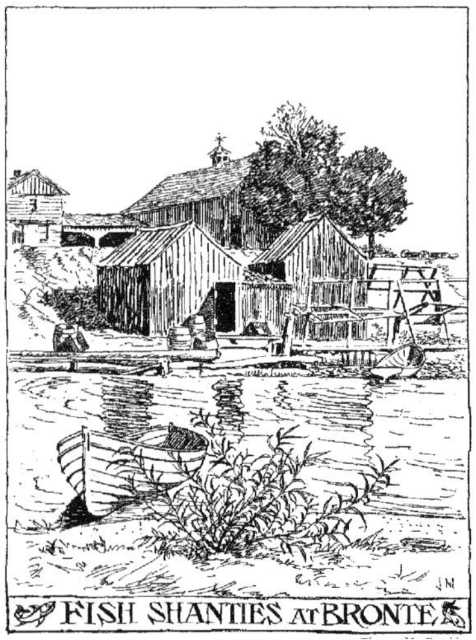

A final example of his commercial work [fig. **B.22**]. He did many diplomas, certificates, presentation pieces, bookplates, etc. This certificate of the Ontario Association of Architects was chosen for obvious reasons. The design was done in 1920....

Of course, his paintings are of major importance. But only four will be shown. No apology is made for choosing the three most commonly reproduced — they are good examples of variation in style and technique. *Tracks and Traffic* was his first important canvas, painted in 1912 [fig. **B.23**]. It is my favourite; perhaps because I am a city man, but also because it reflects that impressionistic quality of mystery which may be apprehended in an unpeopled landscape.

The Tangled Garden was painted at MacDonald's Thornhill farm in 1916

Fig. **B.17**. *Fish Shanties at Bronte*, 1899, pen-and-ink; formerly collection of TM, present whereabouts unknown; reproduced from William Colgate, *Canadian Art* (Toronto: Ryerson Press, [fig. **B.24**]. An impressive example of the imposition of his design skills onto a painting. It drew fierce criticism, particularly from fellow Club member and art critic Hector Charlesworth.

The Solemn Land was painted from sketches made during MacDonald's second boxcar trip to Algoma country in 1919. The large canvas was not completed until two years later [fig. **B.25**].

Belgium, 1914 [fig. **B.26**]. Chosen to be shown because it is an unusual work reflecting MacDonald's revulsion at the horror of war....

This too brief introduction to MacDonald as artist could not be complete without showing examples of his major commission — the interior decoration of St. Anne's Church. A church whose architecture is based on the great St. Sophie [i.e., Santa Sophia] in Constantinople. The entire Byzantine design of the interior was MacDonald's; he supplied scale designs, colour schemes, and materials for all the painters who worked on the project. It was started and completed between 1923 and 1924.

The ceiling of the chancel is quite gorgeous [fig. **B.27**], with a background of dark blue. The paintings are set in wide richly ornamented borders of Byzantine discs and entwined scrolls.

MacDonald contributed two of the paintings for the ceiling of the chancel; one being *The Stilling of the Tempest*, which is shown here [fig. **B.28**], the other being *The Transfiguration* [fig. **B.29**].

The main dome is coloured a strong tone of Venetian red. The four pillars

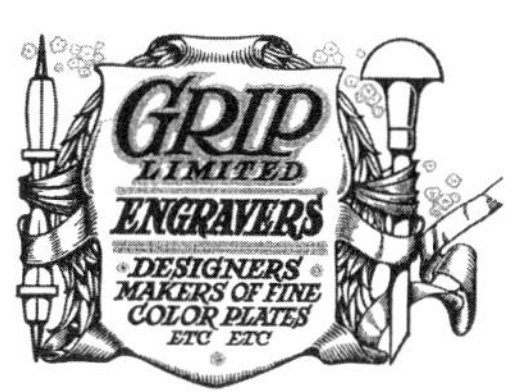

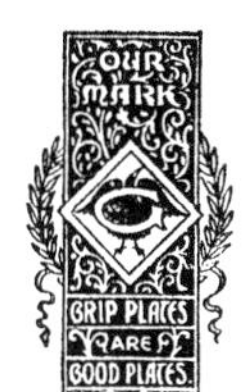

Figs. **B.18-19**. JM, Grip Ltd. invoice logo, 1911; A.H. Howard (?), Grip P. & P. logo, c. 1899; HBP.

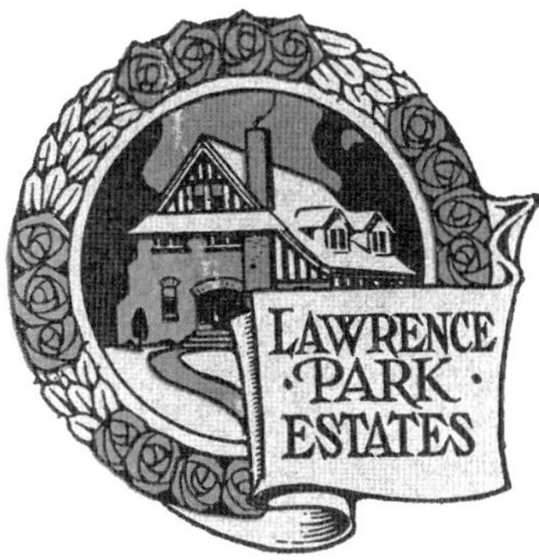

Fig. **B.20**. Envelope logo, Lawrence Park Estates booklet (Toronto: Dovercourt Lands Buildings and Savings Co., n.d. [1911 or '12]), printed by Grip Ltd.; RSc.

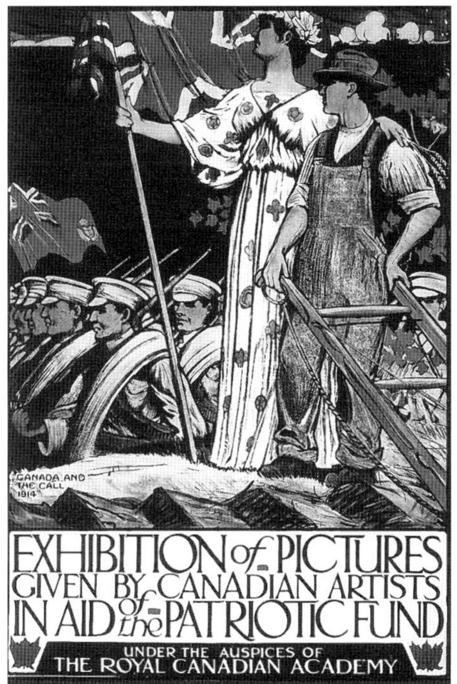

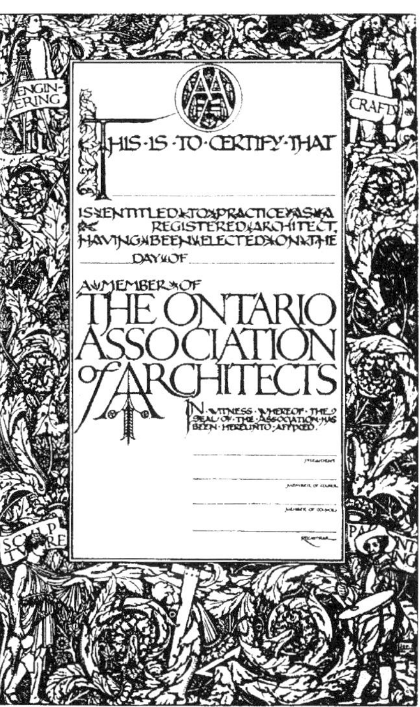

Fig. **B.21**. *Canada and the Call, 1914*, 1914, offset lithograph, printed by Rolph-Smith and Co., Toronto; reproduced in 1914 RCA *Patriotic Fund* exhibition catalogue; RSc. *Note*: for colour reproduction, see **Pl. II:1**.

Fig. **B.22**. Ontario Association of Architects diploma, 1920; withdrawn, 1935.

carry the pendentive paintings, which are approximately 15 feet high by 10 feet wide. One of these four paintings was done by MacDonald. It is titled *The Crucifixion* [fig. **B.30**].

While in his first year as [Arts and Letters] Club president he was appointed principal of the [Ontario] College of Art (March 11th, 1929). The load was a very heavy one, particularly because he continued as head of the Graphics and Design Department.

In 1931 he had a serious illness and was forced to apply for a year's leave of absence. He went to Barbados for the early months of 1932. That fall he was able to return to the College, but he was still far from well.

On November 22nd 1932 he had an argument with a student about locker accommodation. Less than an hour later he suffered a massive stroke and was taken to his home. He never regained his speech. He died four days later. He was fifty-nine years of age.

Fig. **B.23**. *Tracks and Traffic*, 1912, oil on canvas; AGO.

Fig. **B.24**. Sketch for *The Tangled Garden*, 1916, oil on panel; NGC.

Fig. **B.25**. Sketch for *The Solemn Land*, 1921, oil on board; AGO.

Fig. **B.26**. *Belgium, 1914*, 1915, oil on card; AGO.

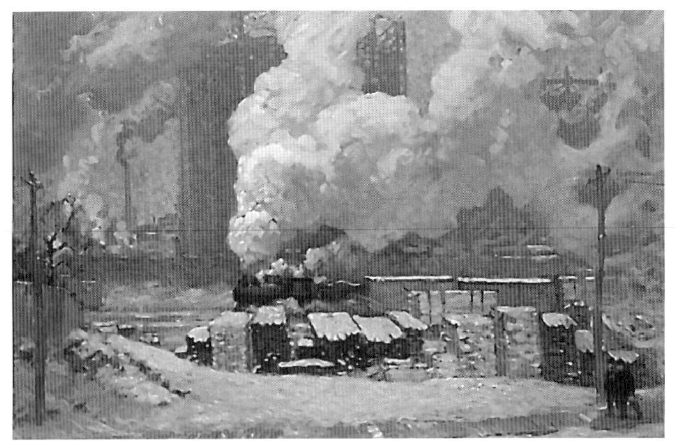

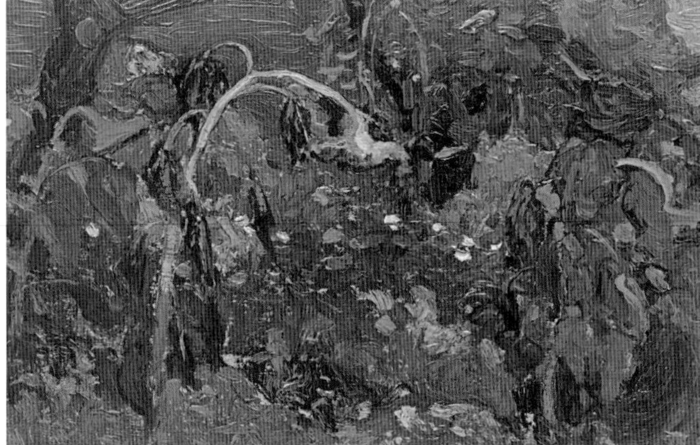

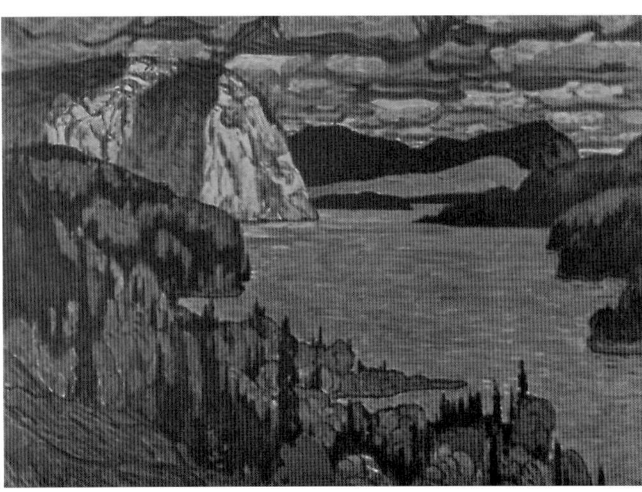

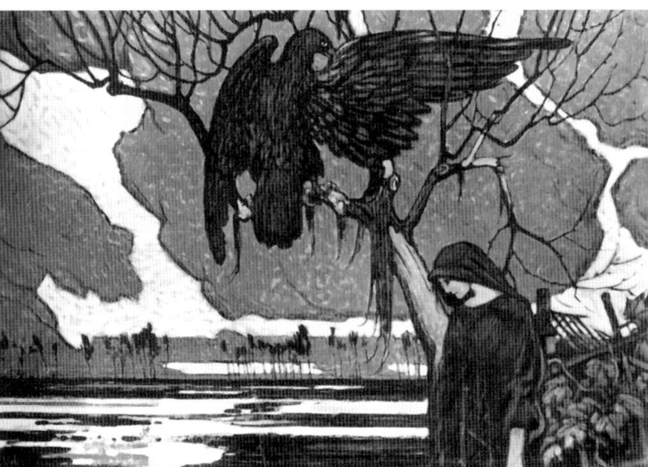

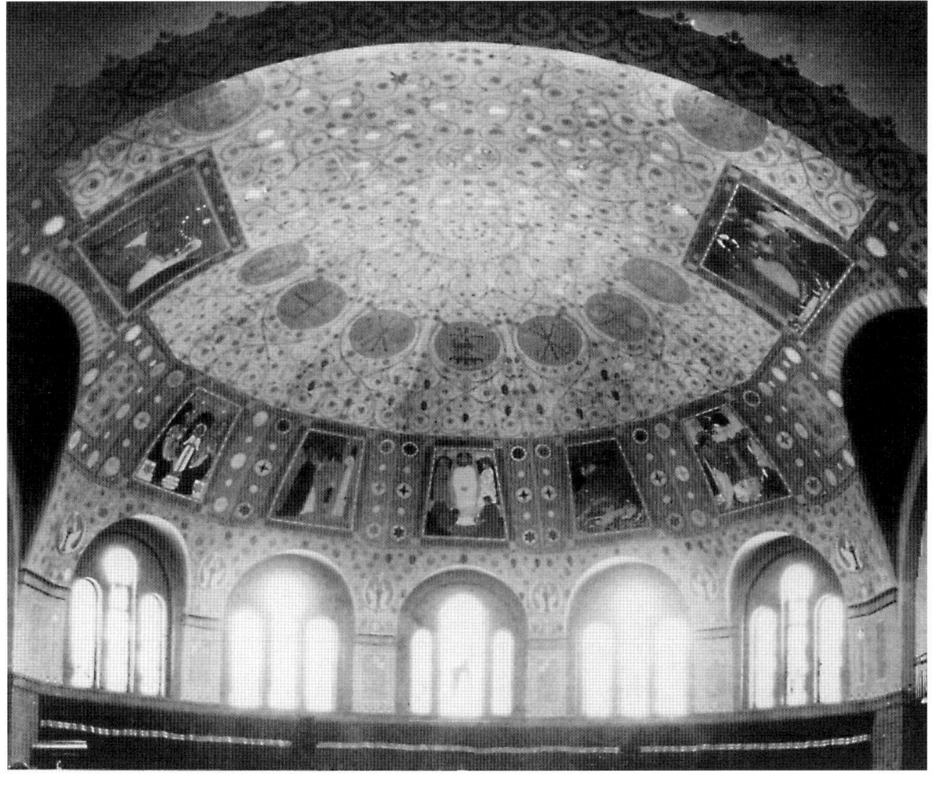

Fig. **B.27**. Chancel ceiling, St. Anne's Church, Toronto, 1923; reproduced from *Journal,* RAIC (May-June 1925).

Fig. **B.28**. *The Crucifixion*, St. Anne's Church, 1923.

Fig. **B.29**. *The Stilling of the Tempest*, St. Anne's Church, 1923.

Fig. **B.30**. *The Transfiguration*, St. Anne's Church, 1923.

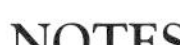

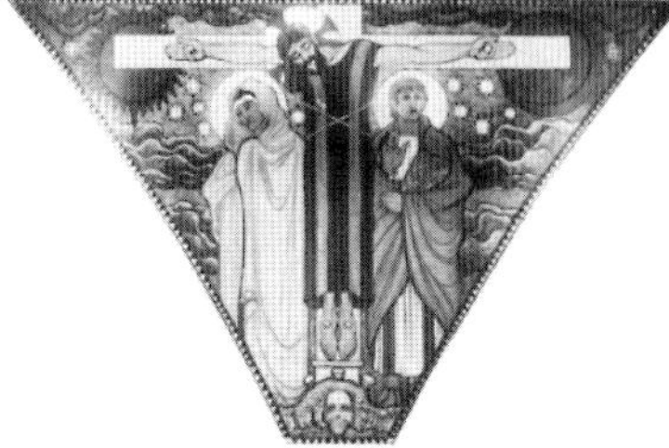

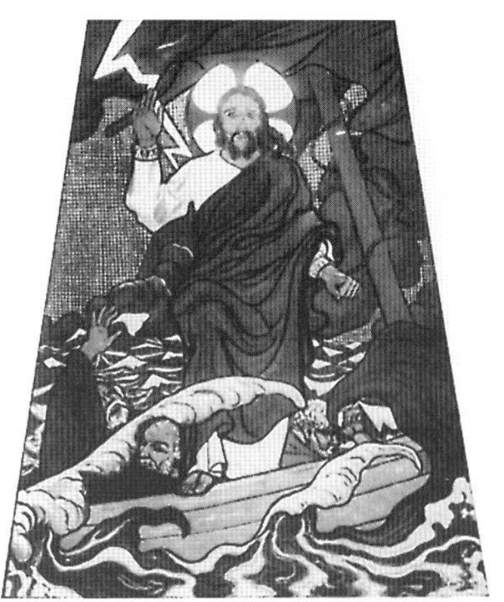

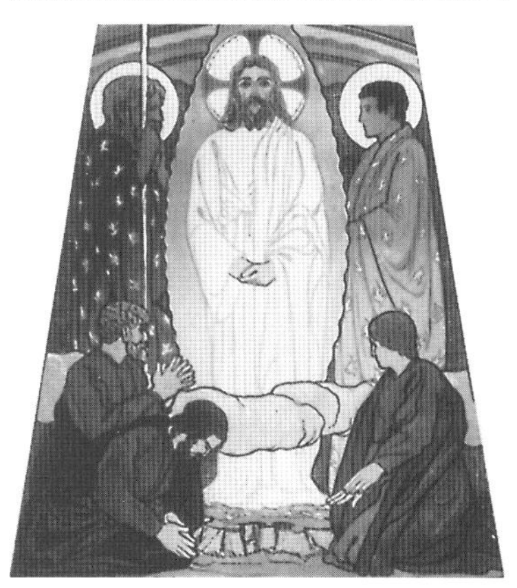

NOTES

1. Typescript, with holograph corrections, January 1937; photocopy in HBP. Written by TM for use by A.H. Robson and E.R. Hunter in their monographs on JM, published by Ryerson Press in 1937 and 1940, respectively.

2. Edited version of foreword to *J.E.H. MacDonald: 1873-1932* (Hamilton: Art Gallery of Hamilton, 1957).

3. Excerpted from "Portrait of a President: A Talk on J.E.H. MacDonald and the Arts and Letters Club," given at an ALC members' dinner, 27 March 1981. Photocopy of typescript with author's corrections, Archives, ALC. For the second half of this talk, see the conclusion to the Appendix, "Designs for the Arts and Letters Club," pp. 112-13.

Colour Plates

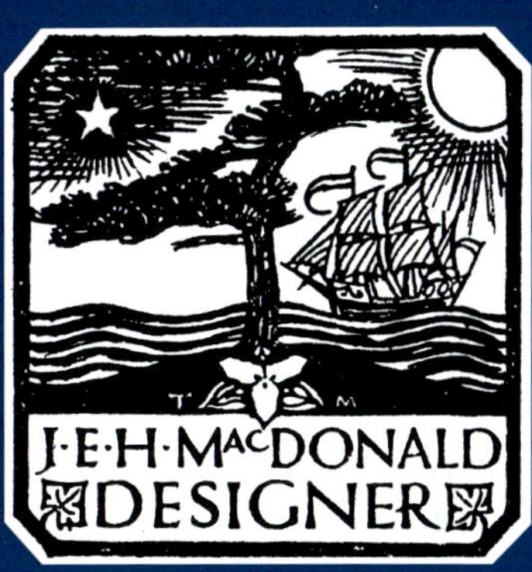

Colour Plates

I: Design for Commerce

Pl. I:1 (a). Title page, *The Atlantic Royals* (Montreal: The Canadian Northern Steamships, n.d. [c. 1910]); RSc. Note: printed by Grip Ltd., Toronto. **(b)**. Front and back cover, brochure, *The Atlantic Royals*.

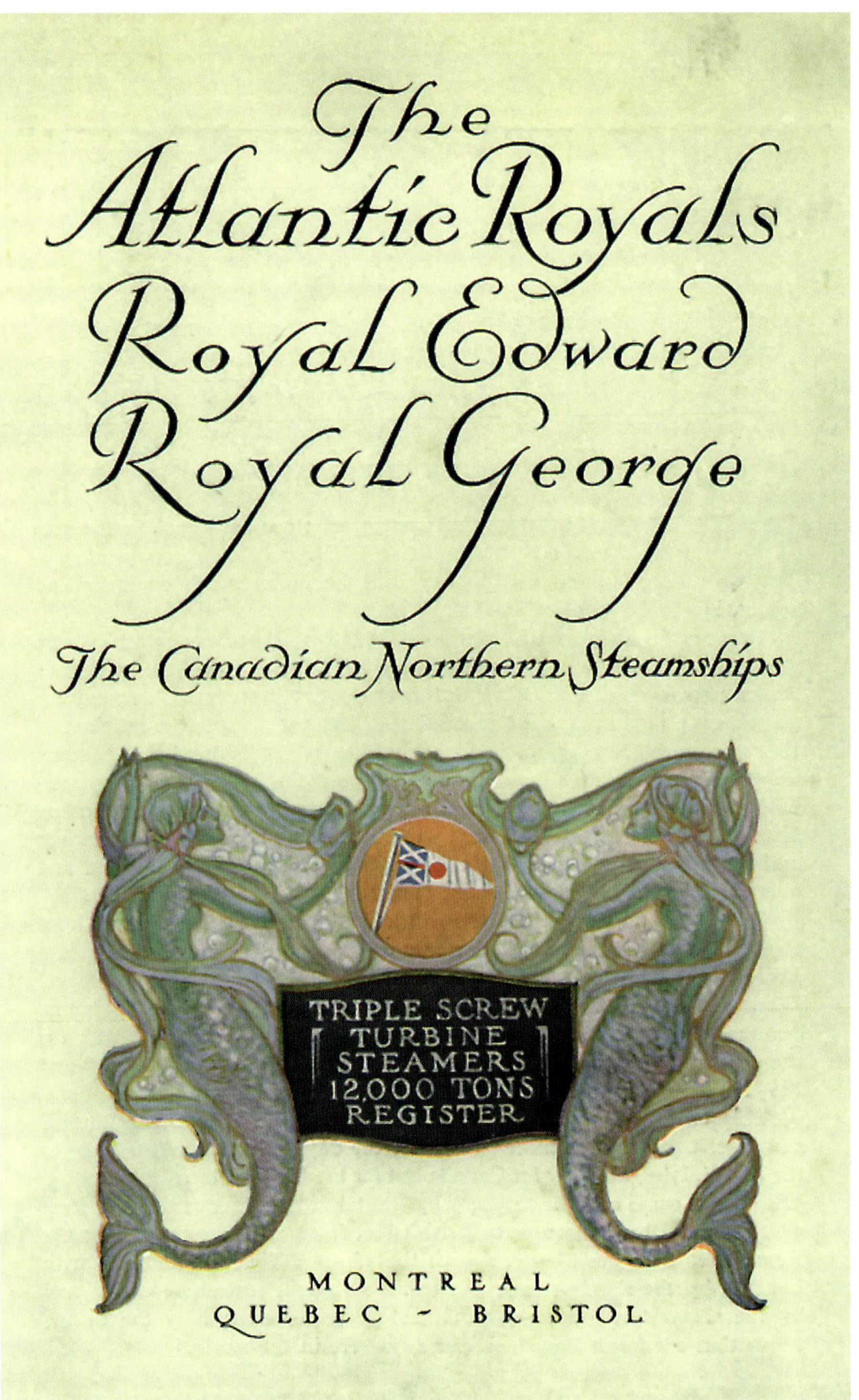

Pl. I:1 (a)

The Royal Line
The Atlantic Royals
The Canadian Northern Steamships

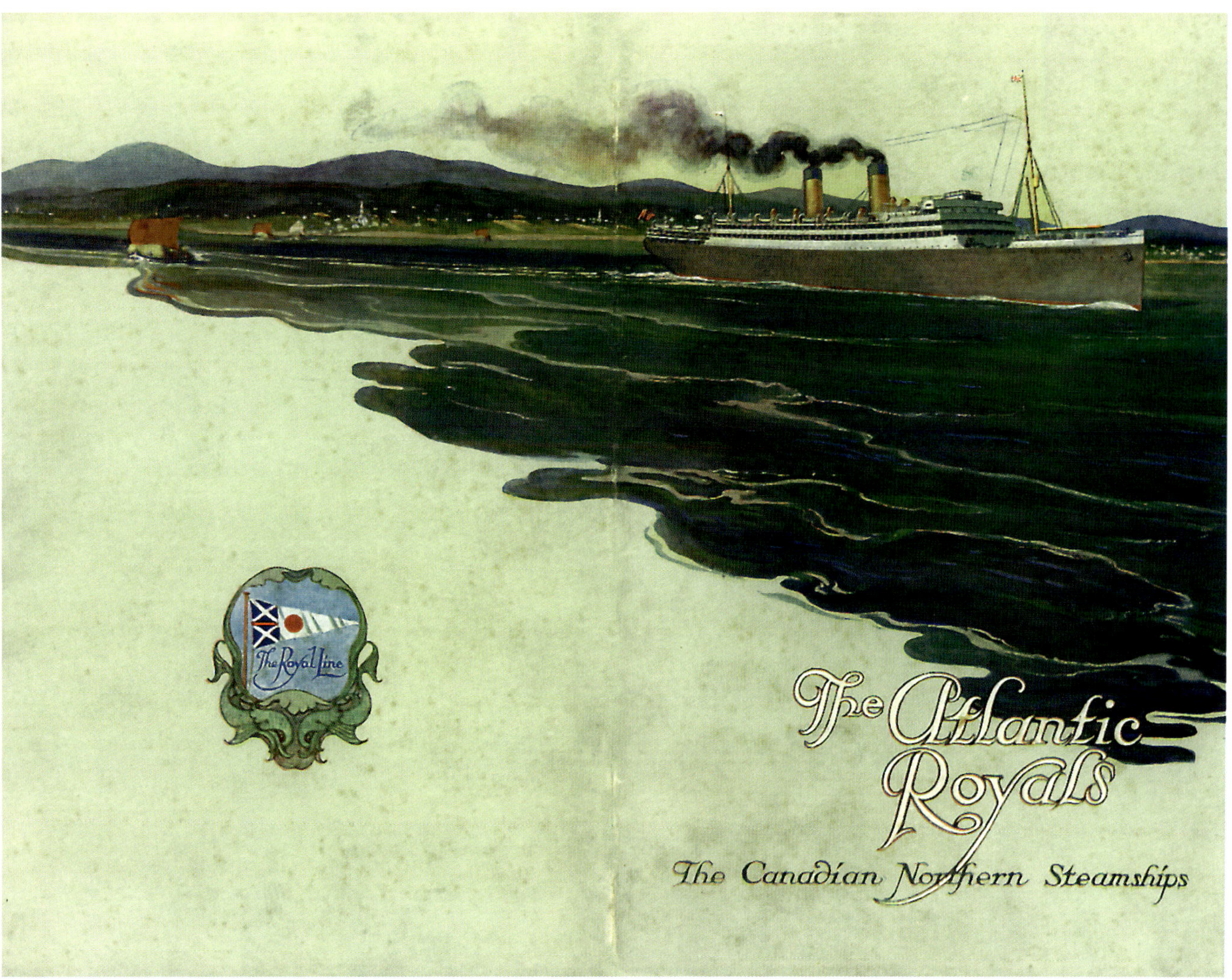

(b)

Colour Plates

Pl. I:2 (a). Back and front cover, brochure, *Quebec and the Chateau Frontenac* (Montreal, Canadian Pacific Railway, 1911); RSc. *Note*: interior illustrations by C.W. Jefferys. **(b)**. Title page, brochure, *Quebec and the Chateau Frontenac*.

Pl. I:3. Front cover, brochure, *Quebec, The Ancient Capital* (Moncton, N.B.: Canadian Government Railway, n.d. [c. 1910s], 2nd ed.); RSc.

Pl. I:4. Front cover, brochure, *Place Viger Hotel, Montreal* (Montreal: CPR, n.d. [1911?]); RSc.

Pl. I:5. Front cover, brochure, *Place Viger Hotel, Montreal* (Montreal: CPR, 1911); RSc.

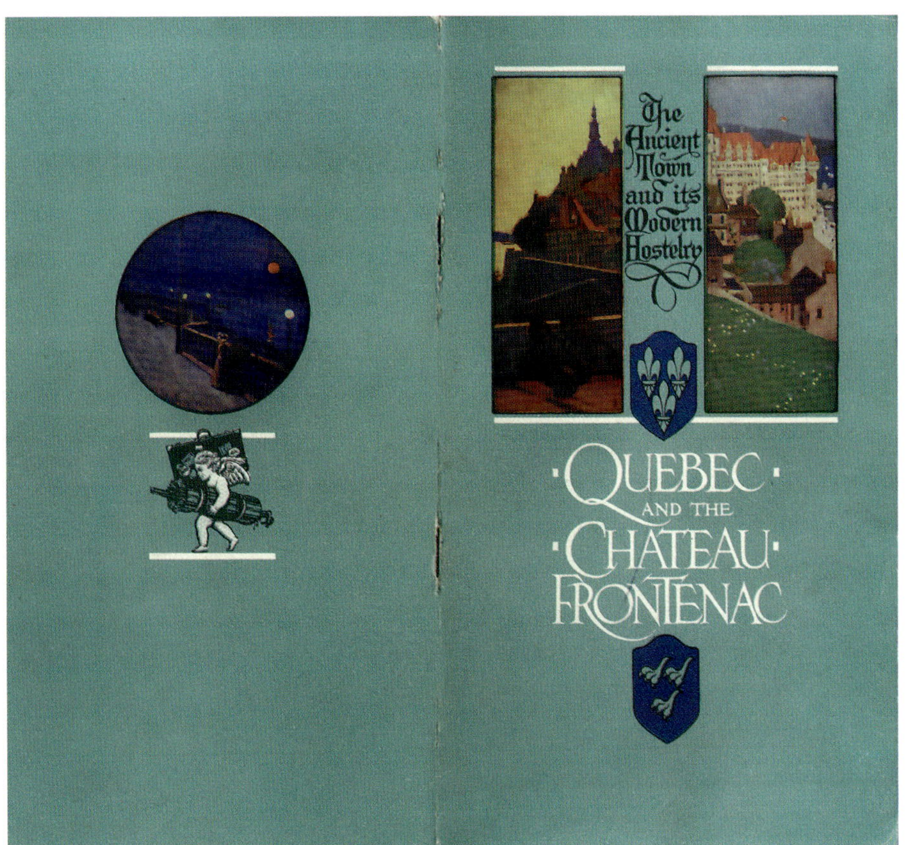

Pl. I:2 (a)

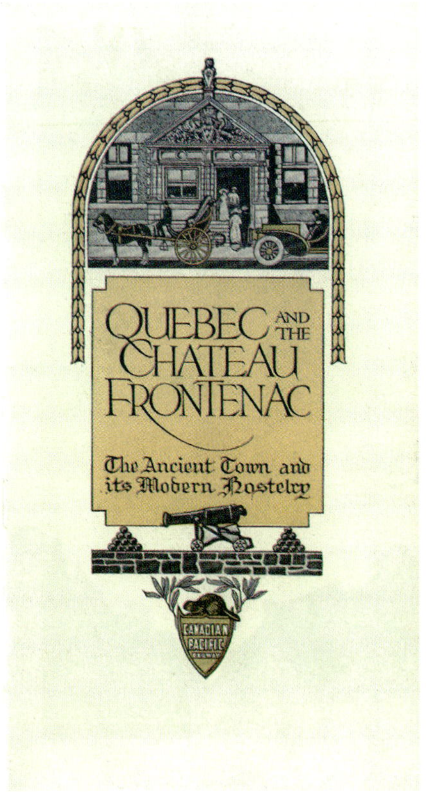

(b)

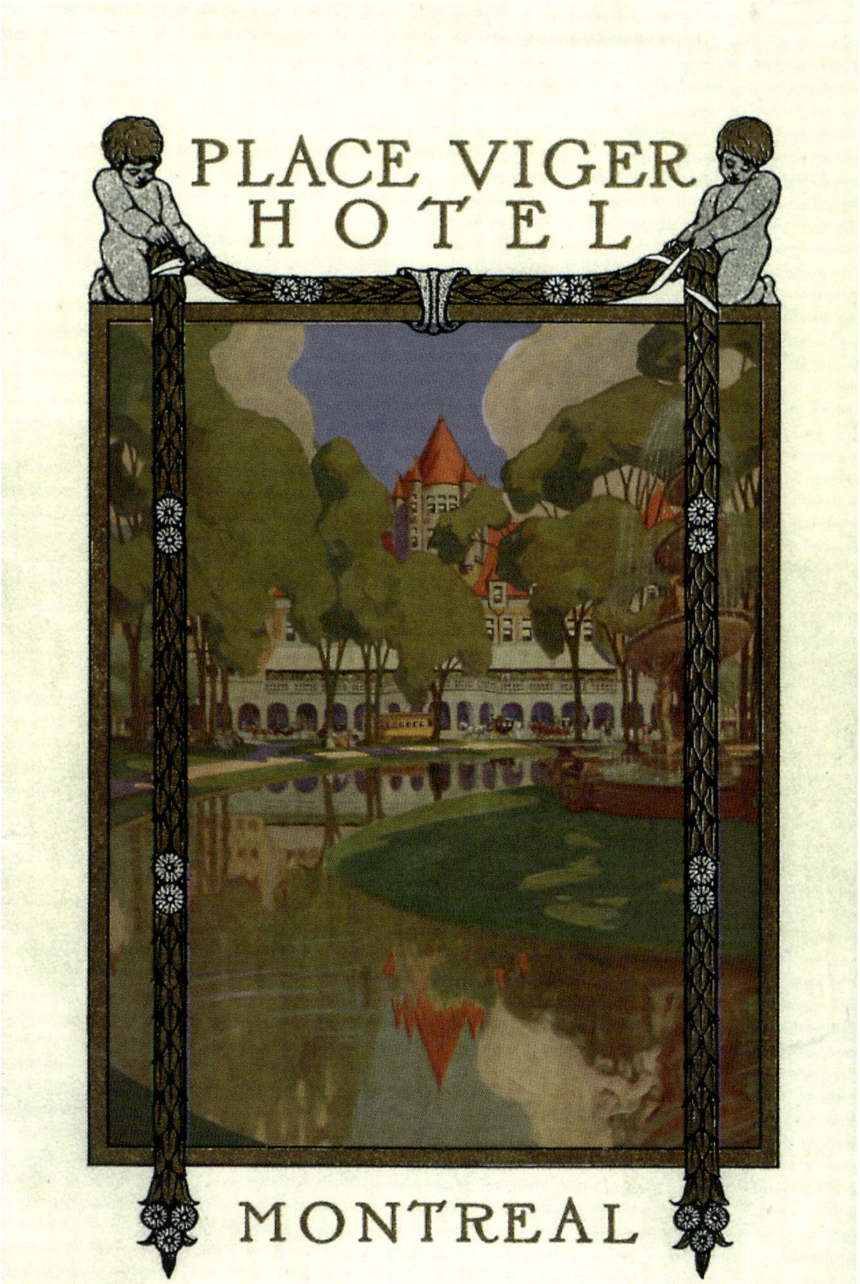

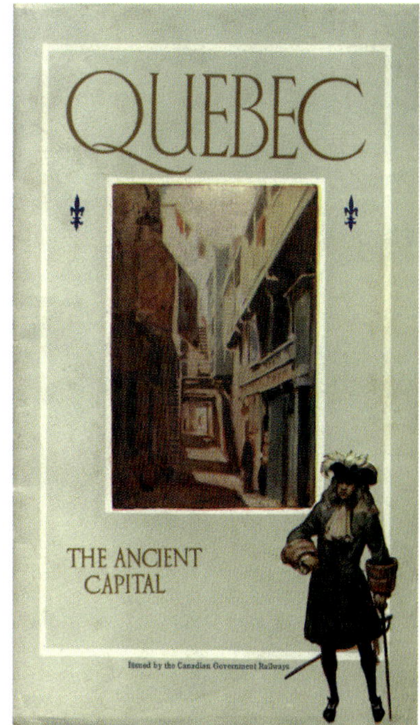

Pl. I:3

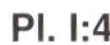

Pl. I:4

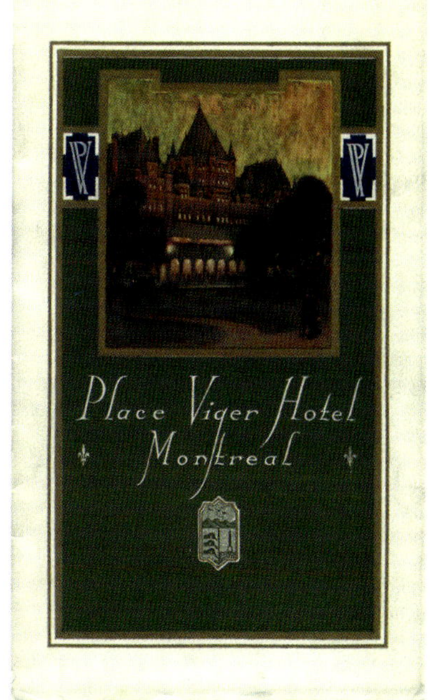

Pl. I:5

Colour Plates

Pl. I:6 (a-b). Front cover and envelope, *Lawrence Park Estates* (Toronto: The Dovercourt Land, Building & Savings Co., n.d. [1911]); RSc. *Note*: printed and engraved by Grip Ltd., Toronto.

Pl. I:7. Front endpaper and title page, brochure, *Lawrence Park Estates.*

Pl. I:8. Back and front cover, brochure, *Lawrence Park Estates* (Toronto: DLBSC, 1911); RSc. *Note*: printed and engraved by Grip Ltd., Toronto.

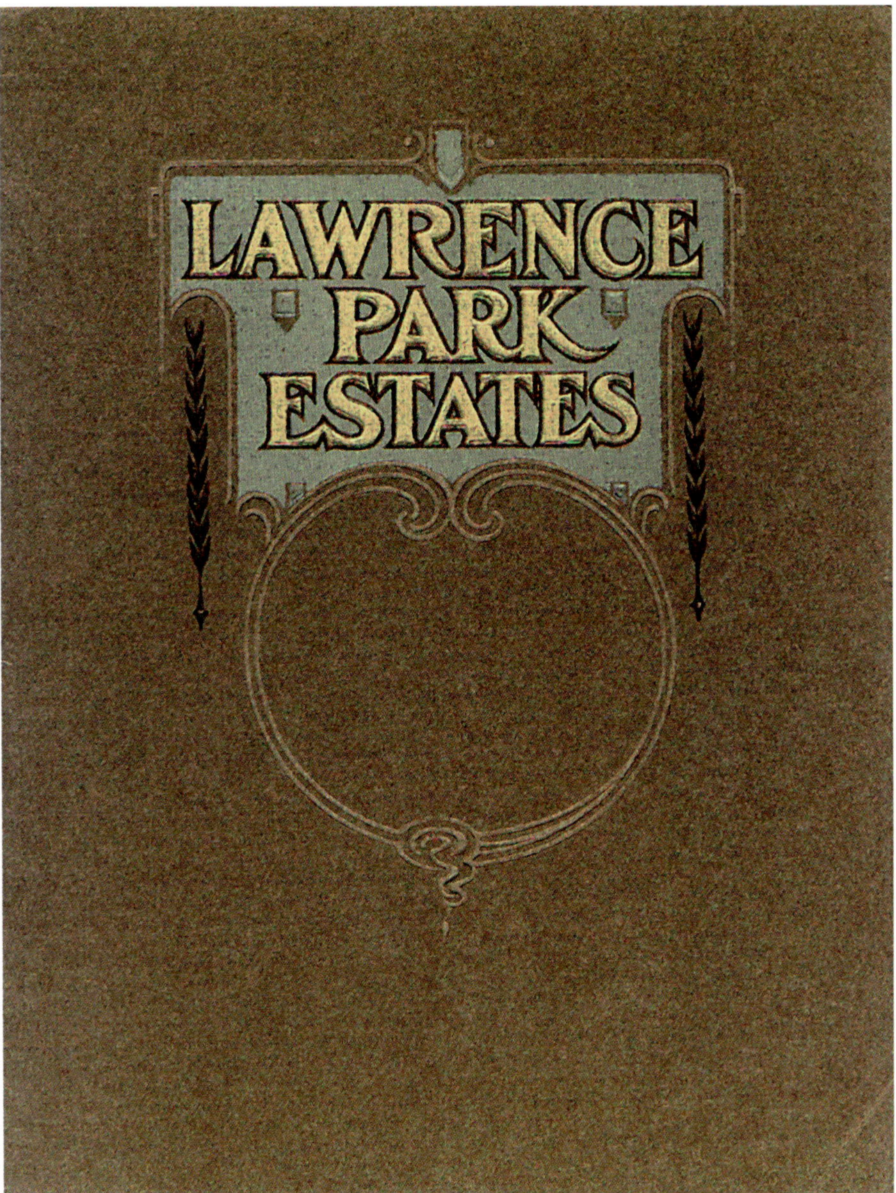

Pl. I:6 (a)

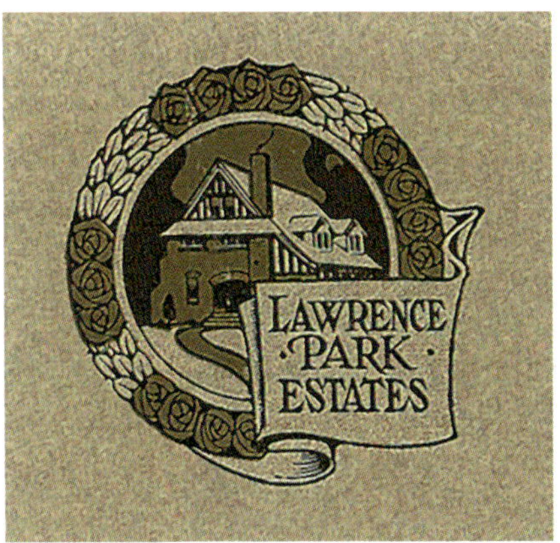

(b)

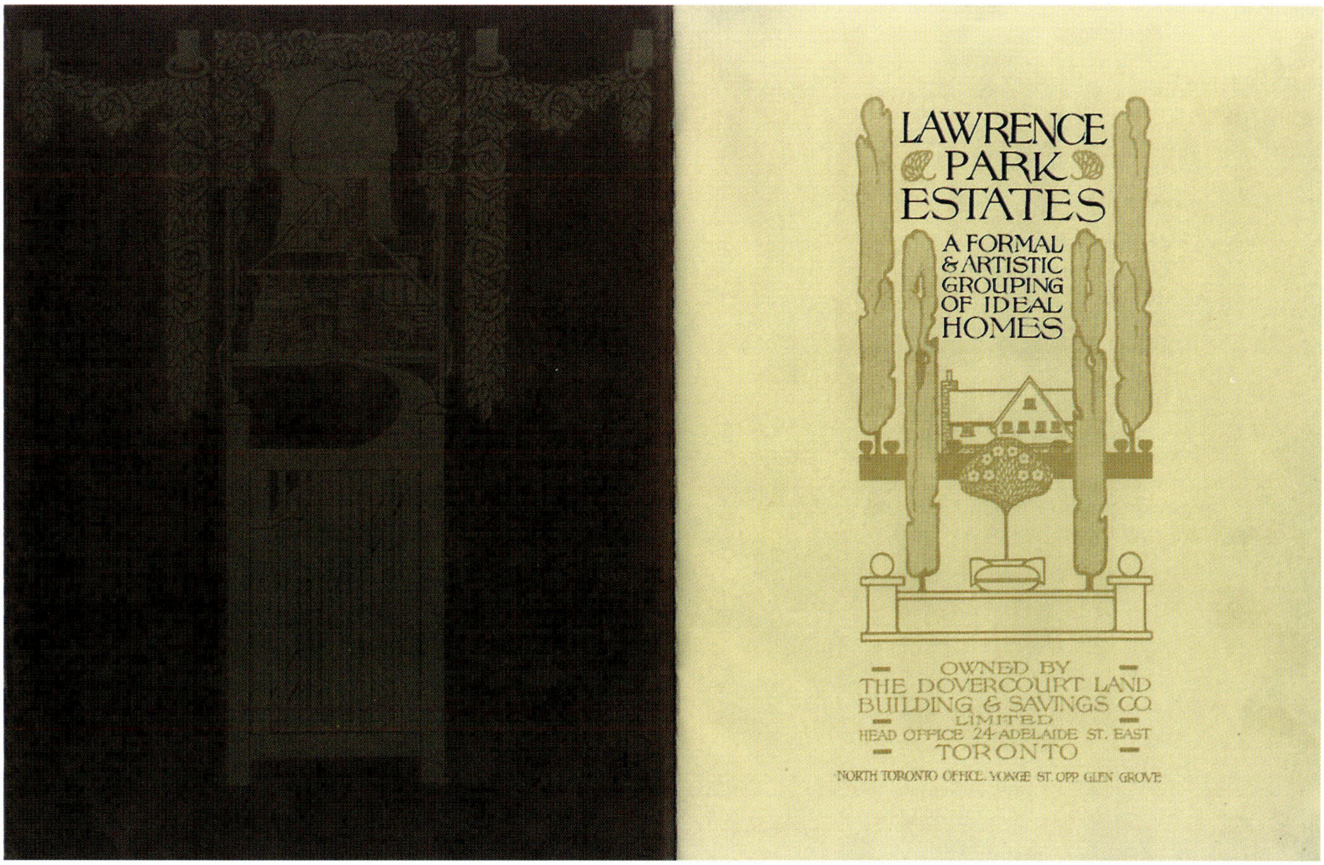

LAWRENCE PARK ESTATES

A FORMAL & ARTISTIC GROUPING OF IDEAL HOMES

OWNED BY THE DOVERCOURT LAND BUILDING & SAVINGS CO. LIMITED

HEAD OFFICE 24 ADELAIDE ST. EAST

TORONTO

NORTH TORONTO OFFICE. YONGE ST. OPP. GLEN GROVE

Pl. I:7

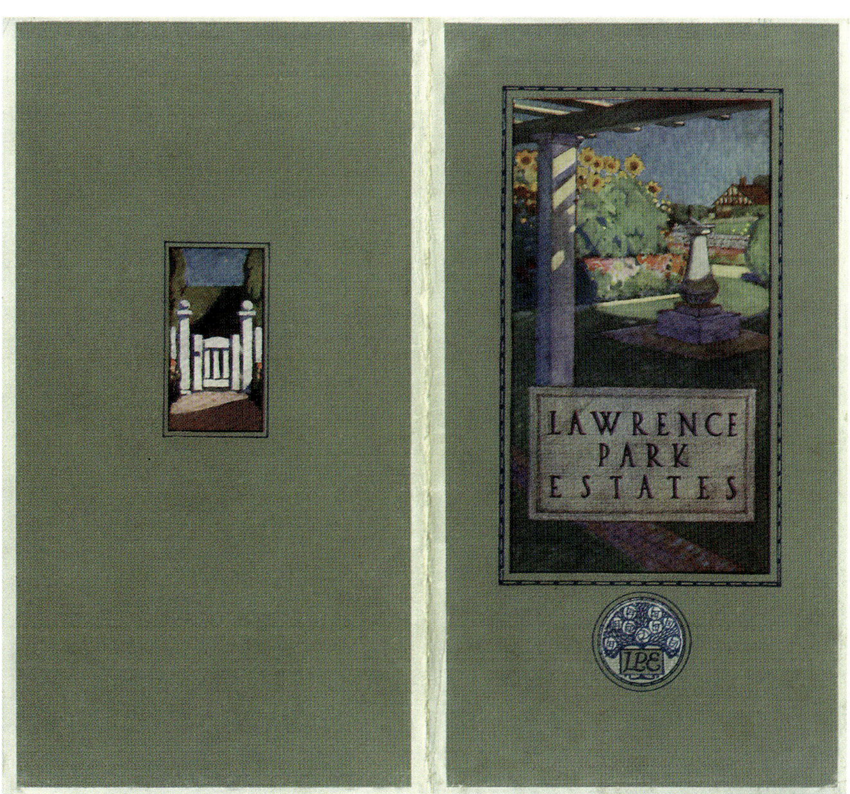

Pl. I:8

Colour Plates

Pl. I:9. Front cover, brochure, *Strathgowan* (Toronto: DLBSC, 1912); RSc. *Note*: printed by Rous & Mann Ltd., Toronto.

Pl. I:10. Front cover, brochure, *Northern Ontario* (Toronto: Clarkson W. James, King's Printer, 1922); RSc.

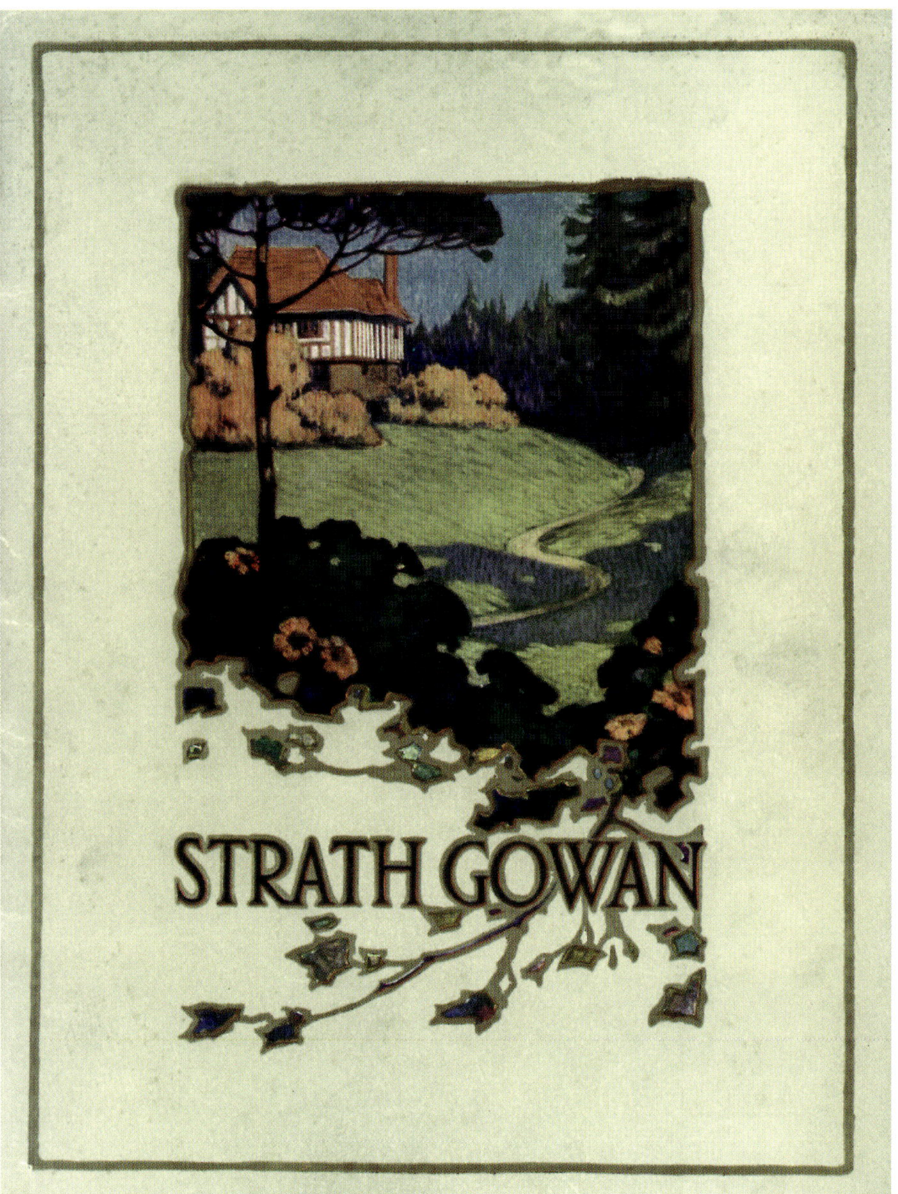

Pl. I:9

Northern Ontario
CANADA
CITIES, TOWNS, VILLAGES
Farming, Fishing,
Mining, Hunting
Lumbering, Touring,
Water Power
Printed by order of
THE LEGISLATIVE ASSEMBLY OF ONTARIO
1922
Northern Ontario
CANADA
A NEW LAND NEARBY
What Settlers say
of the Soil, Climate
Farming & Forest Life
Printed by order of
THE LEGISLATIVE ASSEMBLY OF ONTARIO
1922

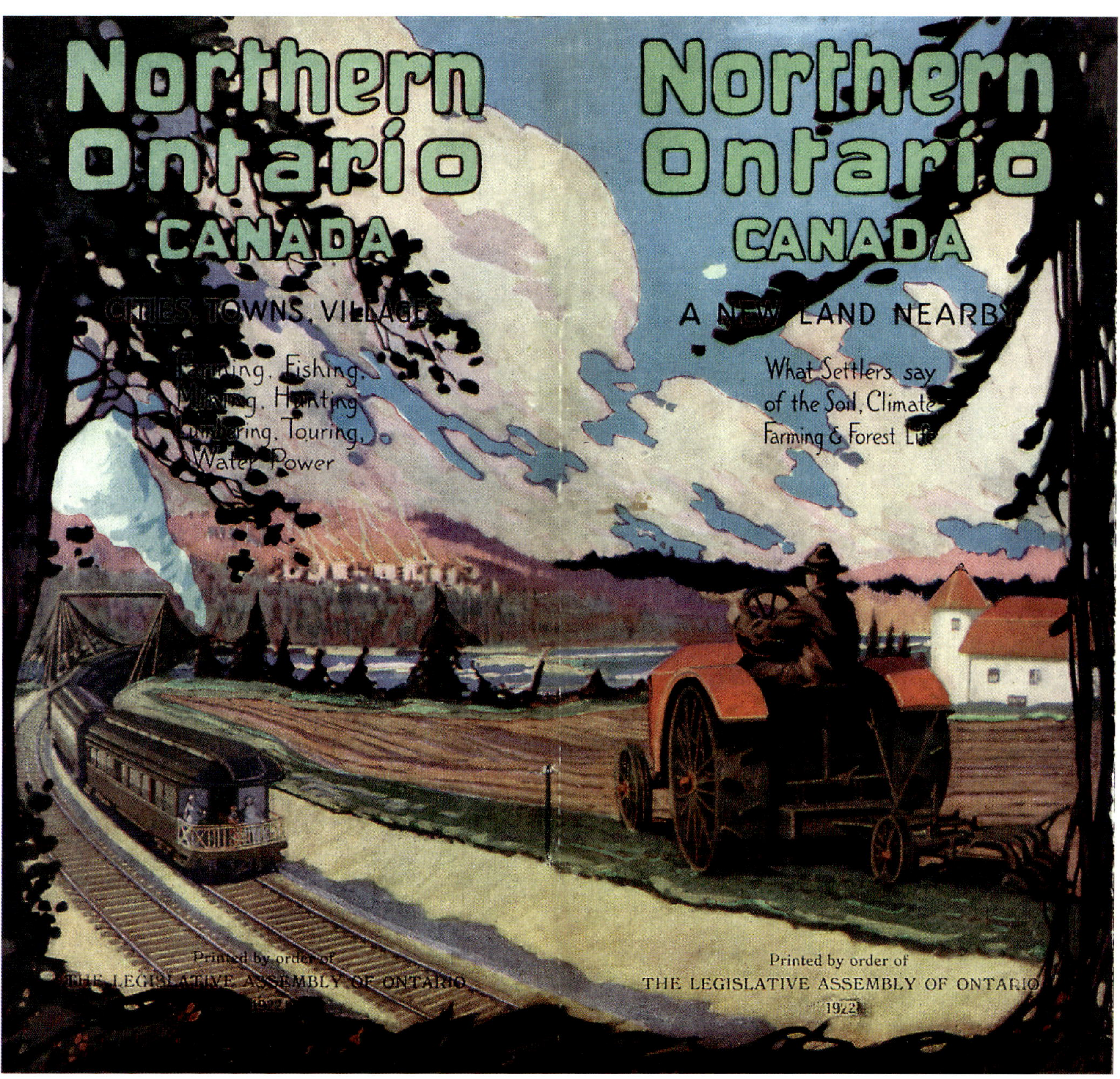

Pl. I:10

Colour Plates

Pl. I:11 (a-b). Front covers, catalogues, *The Sheridan Nurseries Limited* (Toronto: The Sheridan Nurseries Ltd., **a)** 1928; **b)** 1929); Archives, SNL.

Pl. I:12. Front cover, menu, *The Fathers of Confederation* (Montreal: Canadian National Railways, 1927); RSc. *Note: "A mare..."* lettering on coat-of-arms by TM, inset painting by Robert Harris.

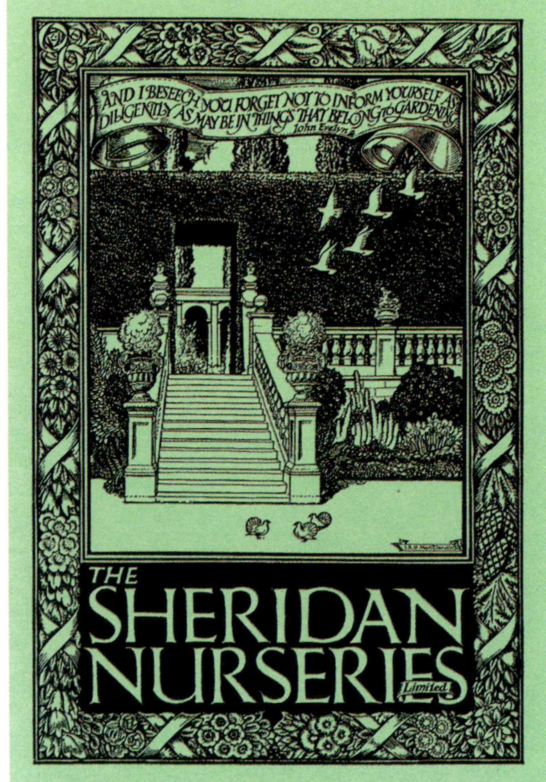

Pl. I:11 (a)

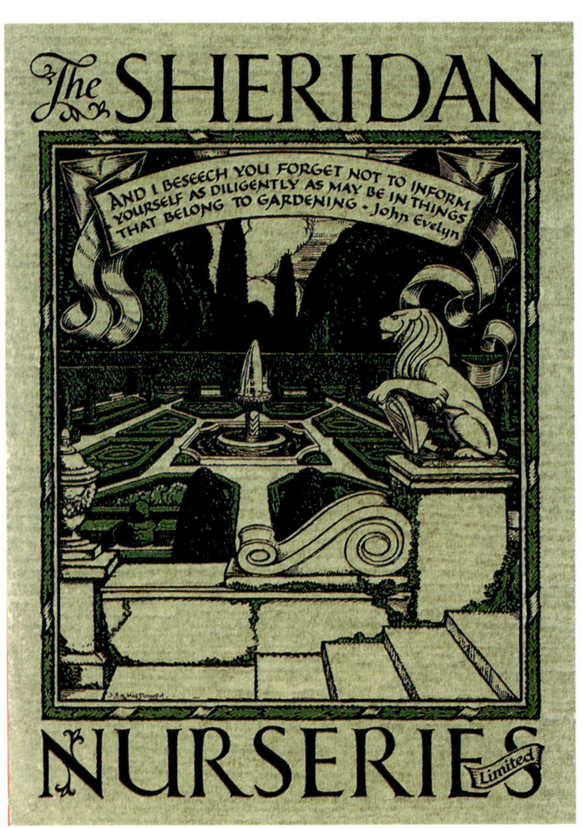

(b)

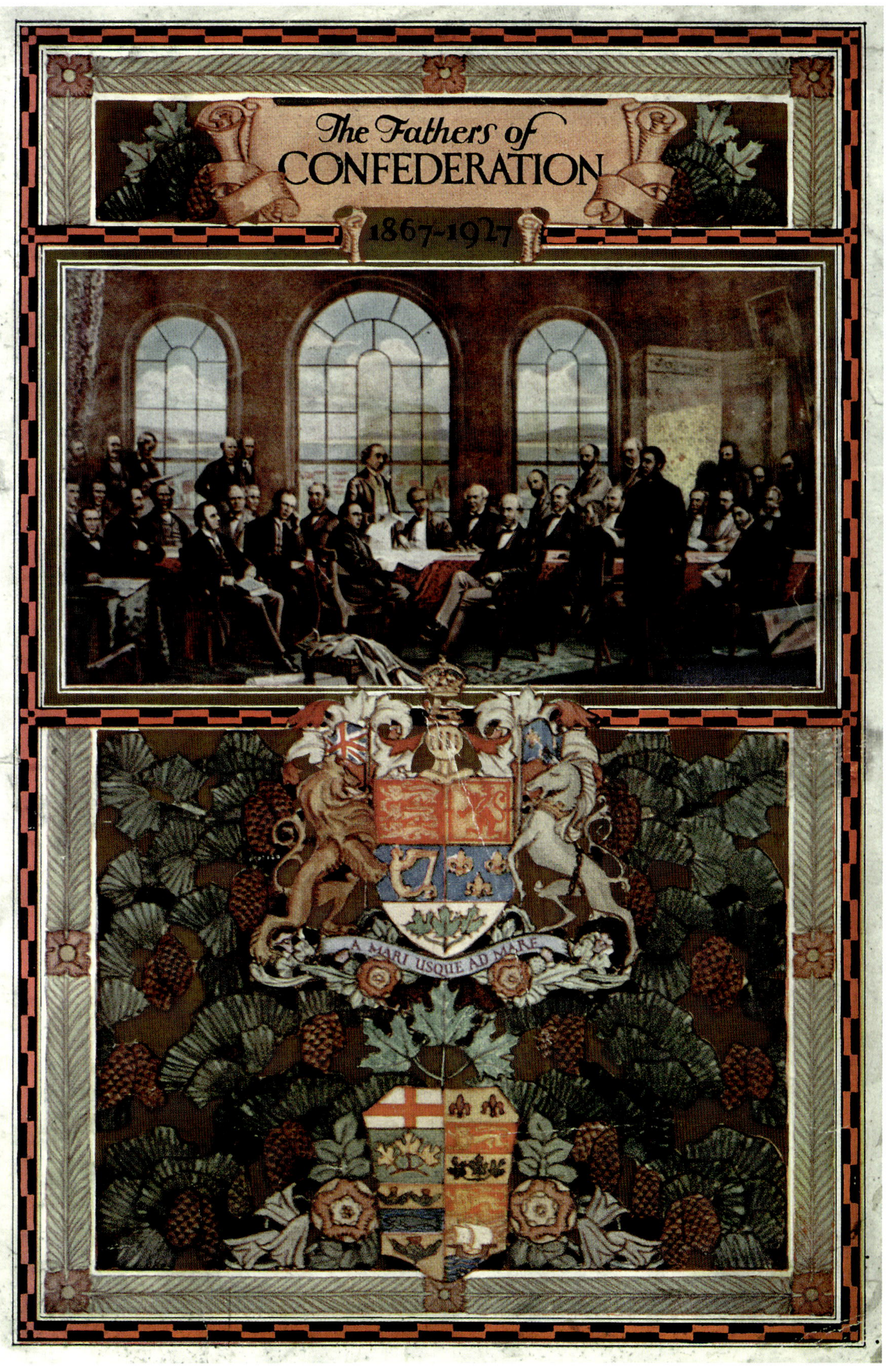

Pl. I:12

Colour Plates

Pl. I:13. Christmas card, *"The starre I see it come againe,"* designed and printed for Vincent and Alice Massey, 1922; RSc. *Note*: design based on JM's back-cloth for *The Chester Mysteries*, 1919, Hart House Theatre; for a photograph of the back-cloth and stage set of this production, see b&w section **II:7**.

Pl. I:14. Christmas card, *A Merry Christmas* (Toronto: Rous & Mann Ltd., n.d. [c. 1922-32]); HBP. *Note*: Rous & Mann launched the Canadian Artists Cards series in 1922 and discontinued it in 1932. The cards were originally printed by a French-patented stencilling process known as the Del Aqua Process (similar to *pochoire*), which proved too expensive; later cards were printed by the letterpress process.

Pl. I:15. Christmas card, *Lake O'Hara Camp* (Toronto: Rous & Mann Ltd., n.d. [c. 1927?]); HBP. *Note*: although this copy is inscribed under the image by TM, "Drawn by J.E.H. MacDonald 1930," it is inscribed and dated inside by JM, "Xmas '27."

Pl. I:16. Christmas card, *The Red Canoe*, serigraph (Toronto: William E. Coutts Co. Ltd, Painters of Canada Series, 1931); Hallmark Cards Canada/NAC (C-132242). *Note*: Encouraged by A.Y. Jackson, William Coutts, who founded his card-printing company in 1916, launched the Painters of Canada Series of Christmas Cards in 1931. They were printed by the serigraph (silkscreen) process by Sampson-Matthews Ltd., Toronto, with Franklin Carmichael supervising production.

II: Design for Culture

Pl. II:1. Poster, *Exhibition of Pictures Given by Canadian Artists in Aid of the Patriotic Fund* (i.e., *Canada and the Call, 1914*), 1914, offset lithography on paper (74.0 x 106.0 cm), printed by Rolph, Smith and Co., Toronto; HA-Cc; photo: John Porter. *Note*: based on JM's first-prize-winning design in poster competition sponsored by the RCA for its special *Patriotic Fund* exhibition, which opened at the Art Museum, Toronto Public Library, on 30 Dec. 1916, then travelled across Canada. For the gouache maquette submitted to the RCA jury, see b&w section **II:3**.

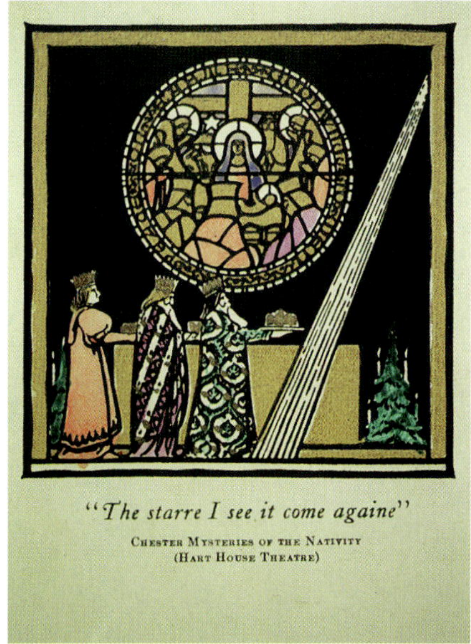

Pl. I:13

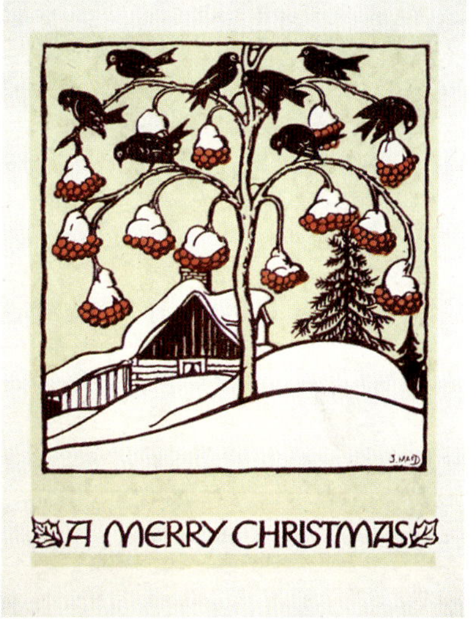

Pl. I:14

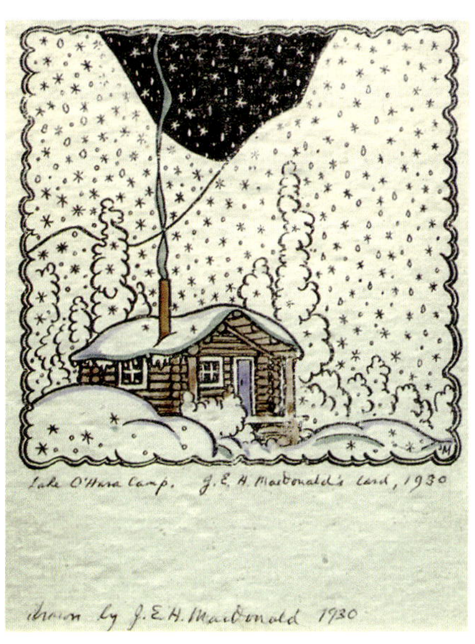

Pl. I:15

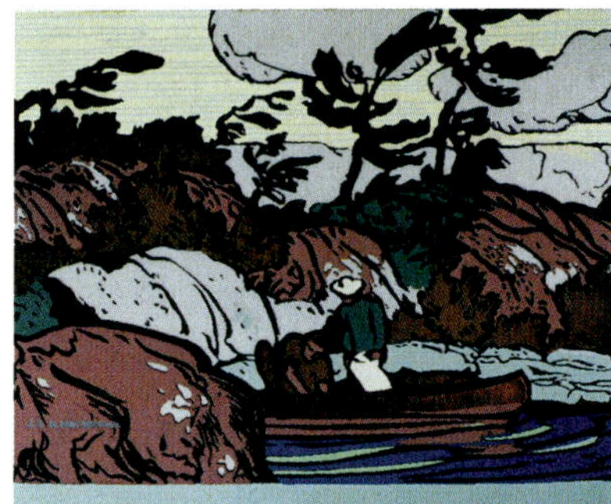

Pl. I:16

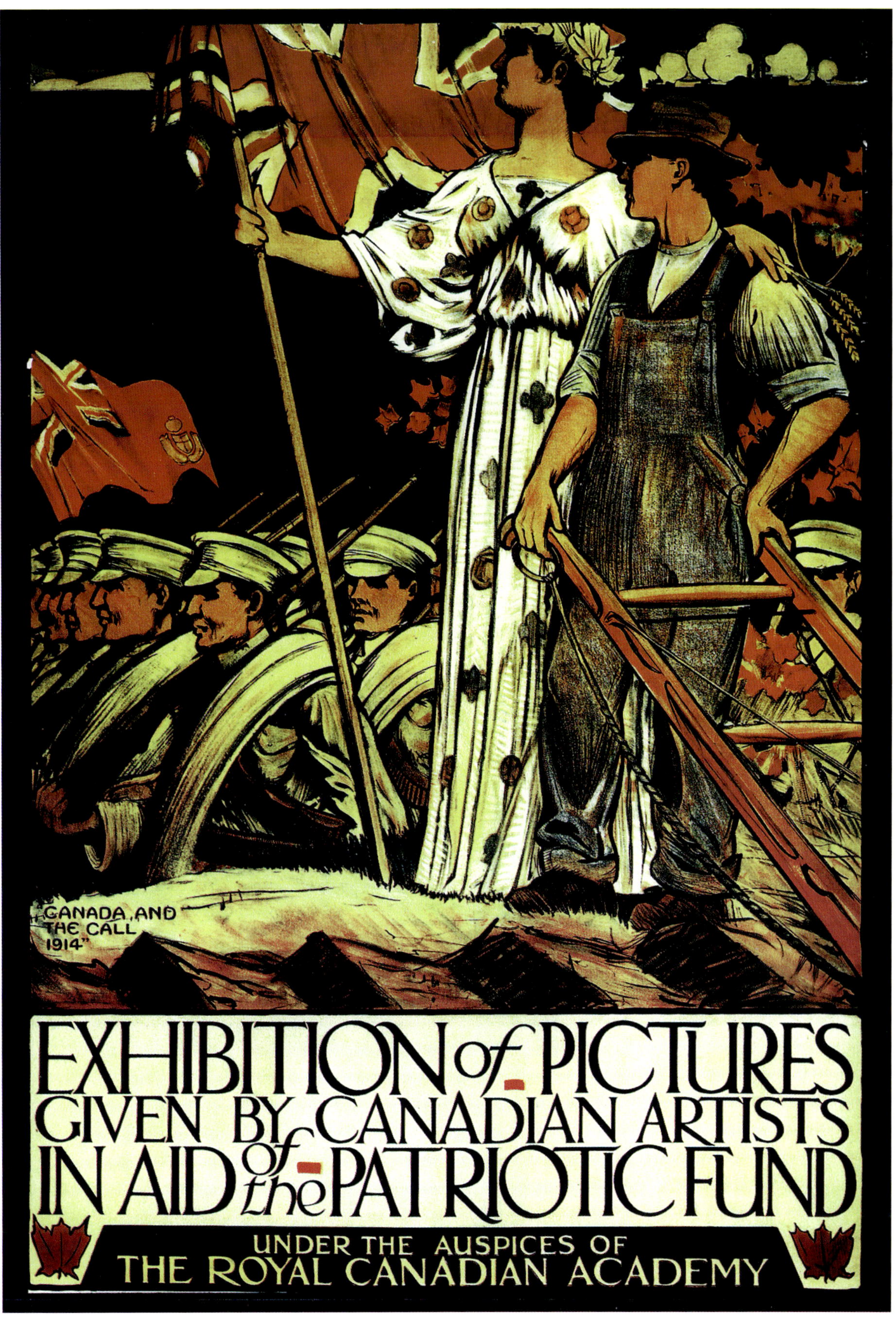
"CANADA AND
THE CALL
1914"
EXHIBITION of PICTURES
GIVEN BY CANADIAN ARTISTS
IN AID of the PATRIOTIC FUND
UNDER THE AUSPICES OF
THE ROYAL CANADIAN ACADEMY

Pl. II:1

Colour Plates

Pl. III:11 (a-b): Dust jacket, *Legends of Vancouver*, by E. Pauline Johnson (Tekahionwake) (Toronto: M&S [1922]); RSc. *Note*: issued in hard-back and paperback formats; the whale motif **(b)** appears only on the paperback issue (*verso*).

Pl. III:12. Endpapers, *Legends of Vancouver. Note*: for sketch for endpapers, see b&w section **III:20**.

Pl. III:13. Dust jacket, *Bliss Carman*, by Odell Shepherd (Toronto: M&S, 1923). *Note*: some lettering by TM.

Pl. III:14. Dust jacket, *Stories of the Land of Evangeline*, by Grace McLeod Rogers (Toronto: M&S, 1923); RSc.

Pl. III:15. Dust jacket, *Old Province Tales*, by Archibald MacMechan (Toronto: M&S [1924]). *Note*: map also printed as endpapers. Lettering by TM.

Pl. III:16. Dust jacket, *Lord of the Silver Dragon*, by Laura Goodman Salverson (Toronto: M&S, 1927); RSc. *Note*: lettering by TM.

B: Periodicals

Pl. III:17. Front cover, *Maclean's Magazine* (July 1917).

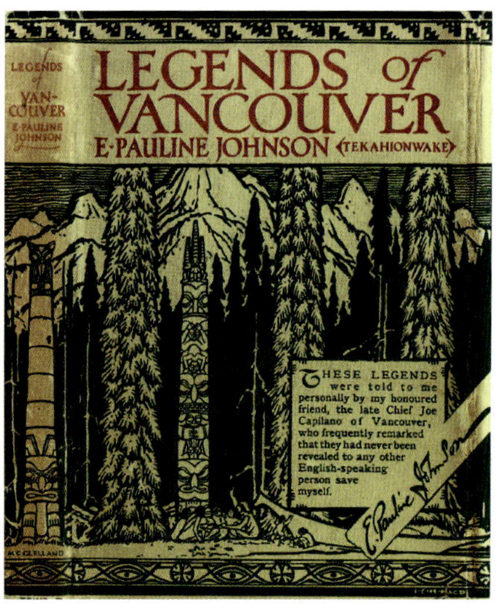

Pl. III:11 (a)

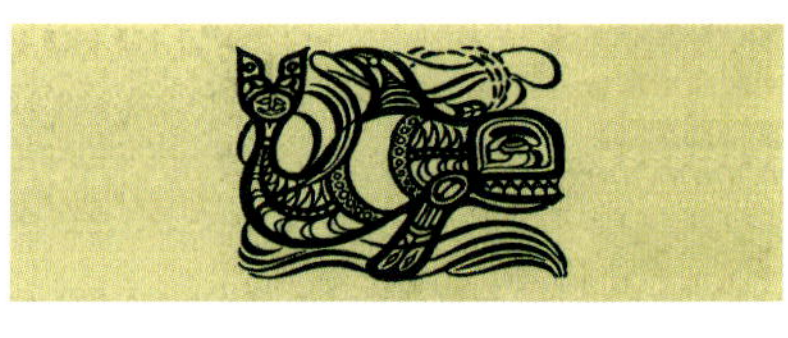

(b)

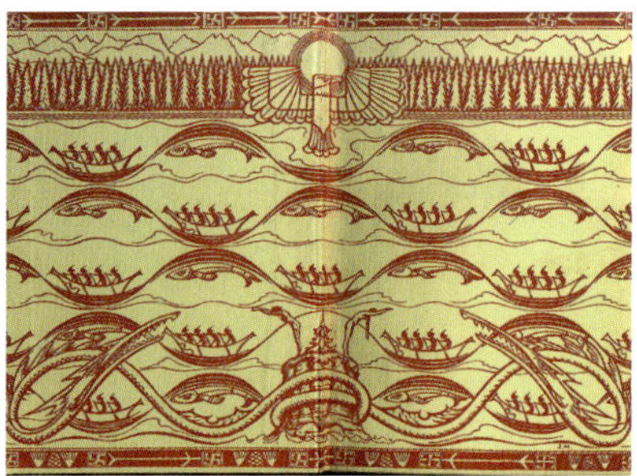

Pl. III:12

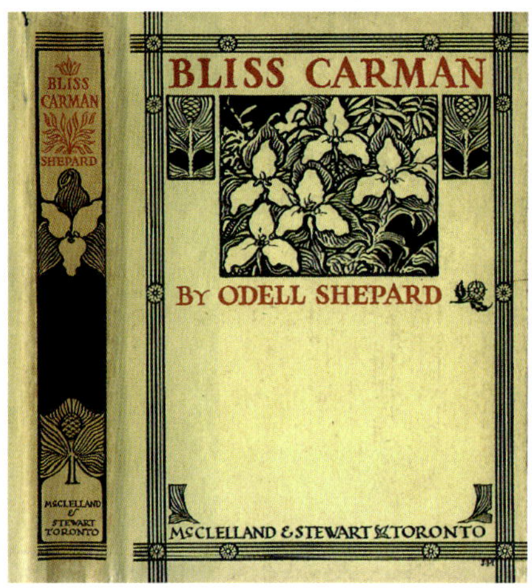

Pl. III:13

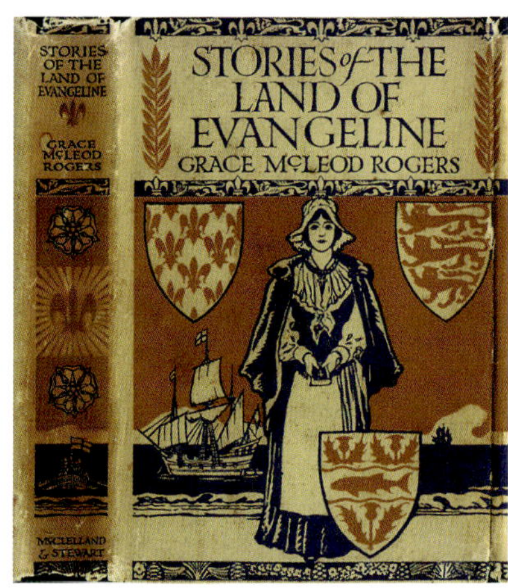

Pl. III:14

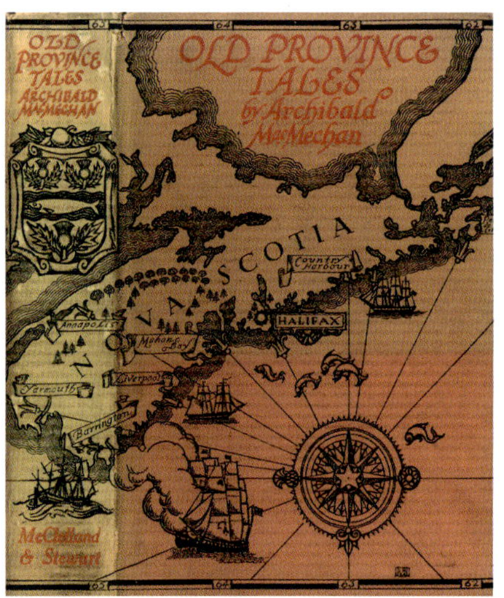

Pl. III:15

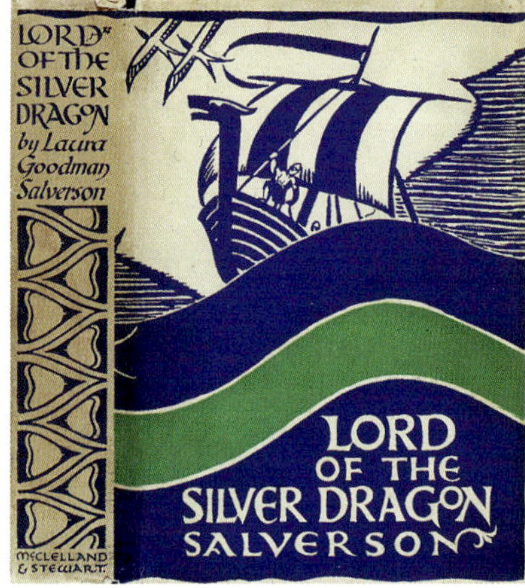

Pl. III:16

Fifteen Cents
MACLEAN'S
CONFEDERATION JUBILEE NUMBER
QUEBEC
ONTARIO
NOVA SCOTIA
SASKATCHEWAN
YUKON
MANITOBA
ALBERTA
PRINCE EDWARD IS
BRITISH COLUMBIA
NEW BRUNSWICK
1917
JULY
1867
THE MACLEAN PUBLISHING COMPANY, LIMITED, TORONTO, CANADA

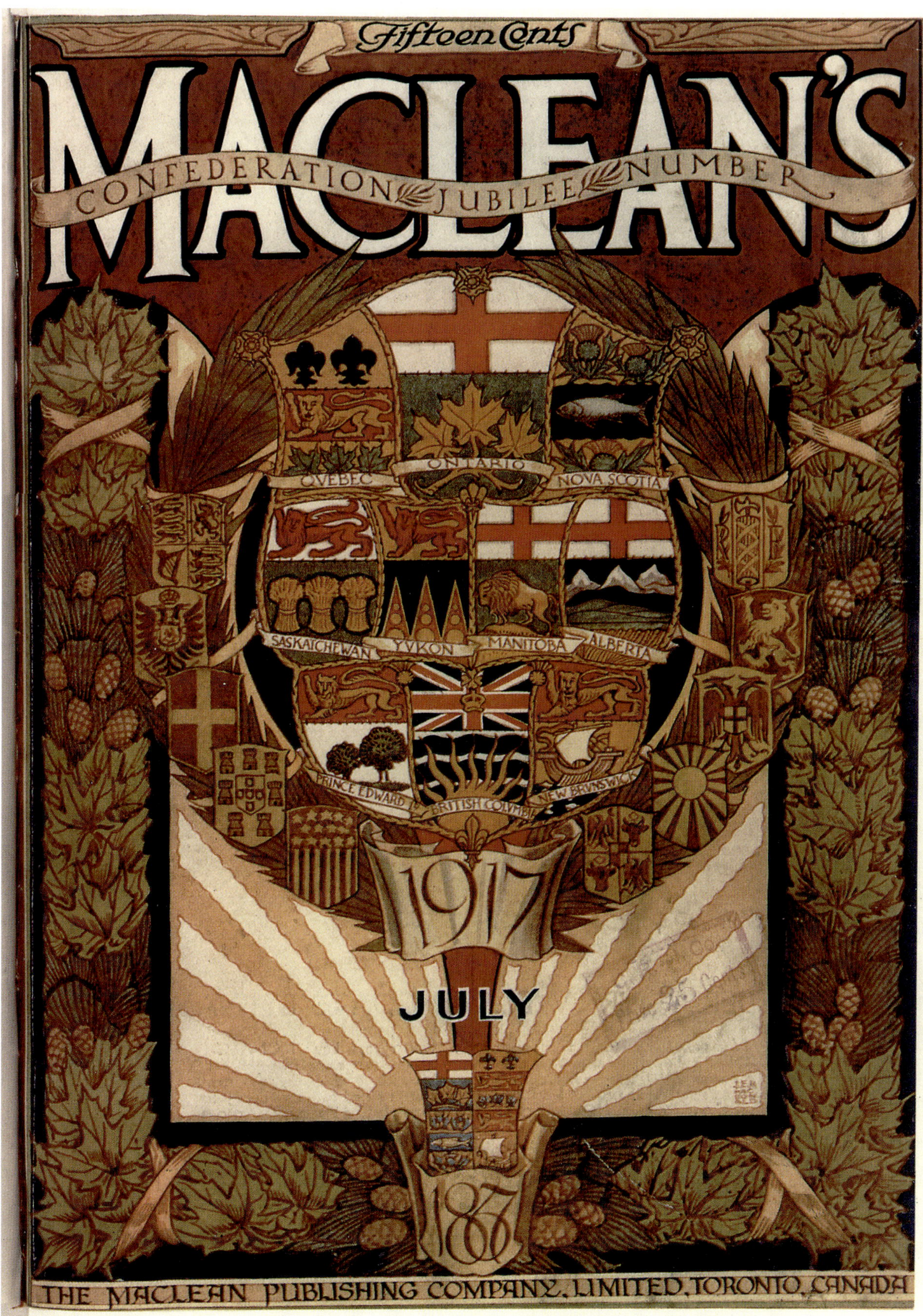

Pl. III:17

Colour Plates

Pl. III:18. Front cover border, *Maclean's Magazine* (May 1924). *Note*: inset painting by M.-A. Suzor-Coté.

Pl. III:19. Front cover border, *Canadian Homes and Gardens* (Oct. 1925).

IV: Lettering

Pl. IV:1. Leaf from *In Memoriam Robert Ford Gagen*, 1926, ink and watercolour on japan imperial paper (22.5 x 14.0 cm); NGC (acc. no. 28004). *Note*: memorial book commissioned by the OSA, 9 March 1926, in honour of the painter Robert F. Gagen (1848-1926), who taught at the Central Ontario School of Art and Design, and who joined the OSA as a foundation member in 1872. He was the author of "Ontario Art Chronicle" (typescript, n.d.). See b&w section **IV:30-32** for front cover and other leaves from this book.

Pl. IV:2 (a-e). *In Memoriam Charles Lewis*, 1926, ink and watercolour on japan imperial paper; private collection, Montreal. Photos: courtesy of Bruce Whiteman. *Note*: although dated 1 Sept. 1925, this memorial presentation address in honour of a deceased Eaton's of Canada employee was completed by JM in 1926, as indicated in the inscription.

Pl. IV:3. *Morning, Cathedral Mountain*, watercolour and coloured inks, in *On Account of Defries*, presentation album, 1924-26, coloured inks on wove paper (21.0 x 18.1 cm); NGC (acc. no. 17921). *Note*: presentation to R.L. Defries, ALC treasurer, on his announced retirement from that office, which he subsequently retained. For title page, see b&w section **VI:18**.

Pl. IV:4. *Let Us Reassure Ourselves*, 1914, coloured ink on parchment (26.0 x 21.0 cm); MSc. *Note*: quotation is from Mary Baker Eddy's *Science and Health* (Boston, 1875), the textbook of the Christian Science movement, of which JM's wife, Joan, was an adherent (as was Doris Speirs, to whom this exercise in calligraphy was given by TM after his mother's death).

Pl. IV:5 (a-b). Title page and leaf, *The Honourable Vincent Massey...*, presentation album, 1927, coloured inks on parchment (unfinished); ALC. *Note*: designed by A. Scott Carter, hand-lettered and illuminated by JM, for presentation to Vincent Massey, ALC president (1920-21), on his moving to Washington, D.C. to assume the office of first minister at the Canadian embassy (1926-30). Each page of the album contained a tipped-in contribution from an ALC member.

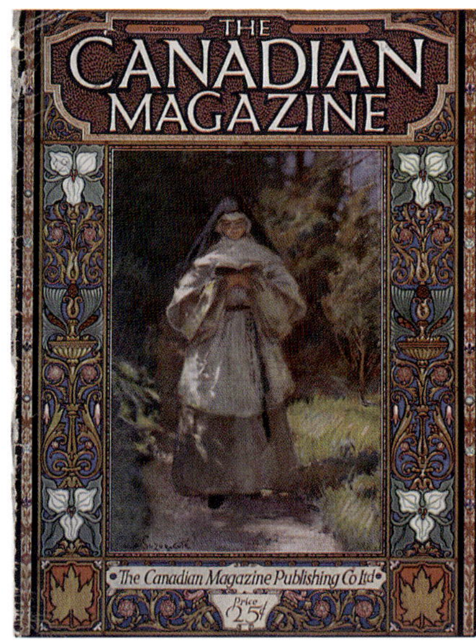

Pl. III:18

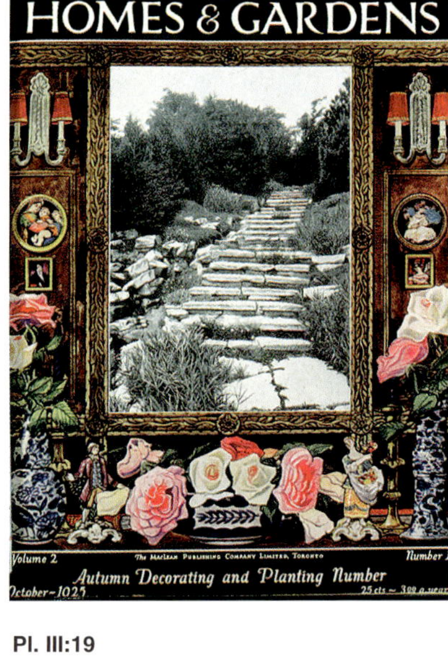

Pl. III:19

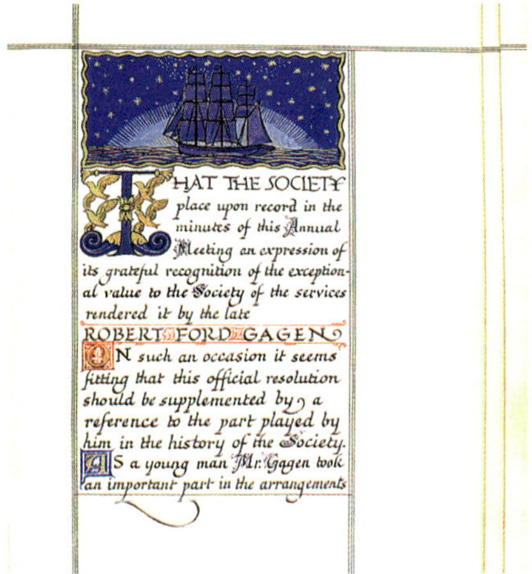

THAT THE SOCIETY place upon record in the minutes of this Annual Meeting an expression of its grateful recognition of the exceptional value to the Society of the services rendered it by the late ROBERT FORD GAGEN. ON such an occasion it seems fitting that this official resolution should be supplemented by a reference to the part played by him in the history of the Society. AS a young man Mr. Gagen took an important part in the arrangements

Pl. IV:1

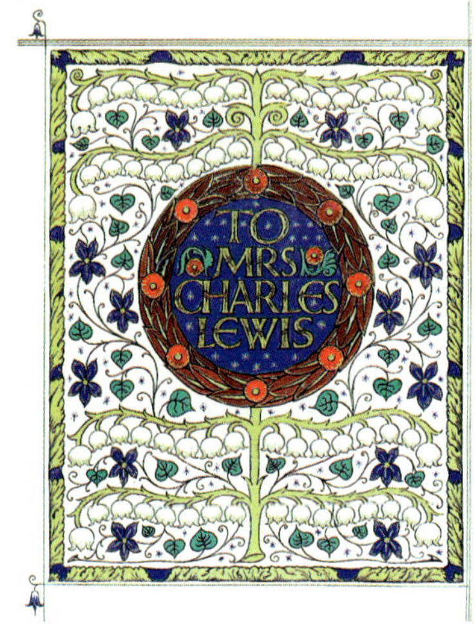

(c)

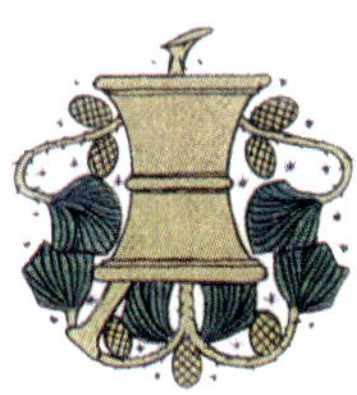

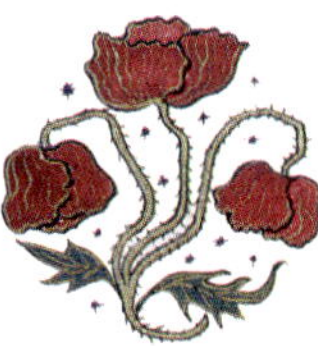

Pl. IV:2 (a-b)

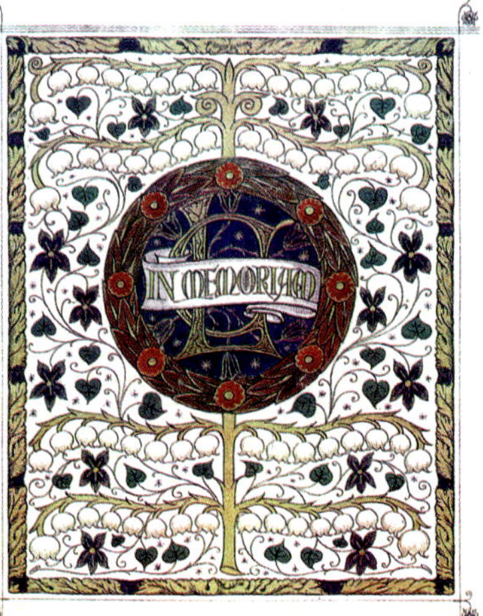

(d)

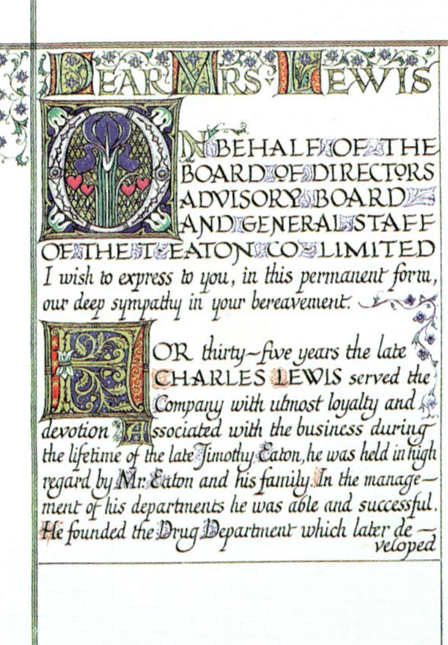

DEAR MRS LEWIS

ON BEHALF OF THE BOARD OF DIRECTORS ADVISORY BOARD AND GENERAL STAFF OF THE T. EATON CO. LIMITED I wish to express to you, in this permanent form, our deep sympathy in your bereavement.

FOR thirty-five years the late CHARLES LEWIS served the Company with utmost loyalty and devotion. Associated with the business during the lifetime of the late Timothy Eaton, he was held in high regard by Mr. Eaton and his family. In the management of his departments he was able and successful. He founded the Drug Department which later developed

(e)

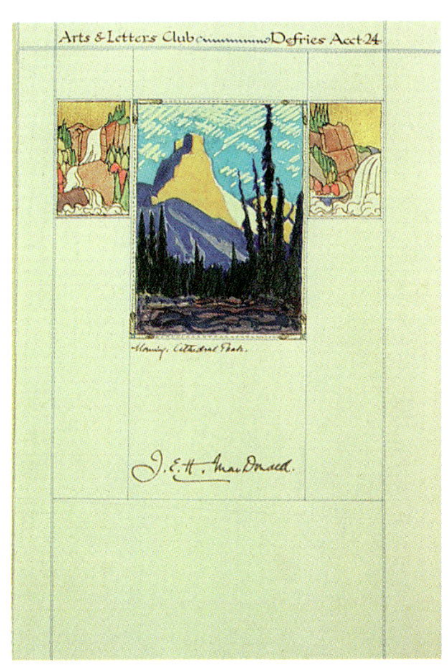

Pl. IV:3

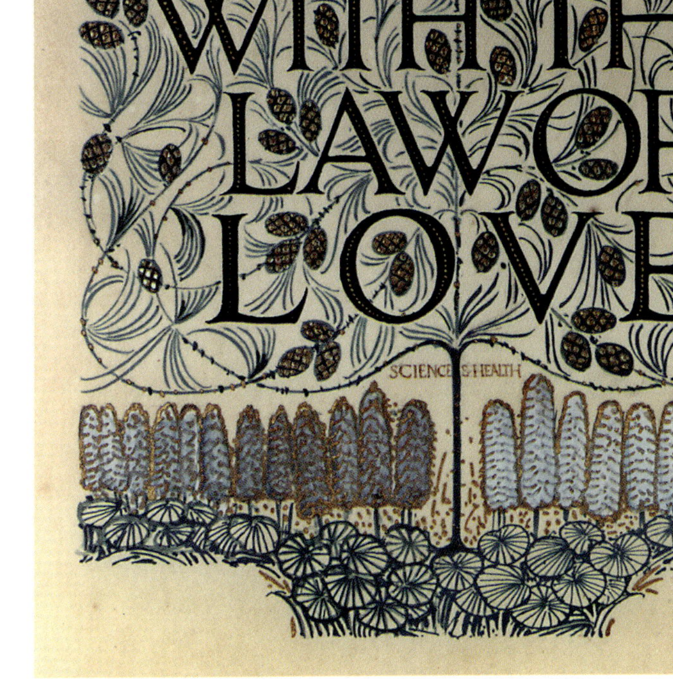

Pl. IV:4

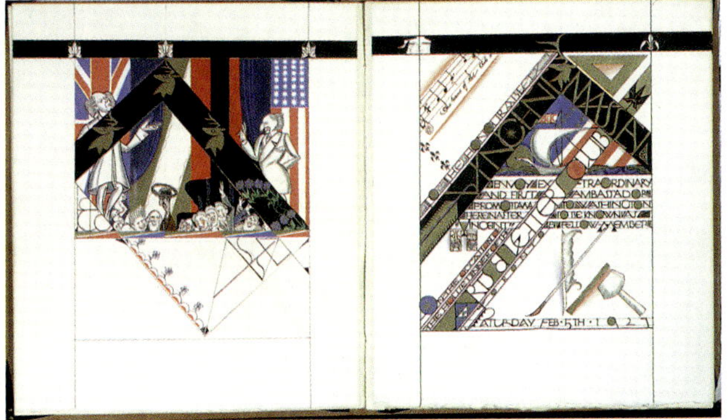

Pl. IV:5 (a)

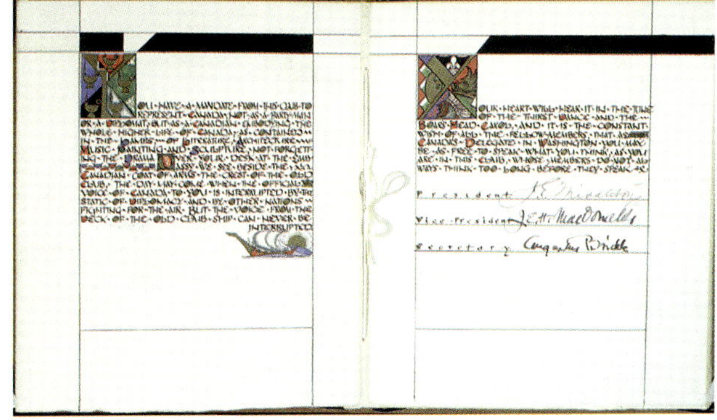

(b)

Colour Plates

VI: Designs for the Arts and Letters Club

Pl. VI:1 (a-h). ALC executive lists, **a)** 1908-09 (1915), **b)** 1909-10 (n.d., i.e., 1915-16?), **c)** 1910-11(1916), **d)** 1912-13 (n.d.), **e)** 1915-16 (1915), **f)** 1916-17 (n.d.; i.e., 1916?), **g)** 1917-18 (1918), **h)** 1920-21 (1922); coloured inks on parchment (various sizes); ALC.

Pl. VI:2 (a-b). "Punning" heraldic shields of ALC presidents Alfred T. Delury and Dr. James E.M. MacCallum (JM, *inv.*), 1920, oil on wood, repainted on masonite, c. 1940s, by Robert and Jim Hubbard; ALC.

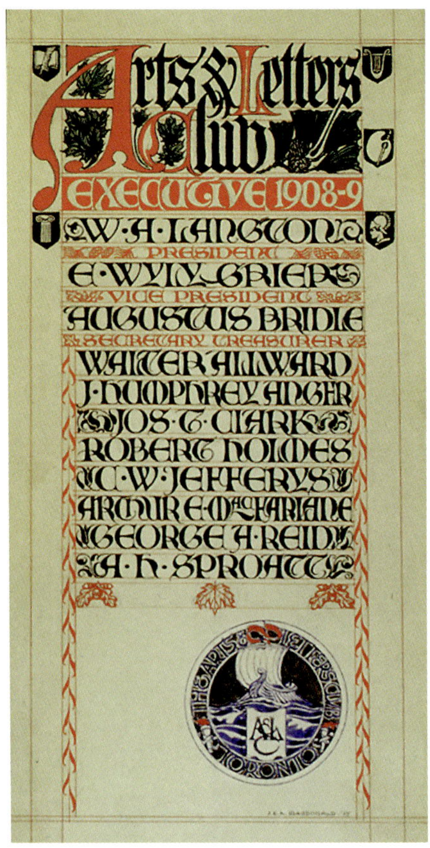

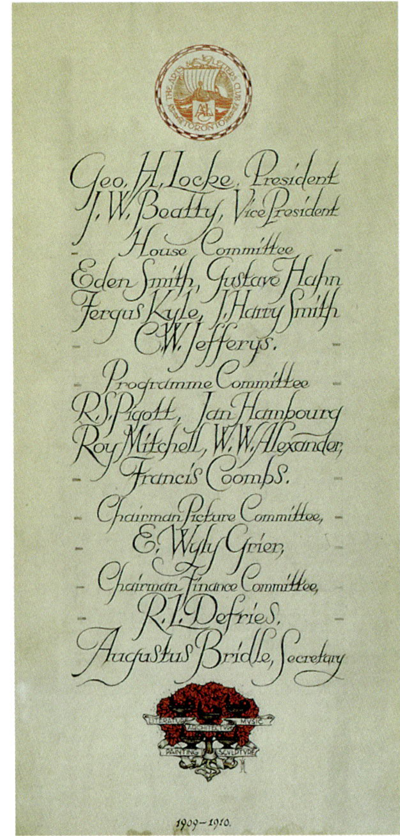

Pl. VI:1 (a)

(b)

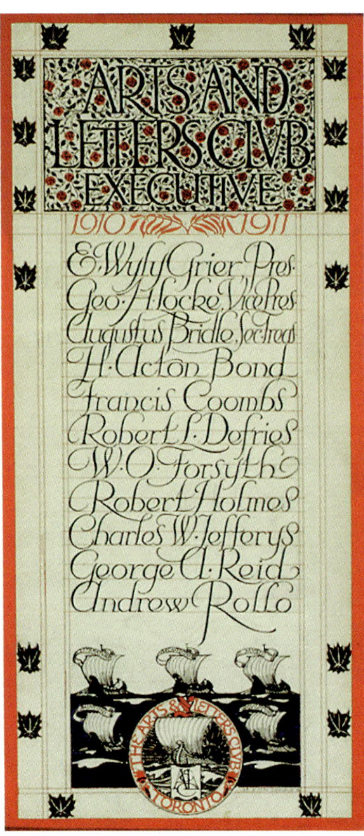

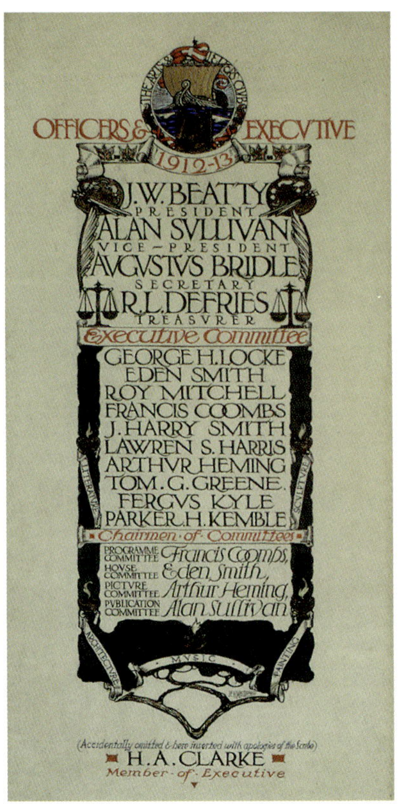

(c)

(d)

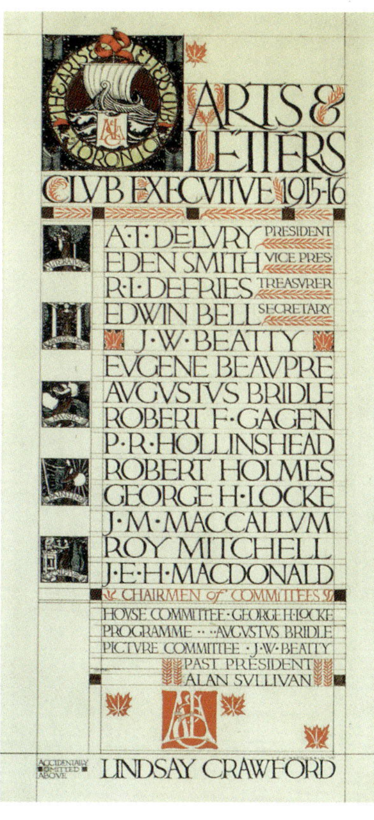

(e)

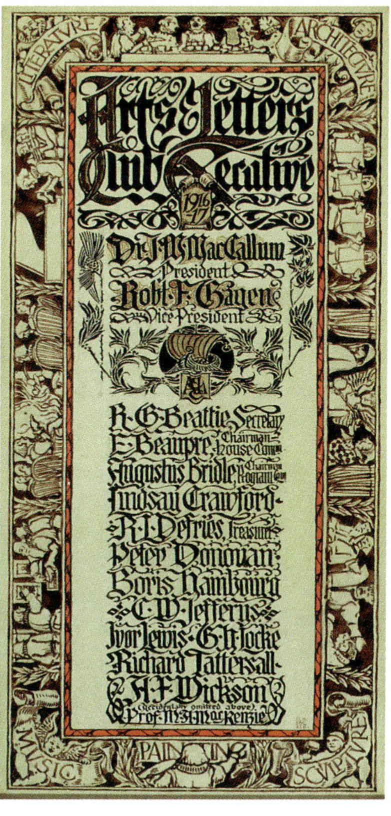

(f)

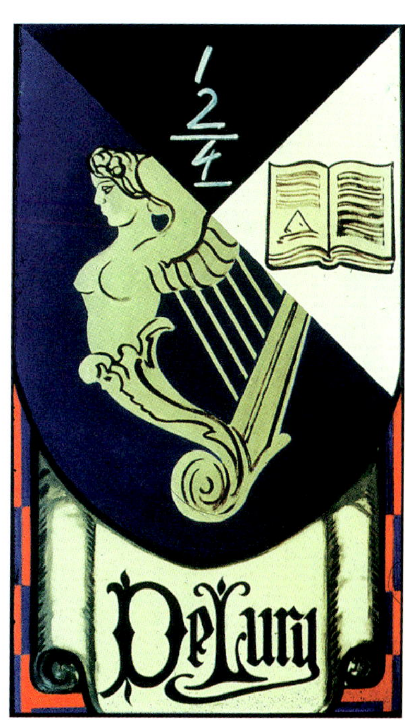

Pl. VI:2 (a)

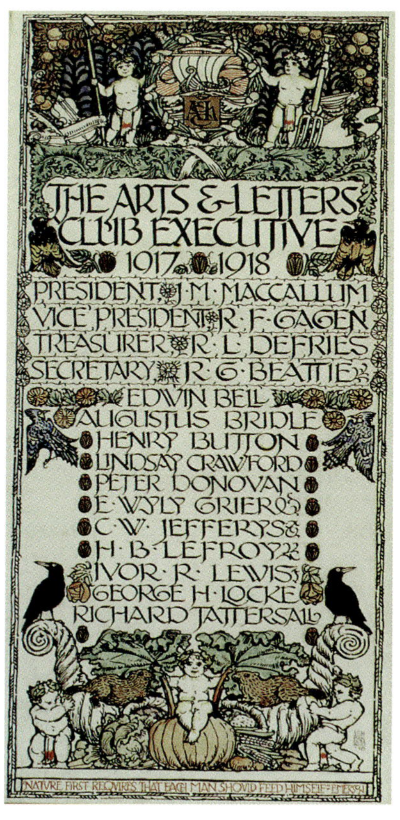

(g)

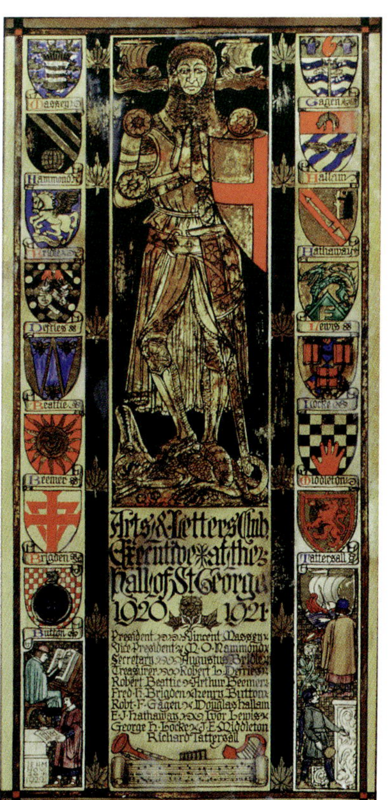

(h)

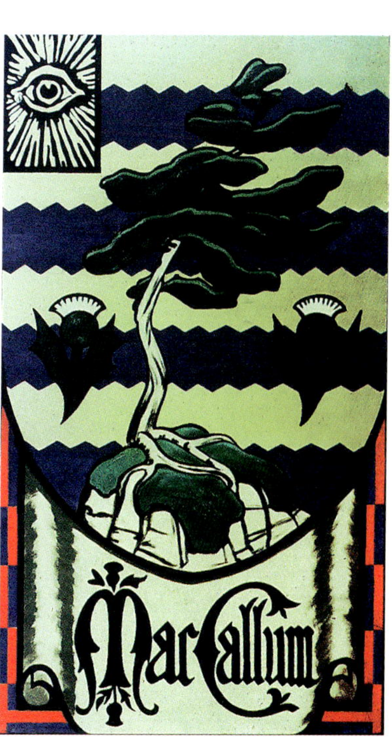

(b)

Colour Plates

VI:2 (c-h). "Punning" heraldic shields of ALC presidents and executive members (JM, *inv.*), 1920, oil on wood, repainted on masonite, c. 1940s, by Robert and Jim Hubbard; ALC. *Note*: painted to hang high on the walls of the new Great Hall of the ALC, 14 Elm St., Toronto. The 9 first presidents were, in chronological order, W.A. Langton (1908-09), George H. Locke (1909-10), E. Wyly Grier (1910-12), J.W. Beatty (1912-13) (see b&w section **VI:15**), Alan Sullivan (1914-15), A.T. Delury (1915-16) (see **VI:2 [a]**), Dr. J.M. MacCallum (1916-28) (see **VI:2 [b]**), Robert F. Gagen (1918-20) (see b&w section **VI:16**), and Vincent Massey (1920-21) **(c)**. The 8 executive members were, in alphabetical order: Augustus Bridle **(d)**, Henry Button, R.L. Defries **(e)**, Boris Hambourg **(f)**, H.B. Lefroy, Roy Mitchell **(g)**, Eden Smith **(h)**, and Richard Tattersall.

VII: Miscellaneous

VII:1. *A Friendly Meeting, Early Canada*, 1923, oil and gold metallic paint on canvas (185.7 x 150.0 cm); MTRL. *Note*: JM's 1st-prize-winning entry in the RCA mural-painting competition held in 1925 to promote the commissioning by builders and architects of murals on Canadian historical themes.

VI: 2 (a-b). *William John Alexander* and *Mavricus Hutton*, 1925, oil on board; University College, U. of T. *Note*: commissioned by students and alumni for the Junior Combinations Room of UC at the behest of Vincent Massey, these caricature portraits were part of 7 original pieces, of which only 4 remain. W.J. Alexander, LL.D. (1855-1944) was professor of English literature at UC from 1889 to 1926; the annual Alexander Lectures were named in his honour. The scoring through of the name of the British writer Charles Doughty (author of *Arabia Deserta* and *The Dawn of Britain*) is a mocking reference to Alexander's disapproval of a favourite author of fellow UC professor Barker Fairley, the founding editor of *Canadian Forum* and a leading supporter of the Group of Seven. The underscoring of "Browning" alludes to Alexander's authorship of *An Introduction to the Poetry of Robert Browning* (Boston, 1888). Maurice Hutton (1856-1940), appointed professor of classics at the college in 1880, became its principal in 1901, and was acting principal of the U. of T. in 1906-07. The date "1925" alludes to the publication in that year of his book *The Greek Point of View*.

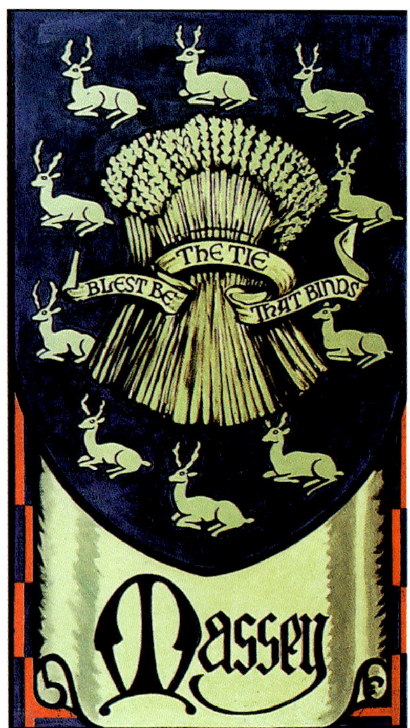

(c)

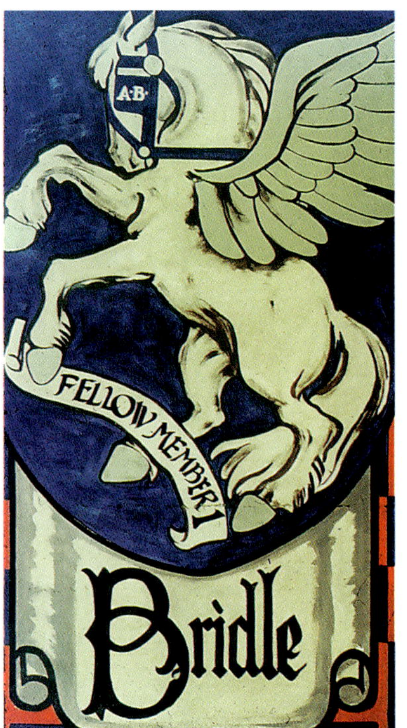

(d)

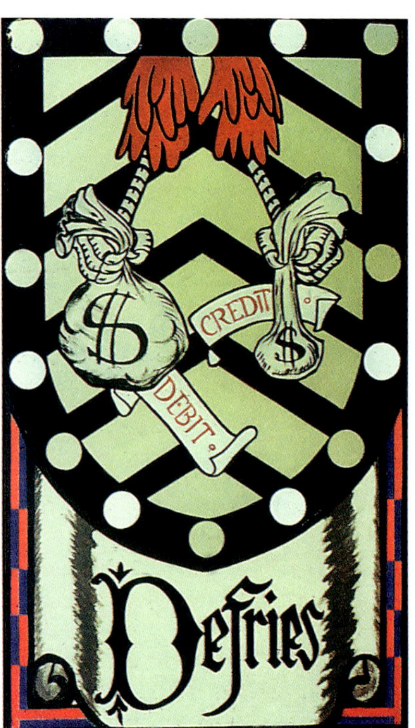

(e)

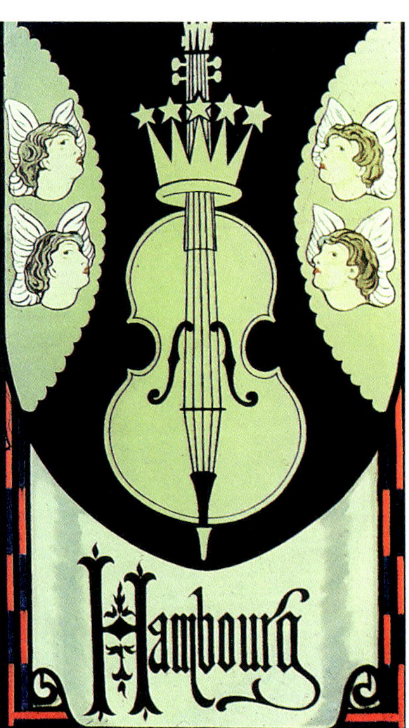

(f)

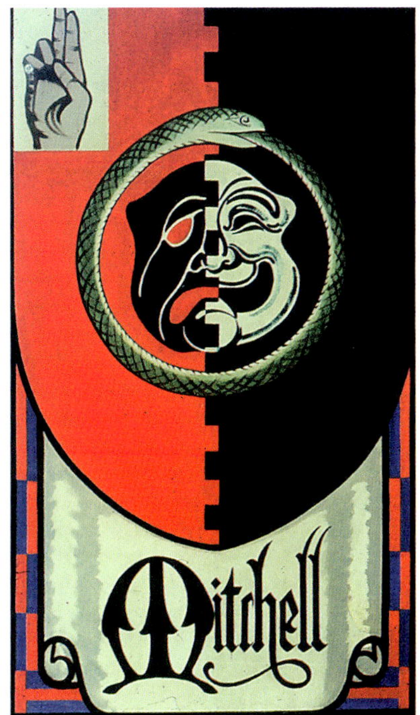

(g)

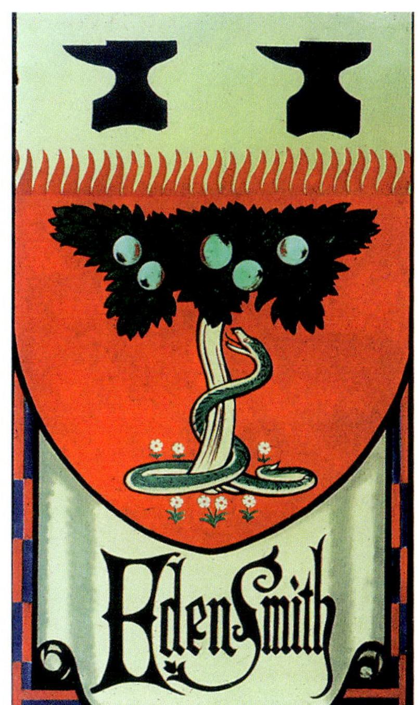

(h)

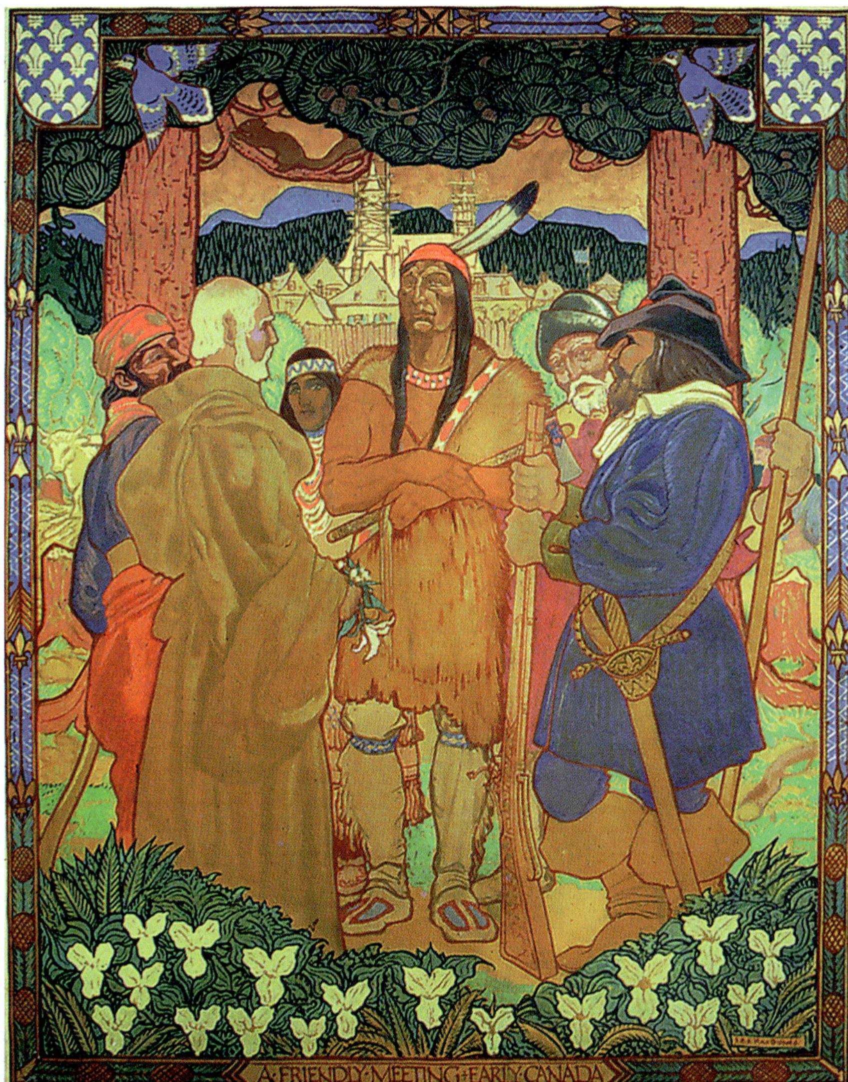

Pl. VII:1

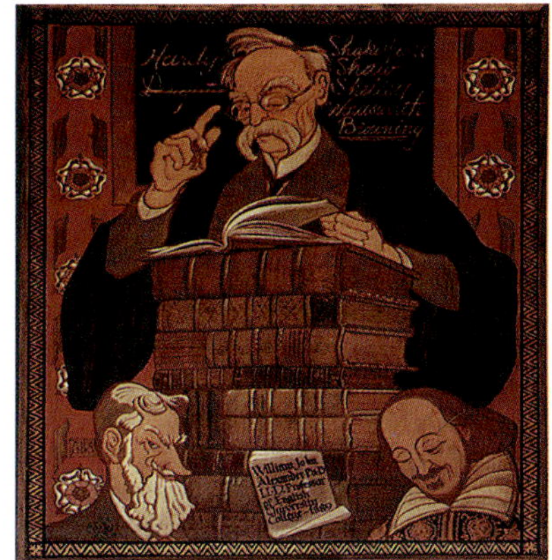

Pl. VII:2 (a)

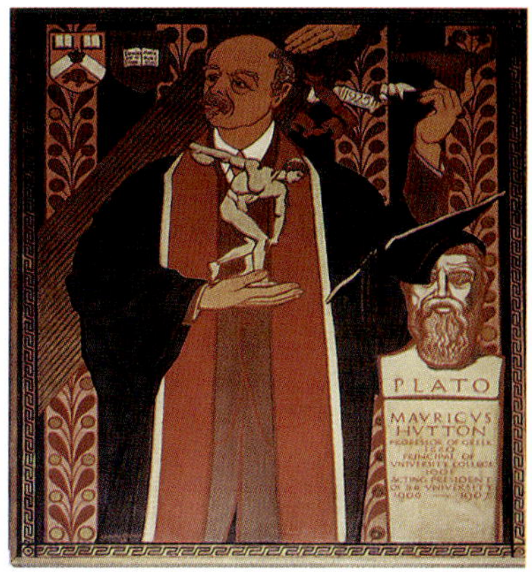

(b)

Design for Commerce

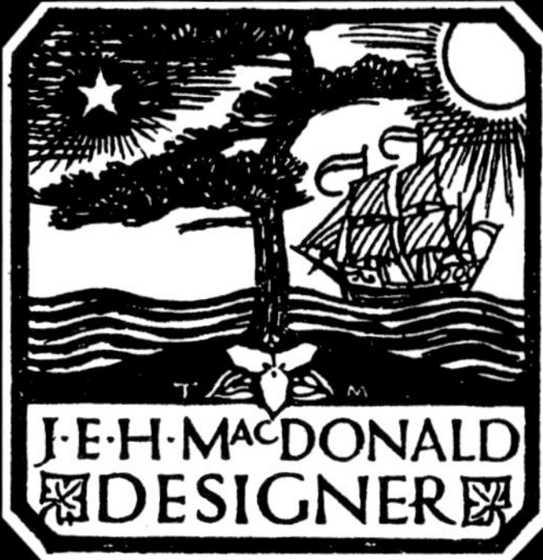

I: Design for Commerce

I:1 (a-c). Advertisement illustrations for King Radiator Co., *Construction* 2 (a: July 1909; b: Aug. 1909; c: Sept. 1909).

I:2. Poster, *The Atlantic Royals* (Montreal: CNS, n.d. [c. 1910]); reproduced in *Complete Course of Instruction, Commercial Design, Lesson II* (Toronto: SCS, 1910).

I:3. Endpapers, brochure, *The Atlantic Royals* (Montreal: CNS, n.d. [c. 1910]); RSc. *Note*: printed and engraved by Grip Ltd., Toronto. For title page and front cover, see colour plates **Pl. I:1-2**.

I:4. Half-title page, brochure, *The Atlantic Royals*.

I:5. Vignette, brochure, *The Atlantic Royals*.

I:6. Title page, brochure, *Chateau Frontenac and Old Quebec* (Montreal: CPR, n.d. [1910?]); RSc. *Note*: in 1910, at the Applied Arts Gallery, CNE, JM exhibited 2 works entitled *Chateau Frontenac*, and 2 "decorative paintings" for CPR hotel brochure covers.

I:7. Title page, brochure, *Quebec, The Ancient Capital* (Moncton, N.B.: CGR, n.d. [c. 1910s], 2nd ed.). *Note*: inset pen-and-ink illustration by C.W. Jefferys.

I:8. Decorative borders, *The "Ocean Limited,"* in brochure, *Quebec, The Ancient Capital*. *Note*: the inset colour illustration is a composite of a retouched photograph and painted artwork, possibly by C.W. Jefferys and/or JM.

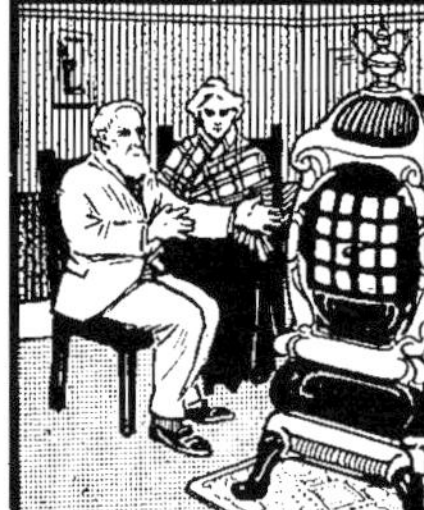

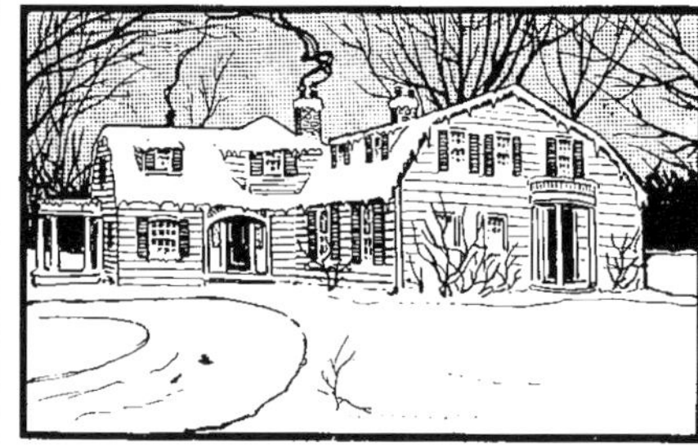

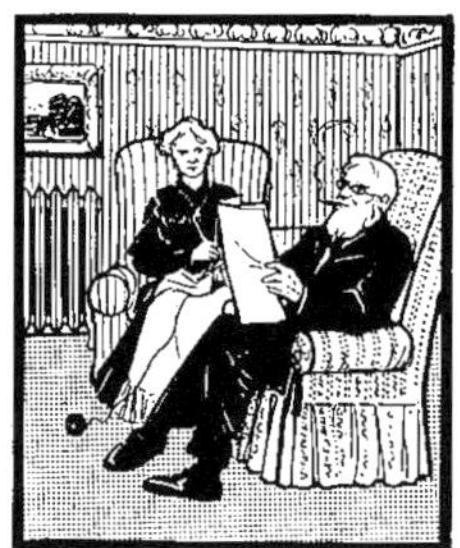

I:1 (a)

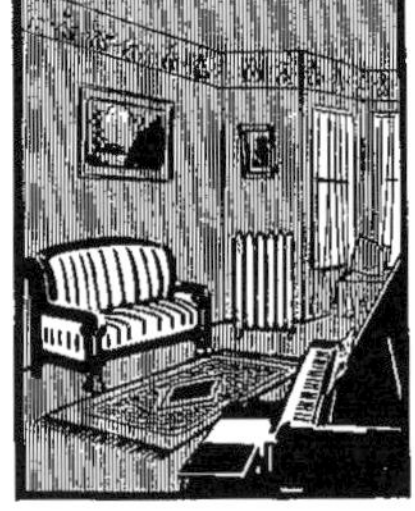

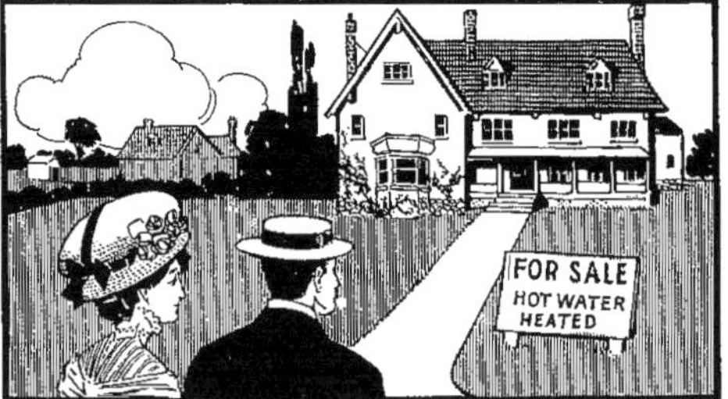

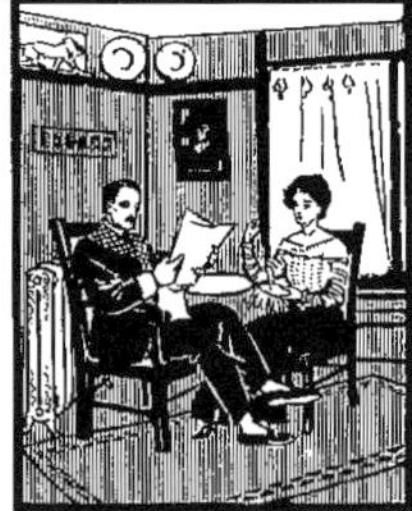

(b)

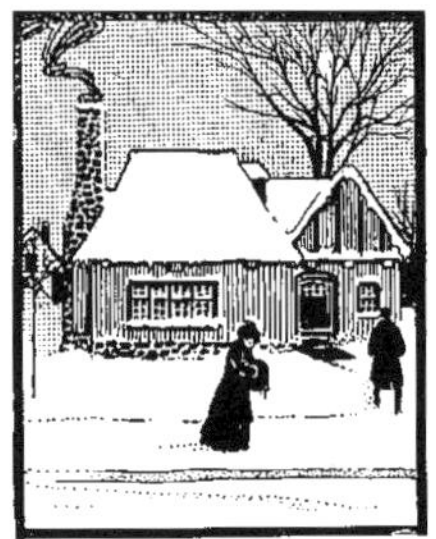

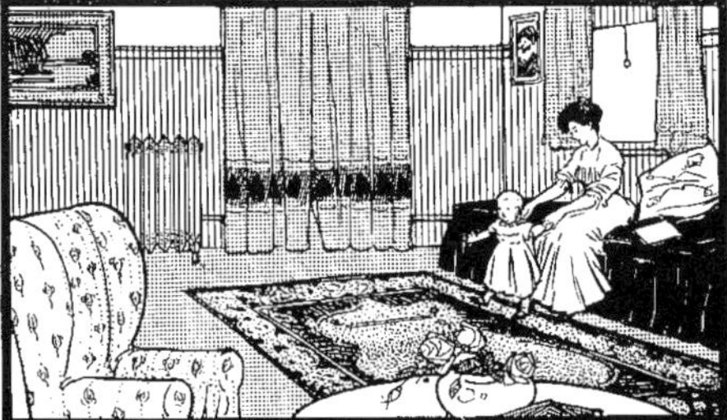

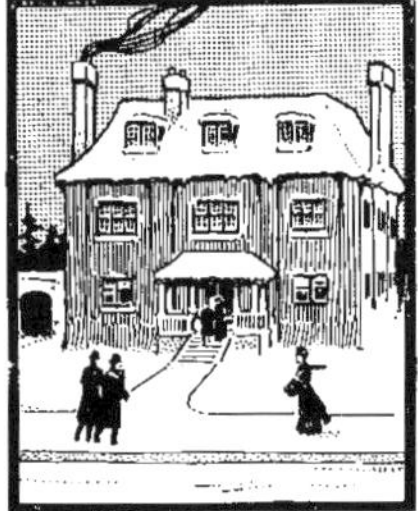

(c)

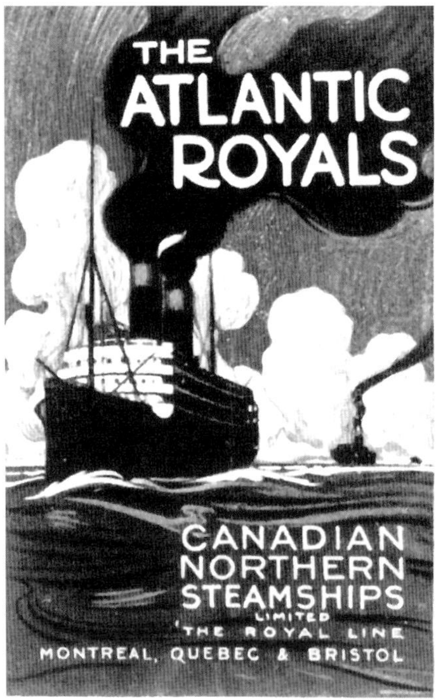

I:2

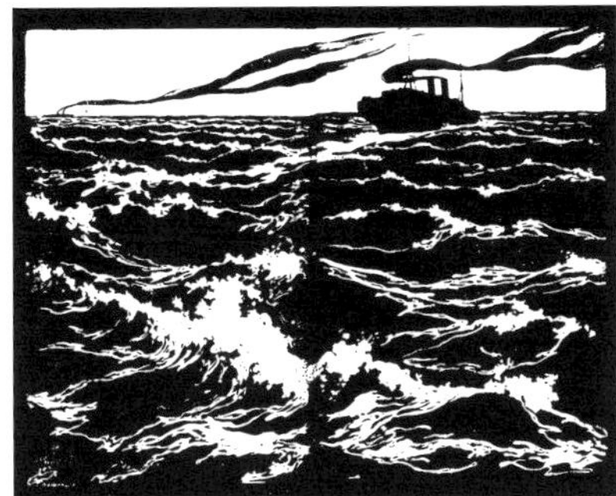

I:3

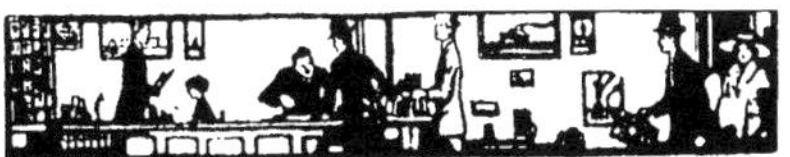

I:5

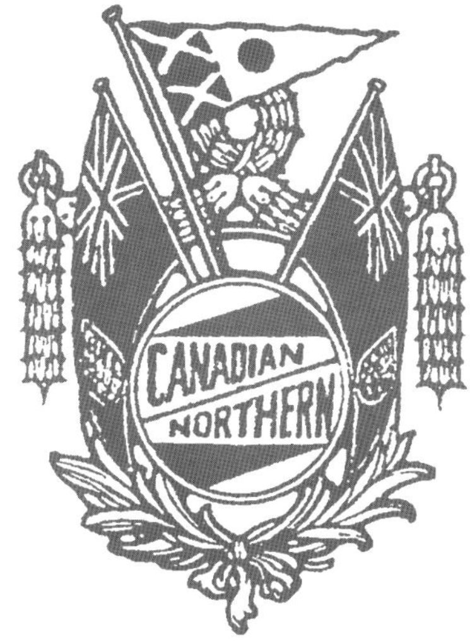

I:4

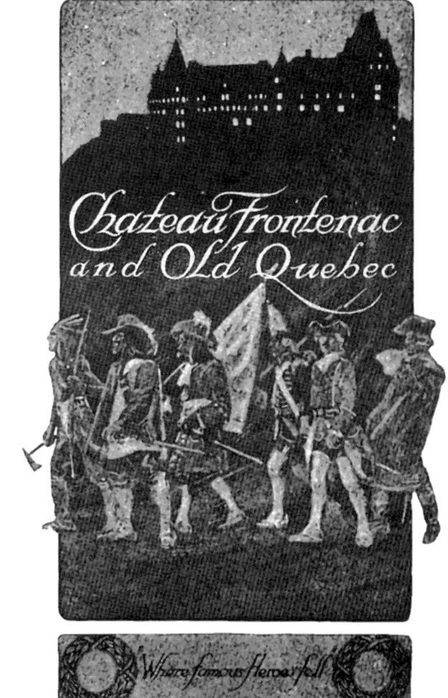

I:6

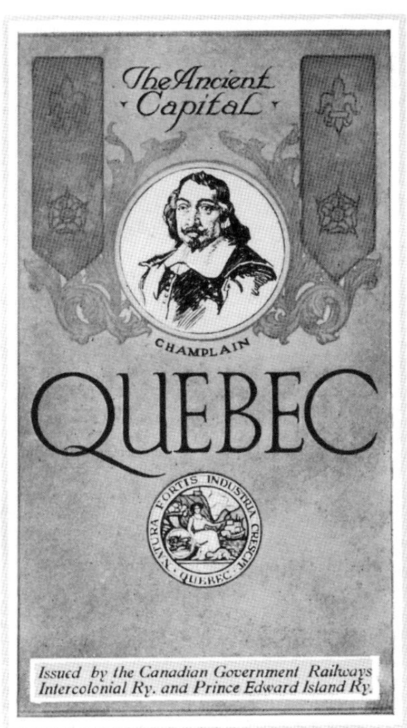

I:7

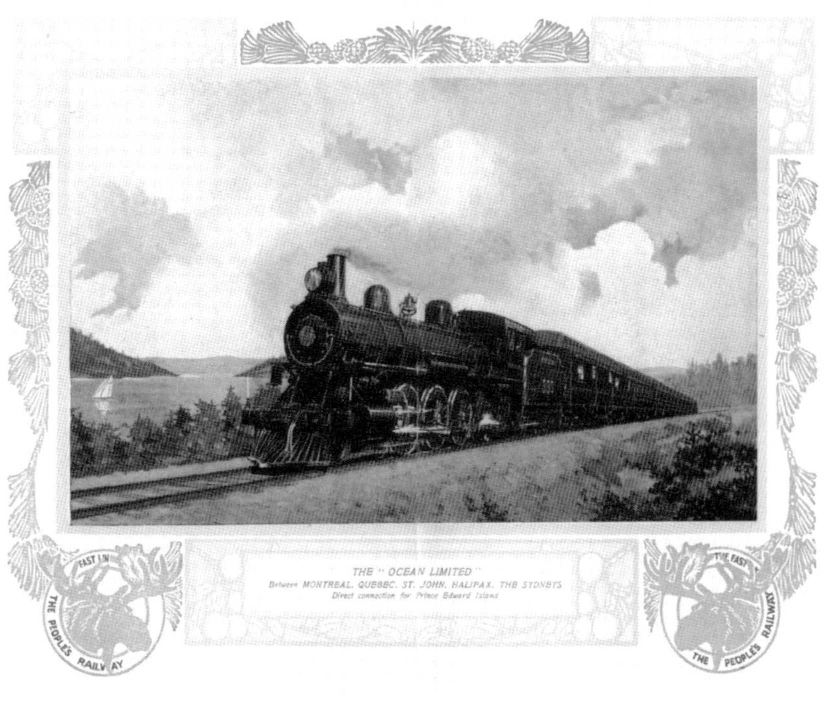

I:8

I: Design for Commerce

I:9. Half-title page, brochure, *Place Viger Hotel, Montreal* (Montreal: CPR, 1911); RSc. *Note*: the interior pen-and-ink illustrations for this brochure are by C.W. Jefferys. For front covers, see colour plates **Pl. I:4-5**.

I:10. Title page, brochure, *Place Viger Hotel, Montreal.*

I:11 (a-b). Vignettes, brochure, *Lawrence Park Estates* (Toronto: DLBSC, n.d. [1911]); RSc. *Note*: printed and engraved by Grip Ltd., Toronto. Interior pen-and-ink illustrations for this brochure are by C.W. Jefferys. For front cover, mailing envelope, frontispiece and title page, see colour plates **Pl. I:6-7**.

I:12. "Foreword" page, brochure, *Lawrence Park Estates.*

I:13. *Bird's Eye View of Lawrence Park Estates*, with decorative borders, brochure, *Lawrence Park Estates.*

I:14 (a-b). Frontispiece and title page, brochure, *Lawrence Park Estates* (Toronto: DLBSC, 1911); RSc. *Note*: printed and engraved by Grip Ltd., Toronto. Interior wash illustrations for this brochure are by C.W. Jefferys. For front and back covers, see colour plate **Pl. I:8**.

I:15 (a-b). *Italy* and *London*, sketches for series of window displays on theme of "Capitals of the Allies," for the Robert Simpson Co., Toronto, 1915, graphite on wove paper (each: 26.6 x 18.0 cm); in "Sketchbook, 1914-22," NGC (acc. no. 18906).

I:16. Advertisement for Ely Ltd., Toronto, n.d. (c. 1919).

I:17. Advertisement for Ely Ltd., *The Lamps* (1919); RSc.

I:18. Advertisement for Nordheimer Piano Co., Toronto, *The Lamps* (1919).

I:19. Advertisement for The E. Harris Co. of Toronto Ltd., *The Lamps* (1919).

I:20. Advertisement for A.J. Boughton, Gilder & Picture Frame Maker, Toronto, *The Lamps* (1919).

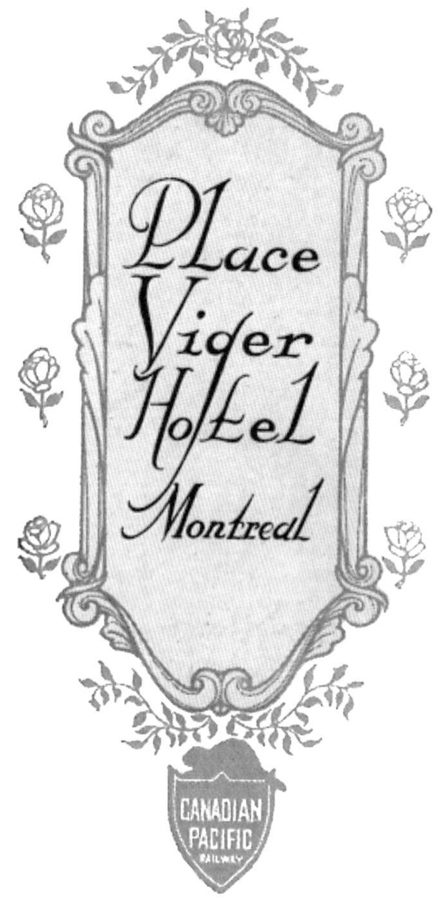

I:9

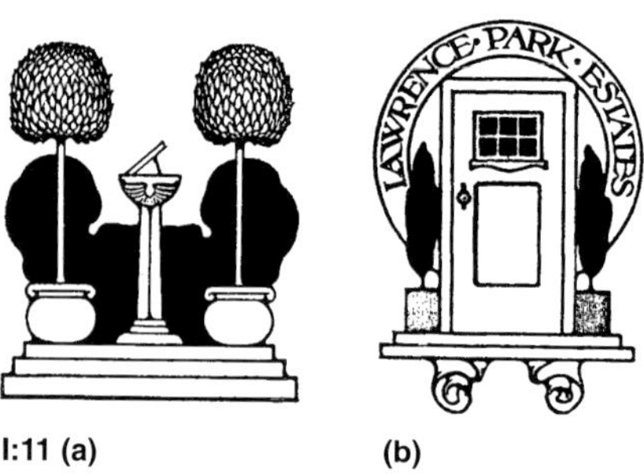

I:11 (a) (b)

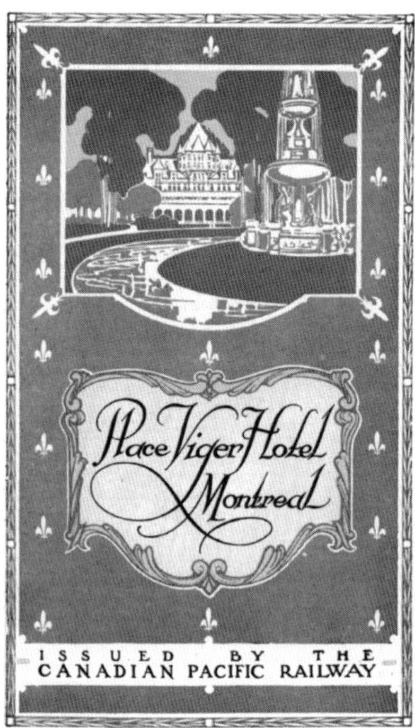

I:10

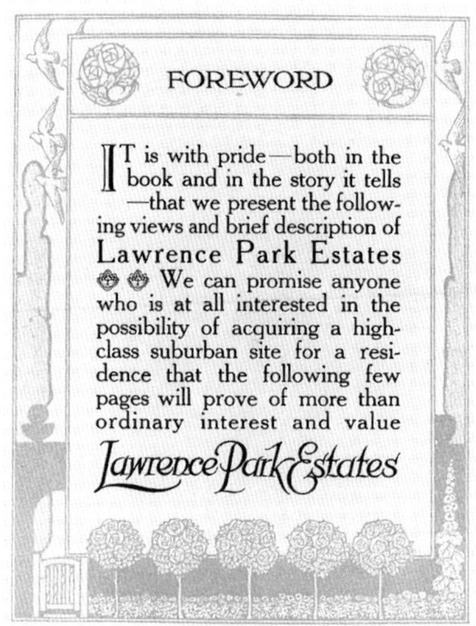

FOREWORD

IT is with pride—both in the book and in the story it tells—that we present the following views and brief description of Lawrence Park Estates. We can promise anyone who is at all interested in the possibility of acquiring a high-class suburban site for a residence that the following few pages will prove of more than ordinary interest and value

Lawrence Park Estates

I:12

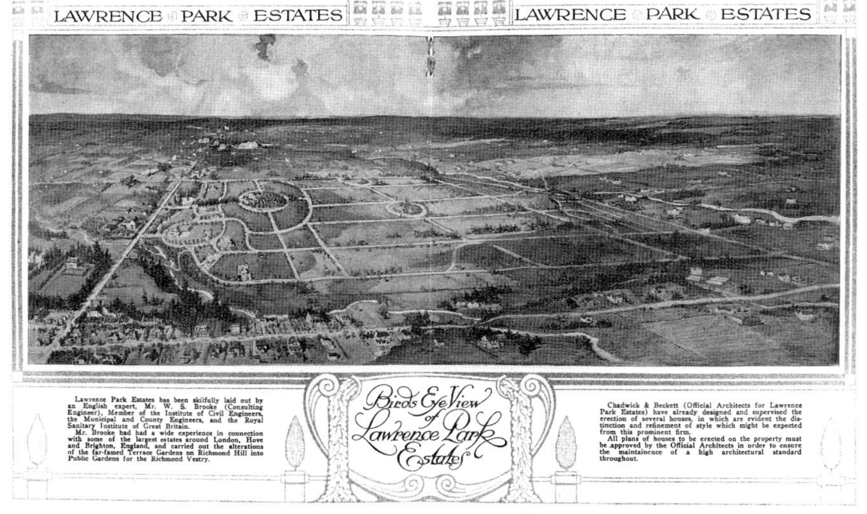

I:13

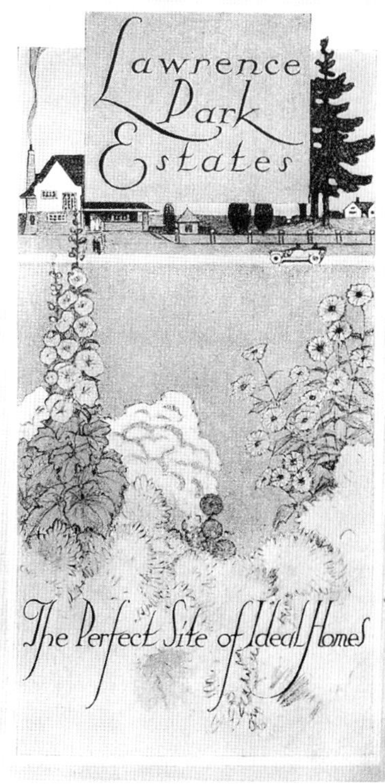

I:14

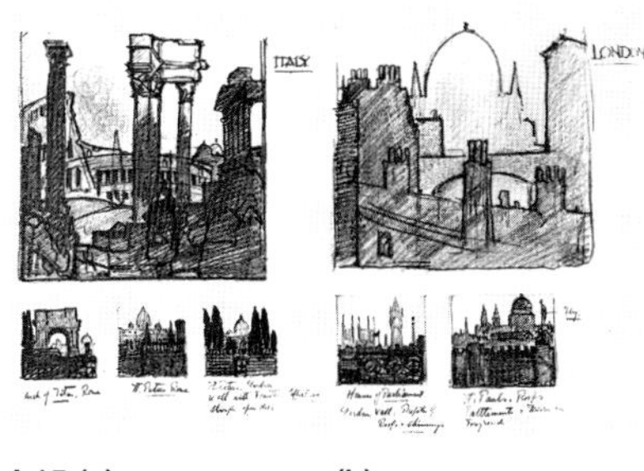

I:15 (a) (b)

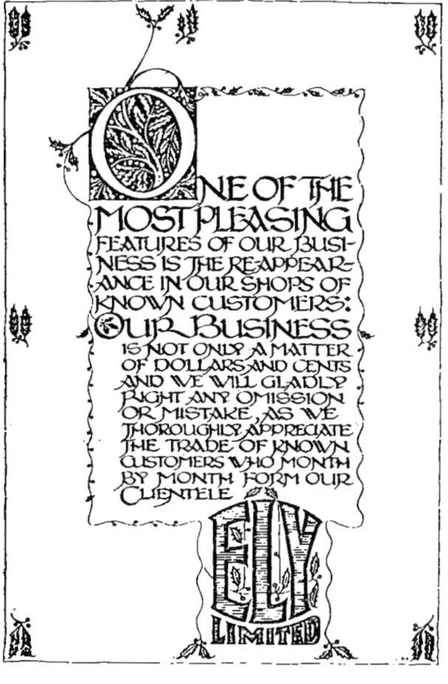

I:17

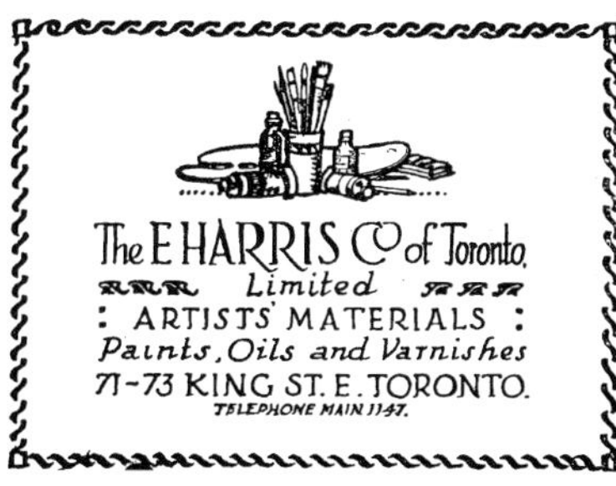

I:19

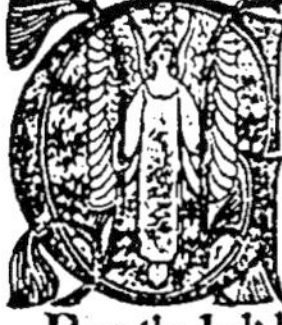

OOD WILL is a thing
that we cherish
It's a part of our every day
code.
But the holiday season
Affords us a reason
To convey our Good Will a la mode.
So we wish you a jolly good Xmas
And a New Year that's happy and gay
May success stay beside you
And Dame Fortune guide you;
As the year travels on day by day.
28 KING ST WEST, TORONTO

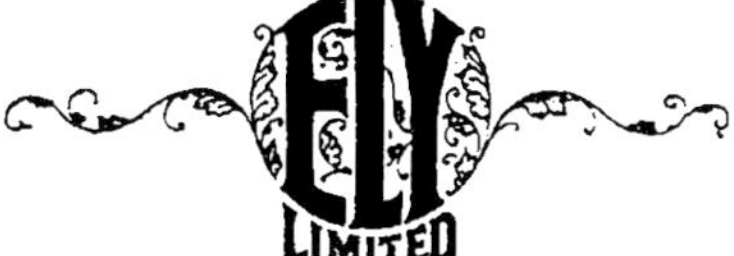

I:16

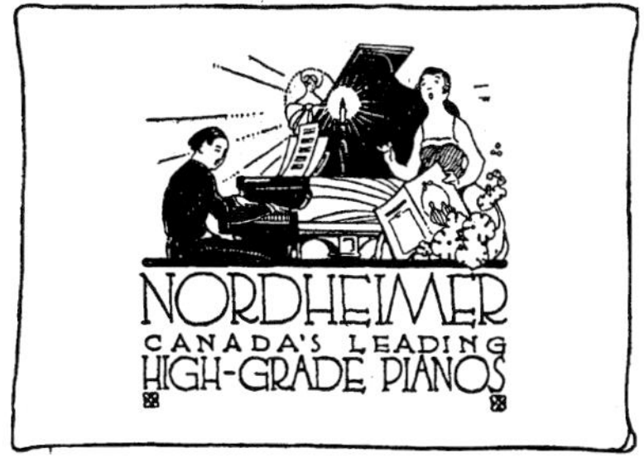

I:18

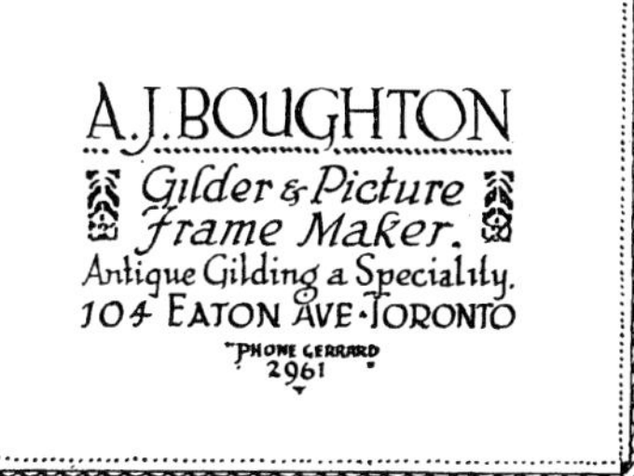

I:20

I: Design for Commerce

I:21. Front cover, booklet, *The Old Fashioned Executor: A Series of Advertisements* (Montreal: National Trust Co. Ltd., n.d. [1919-20?]); NDc. Photo: McCullough Studio. *Note*: the contents were first published as press advertisements in 1919-20, then in booklet form.

I:22. Title page, booklet, *The Old Fashioned Executor.*

I:23. Illustration, *When Personal Executorship Flourished*, in booklet, *The Old Fashioned Executor.*

I:24. Sketch for illustrations for *The Old Fashioned Executor*, c. 1919, graphite on wove paper (26.6 x 18.0 cm); in "Sketchbook, 1914-22," NGC (acc. no. 18906).

I:25. Illustration, *The Lost Will*, in booklet, *The Old Fashioned Executor.*

I:26. Illustration, in booklet, *The Old Fashioned Executor.*

I:27. Christmas card, *A Glad Christmas* (Toronto: Rous & Mann Ltd., Canadian Artists' Cards, n.d. [c. 1922-32]); HBP. *Note*: Rous & Mann launched the Canadian Artists Cards series in 1922 and discontinued it in 1932.

I:28. Christmas card, *A Merry Xmas* (Toronto: Rous & Mann Ltd., Canadian Artists' Cards, n.d. [c. 1922-32]).

I:29. Christmas card, *Christmas Eve, University Avenue, Toronto*, n.d. (c. 1926?), oil, reproduced by quadra-colour process by Reliance Engravers, Toronto, 1926; ALC. *Note*: identified as JM's work by TM, 1976.

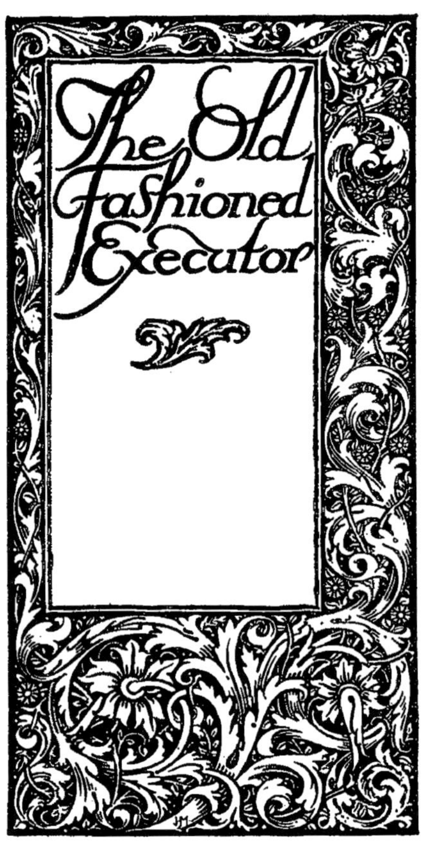

I:21

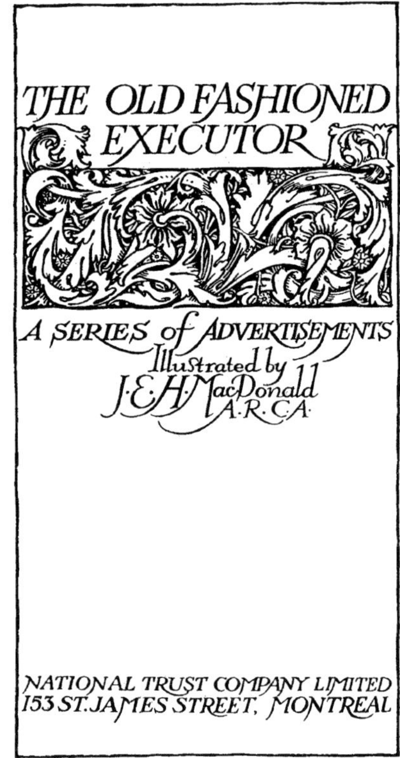

I:22

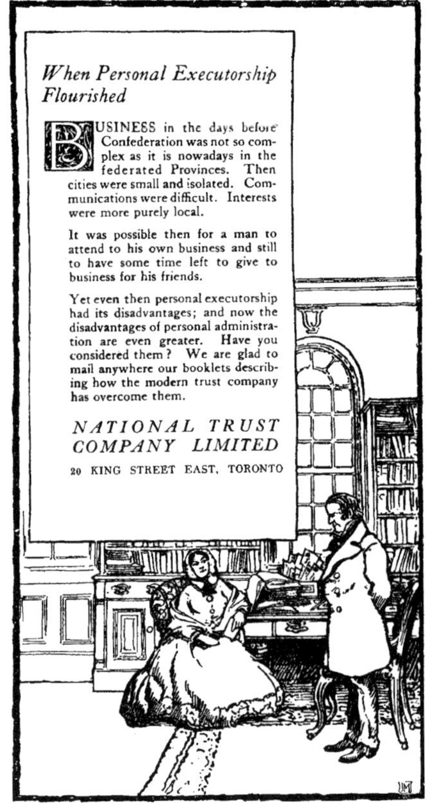

I:23

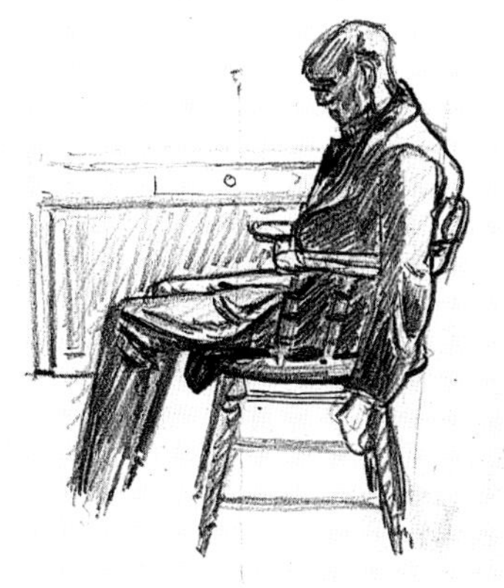

I:24

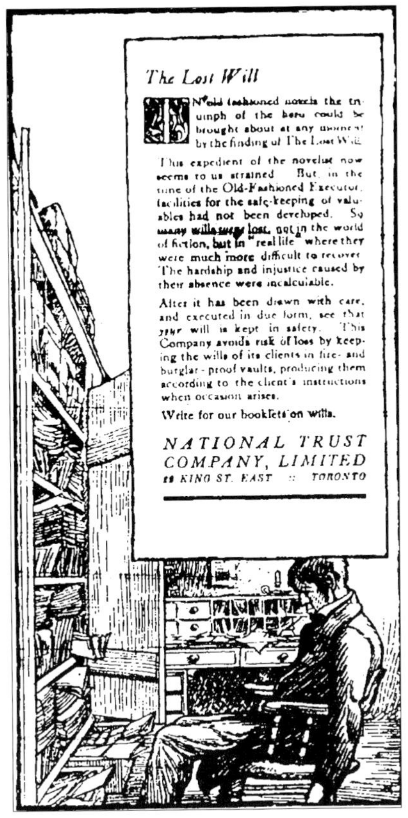

I:25

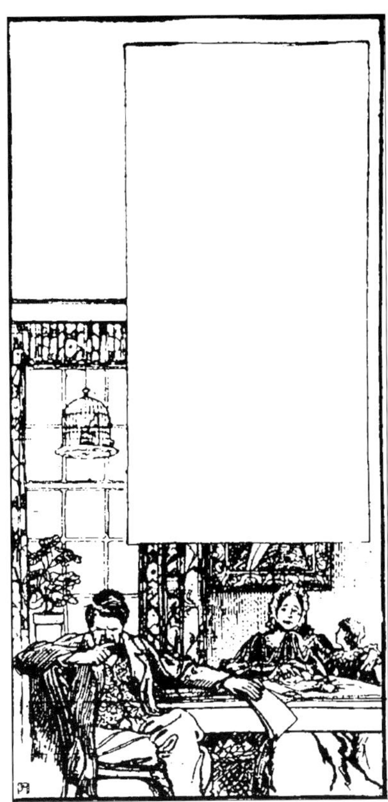

I:26

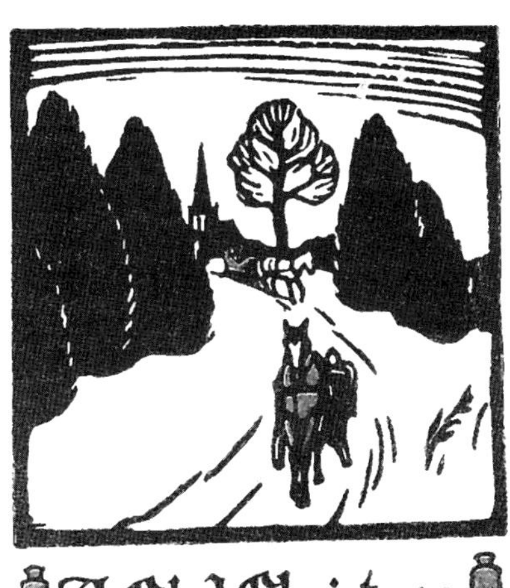

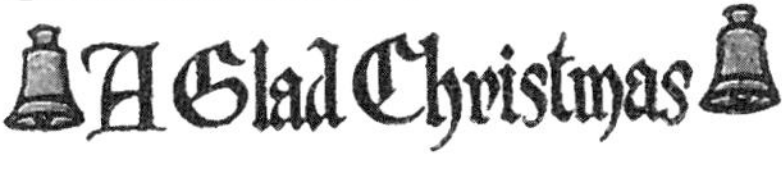

I:27

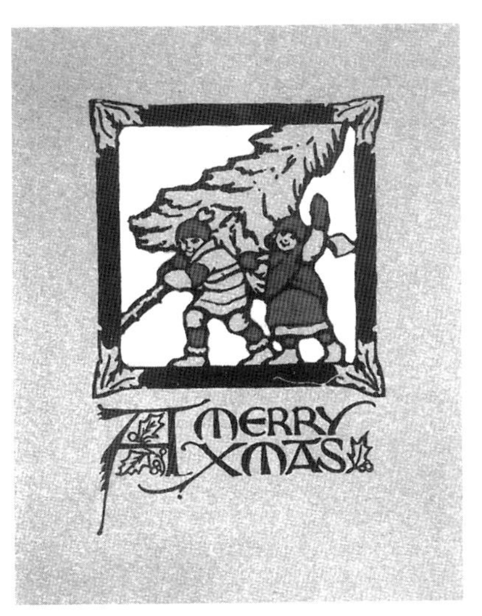

I:28

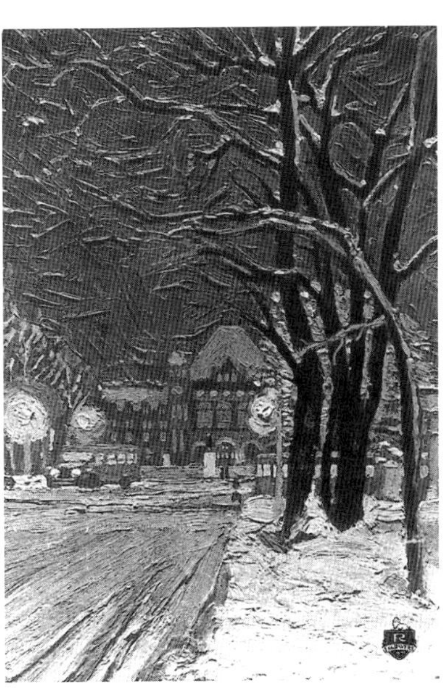

I:29

I: Design for Commerce

I:30 (a-g) Pen and brush-and-ink illustrations for booklet, *Jasper National Park* (Montreal: CNR, 1927); RSc. *Note*: titles of drawings, in order of appearance: **a)** *Mount Kerkeslin and Athabaska Falls;* **b)** *Jacques Lake;* **c)** *Shovel Pass;* **d)** *Mount Erebus and the Astoria River;* **e)** *Mount Tekarra;* **f)** *Pyramid Mountain;* **g)** *Medicine Lake.*

I:31 (a-c). Catalogue, *The Sheridan Nurseries Limited*, (Toronto: SNL, 1929); Archives, SNL. **a)** Sketch for front cover, c. 1929, brush-and-ink on card; **b)** finished artwork for front cover, catalogue, pen and brush-and-ink on card; **c)** photo-engraved zinc plate used to print front cover, catalogue. *Note*: for printed front cover, see colour plate **Pl. I:11 (b)**.

I:32. Front cover, *The Art of Garden Design* (Toronto: Sheridan Nurseries Ltd., n.d [c. 1929?]); Archives, SNL.

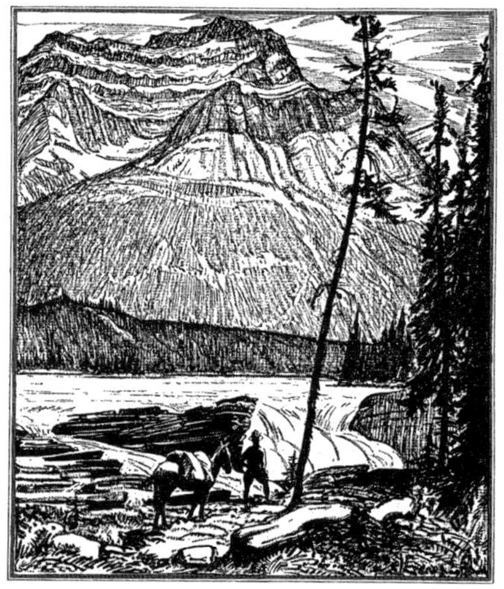

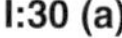

I:30 (a)

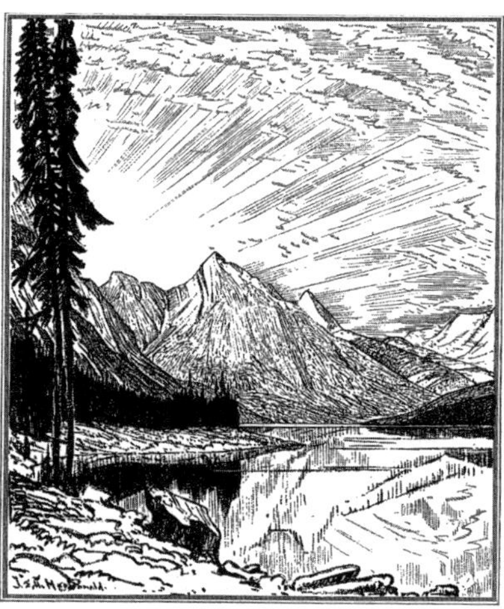

(b)

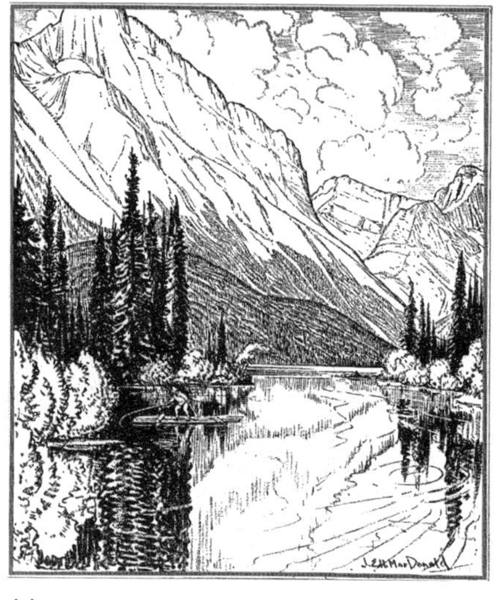

(c)

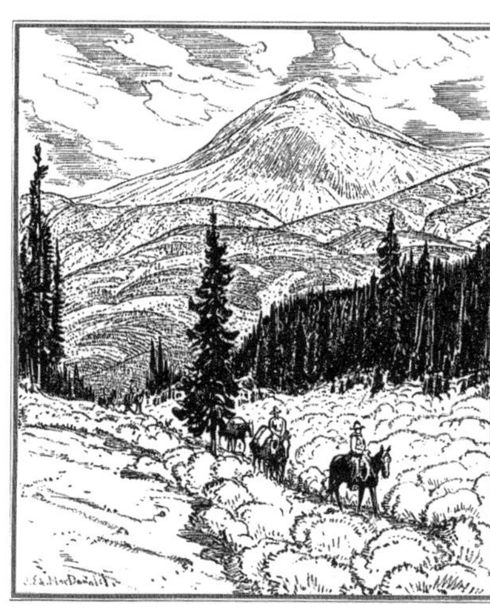

(d)

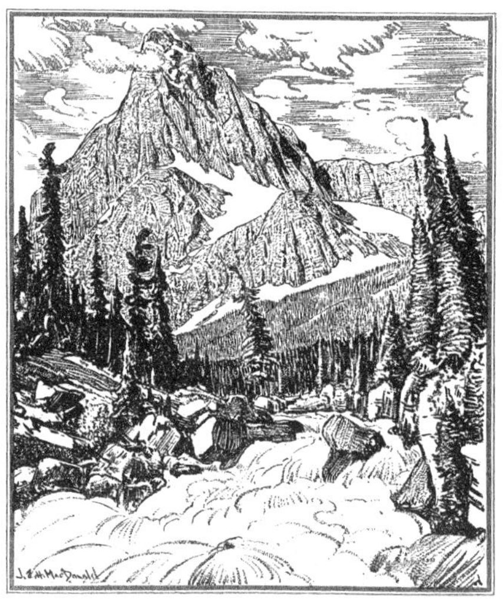

(e)

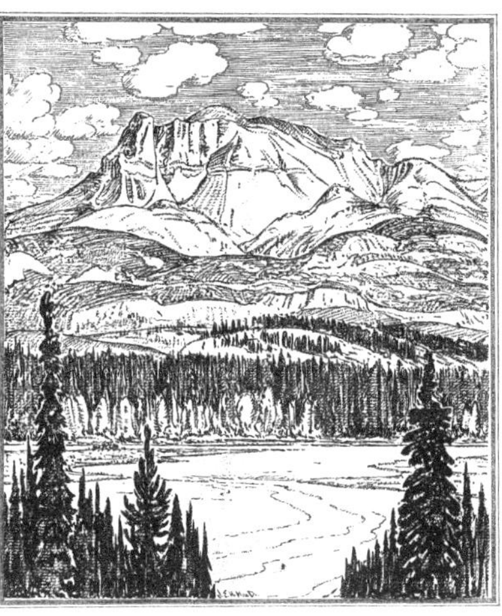

(f)

(g)

The SHERIDAN
NURSERIES

I:31 (a)

The SHERIDAN
AND I BESEECH YOU FORGET NOT TO INFORM YOURSELF AS DILIGENTLY AS MAY BE IN THINGS THAT BELONG TO GARDENING - John Evelyn
NURSERIES
Limited

(b)

(c)

SHERIDAN NURSERIES
THE ART OF
GARDEN
DESIGN
SHERIDAN NURSERIES TORONTO

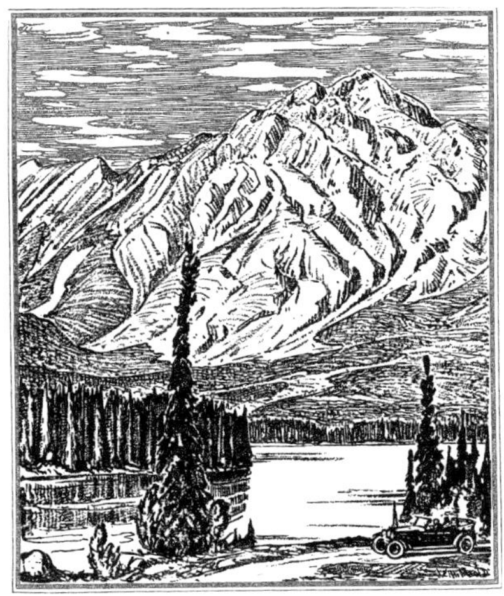

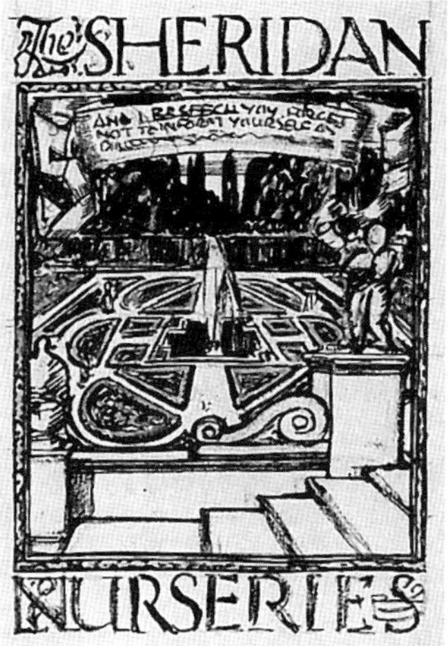

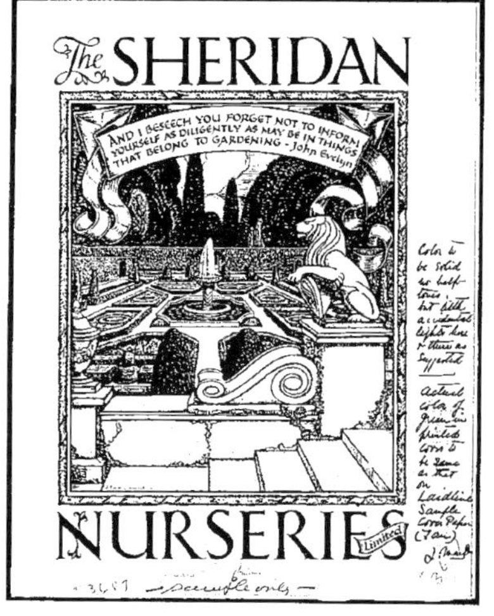

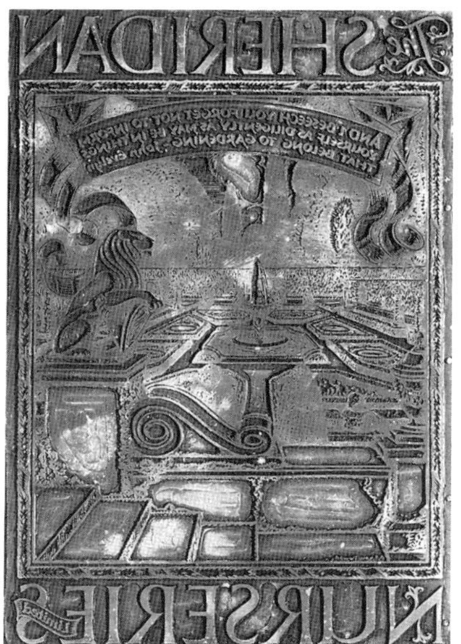

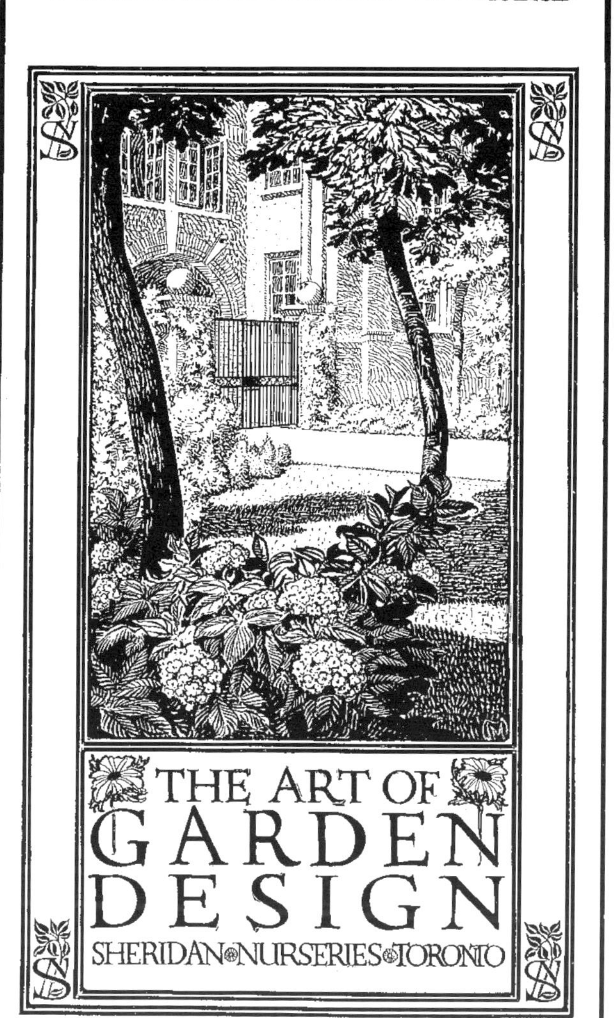

I:32

II: *Design for Culture*

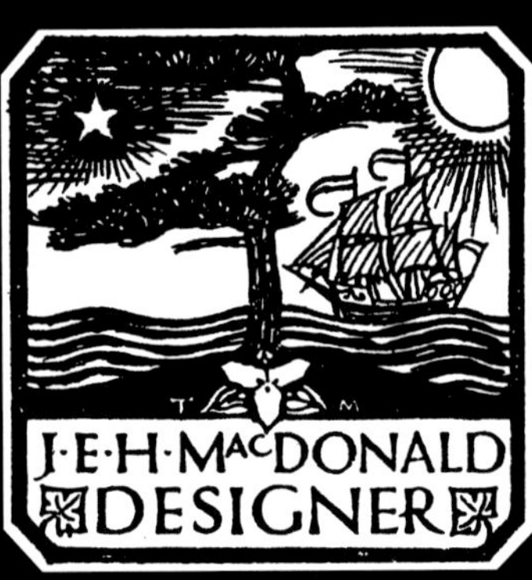

III: Illustration

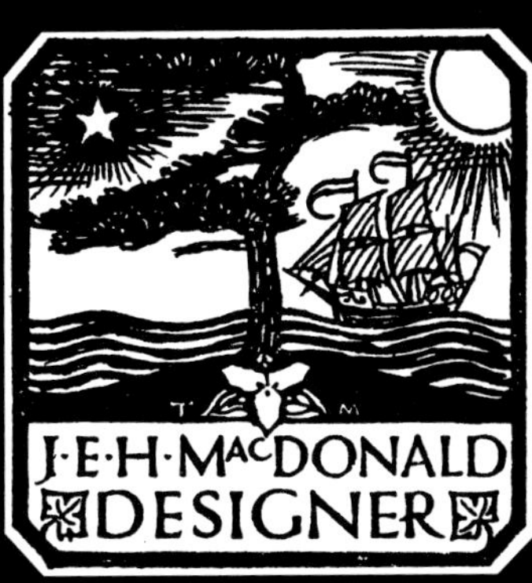

III: Illustration

Books

III:1. Title page publisher's mark, *The Royal Navy*, by H.L. Swinburne (London: A. & C. Black, 1907). *Note*: this decorative element also appears on the cloth cover of this book, which JM identifies as his own work in *Complete Course of Instruction, Commercial Design: Lesson I* (Toronto: SCS, 1910), p. 6.

III:2 (a-c). Vignettes, *Printing Papers: A Handbook for the Use of Publishers & Printers* (London: Spalding & Hodge, n.d.[c. 1905-07?]). *Note*: attributed to JM on stylistic grounds. This book of paper samples was designed and illustrated by members of the Carlton Studio.

III:3. Front cover, *A Backwoods Christmas*, by Augustus Bridle (Toronto: R.G. McLean, Printers, 1910). *Note*: for back cover, see colour plate **Pl. III:5**.

III:4. Half-title, *A Backwoods Christmas*.

III:5. Title page, *A Backwoods Christmas*.

III:6. Decorative border and vignettes, "Illustrated Chart of Canadian History," *Index and Dictionary of Canadian History*, ed. L.J. Burpee and A.G. Doughty (supplement to *The Makers of Canada* series) (Toronto: Morang & Co., 1912). *Note*: other illustrations on this chart are by C.W. Jefferys.

III:7. Front cover, *Come Back Old Pal*, sheet music (Toronto: Leo Feist Ltd., n.d. [c. 1917-18 or later?]); RSc. *Note*: The Dumbells were a popular WWI vaudeville troupe, formed from the Canadian Army's Third Division Concert Party. Named by its founder, Capt. Merton Plunkett, after the division's symbol, the group went from entertaining the troops at Vimy Ridge in Aug. 1917 to performing 4 weeks in London and 12 in New York. The Dumbells toured in Canada and abroad until disbanding in 1929. One of the 8 original players was the artist, cartoonist and ALC member Jack McLaren.

III:8. Front cover, *Shakespeare for Community Players*, by Roy Mitchell (London & Toronto: J.M. Dent & Sons Ltd., 1919).

III:9. Frontispiece, *Shakespeare for Community Players*.

III:10. "Musical instruments," illustration for *Shakespeare for Community Players*.

III:11. "Puck," illustration for *Shakespeare for Community Players*.

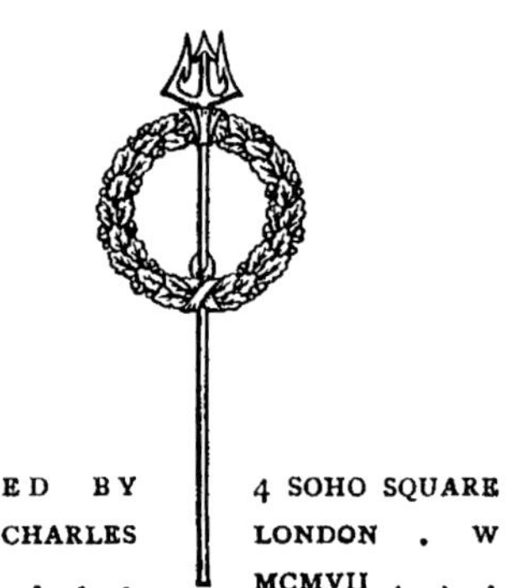

III:1

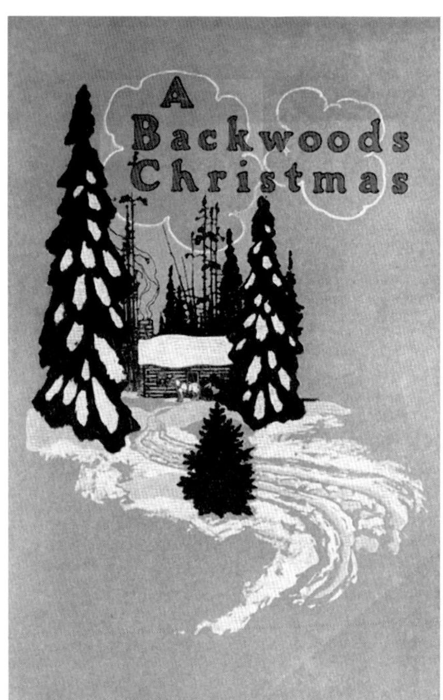

III:3

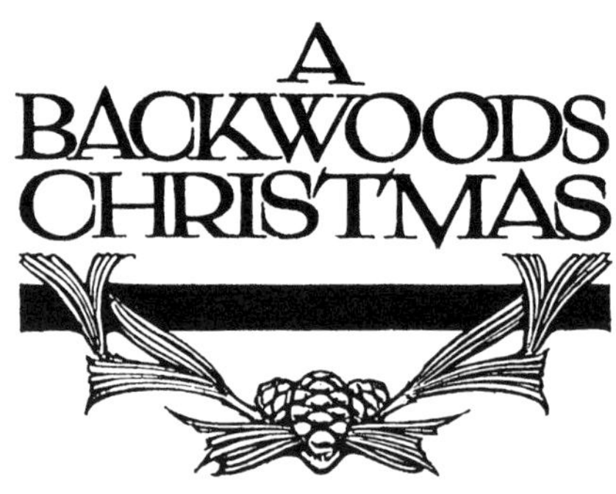

III: 4

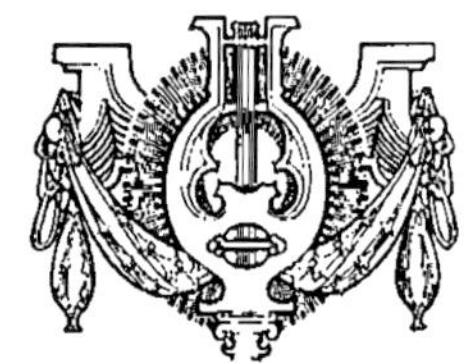

III: 2 (a)

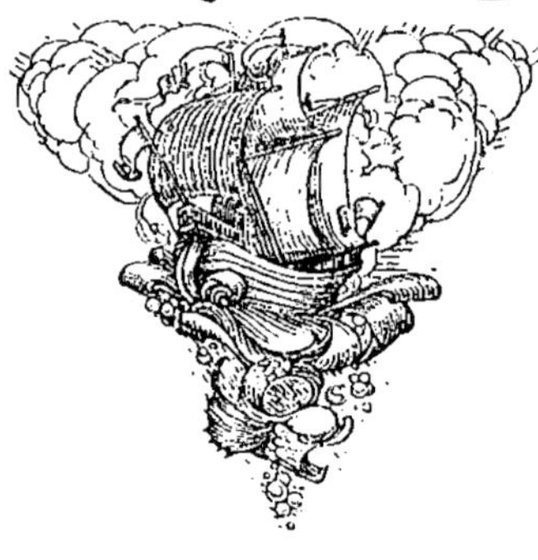

(b)

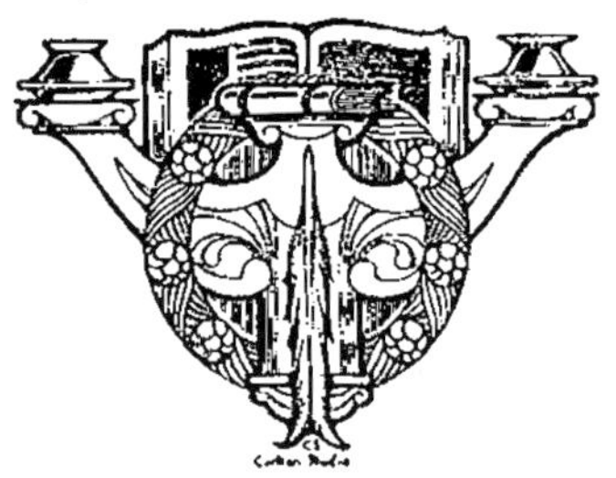

(c)

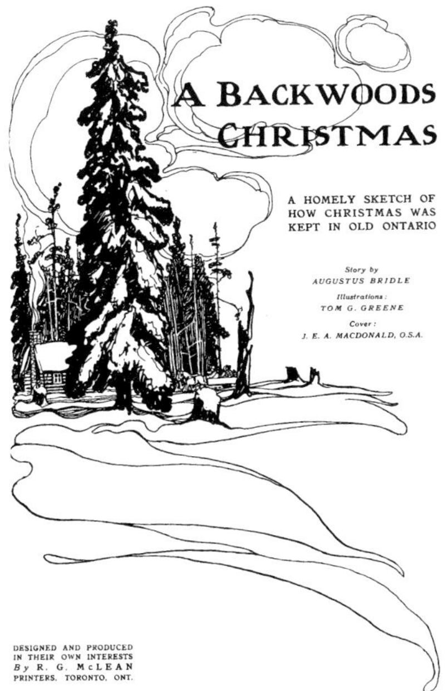

III: 5

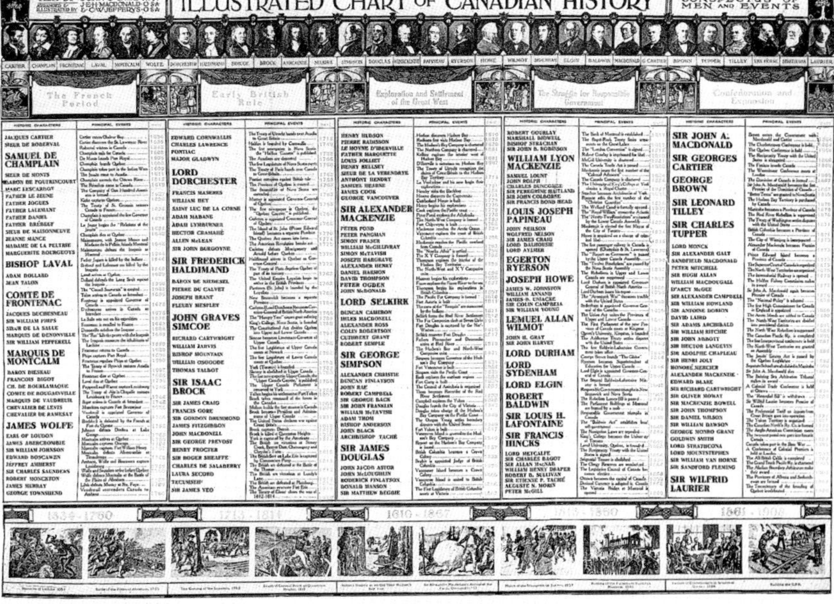

III: 6

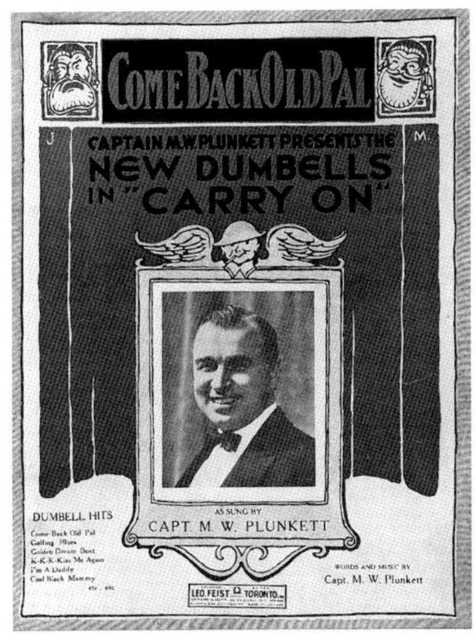

III: 7

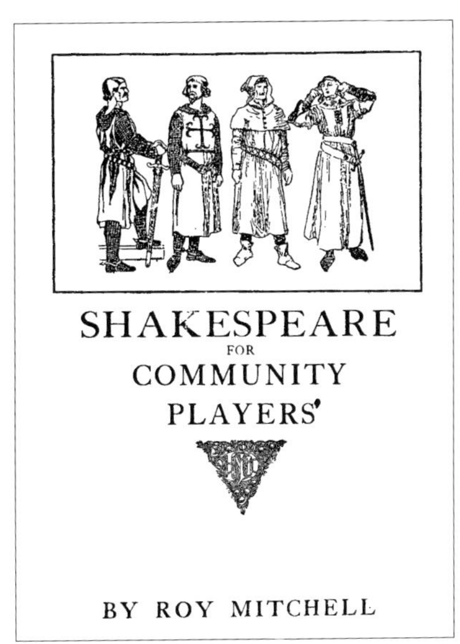

III: 8

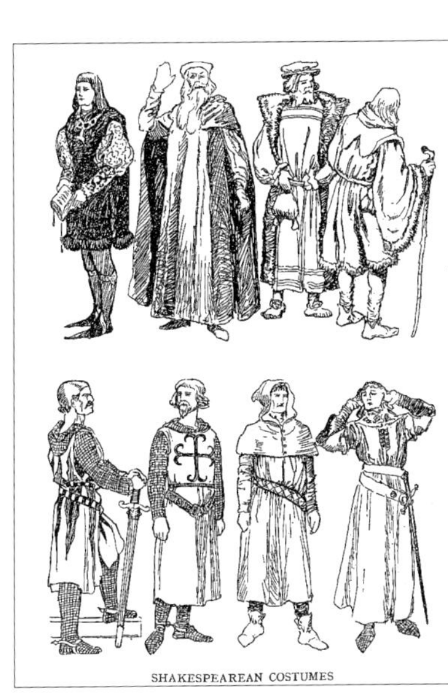

III: 9

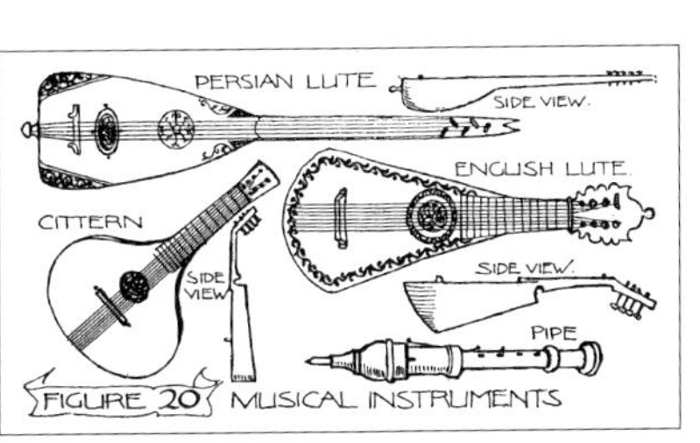

III: 10

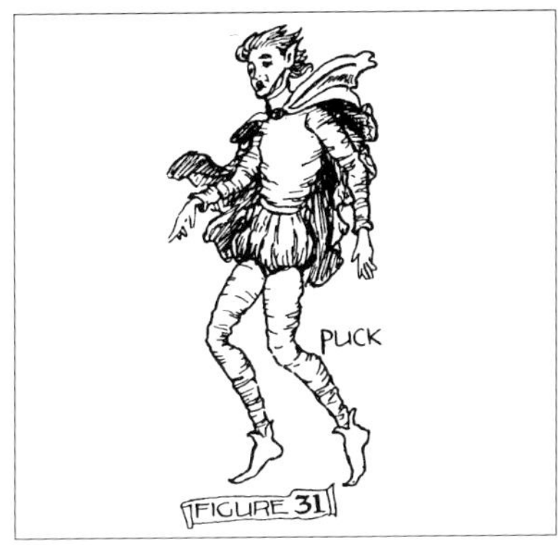

III: 11

III: Illustration

III:12. Title page, *University of Toronto Roll of Service: 1914-1918* (Toronto: University of Toronto Press, 1921). *Note*: lettering on coat of arms by TM.

III:13. Front cover, *Later Poems*, by Bliss Carman, embossed cloth (Toronto: McClelland & Stewart [1921]). *Note*: also used on Carman's *Ballads and Lyrics* (Toronto: M&S [1923]).

III:14. Endpaper border, *Later Poems*, by Bliss Carman. *Note*: reprinted in Carman's *Ballads and Lyrics*.

III:15. Title page, *Later Poems*, by Bliss Carman. *Note*: reprinted in Carman's *Ballads and Lyrics*. Some of the lettering is by TM.

III:16. Endpapers, *Fires of Driftwood*, by Isabelle Ecclestone Mackay (Toronto: M&S [1922]).

III:17. Title page, *Fires of Driftwood*. *Note*: lettering by TM.

III:18. Gilt-embossed, paper-covered card cover, *Legends of Vancouver*, by E. Pauline Johnson (Tekahionwake) (Toronto: M&S [1922]).

III:19.Title page, *Legends of Vancouver*. *Note*: lettering by TM.

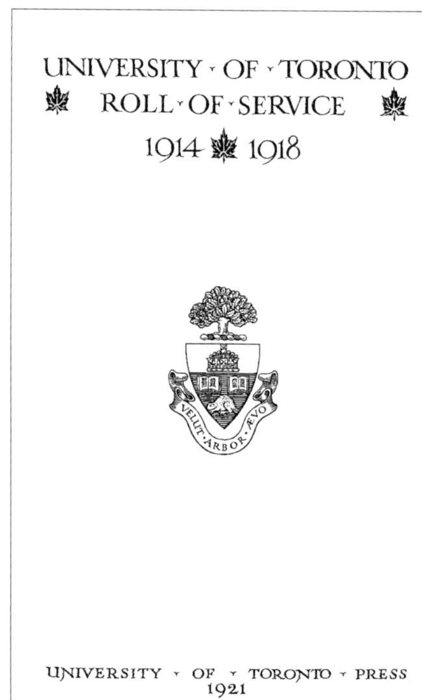

III: 12

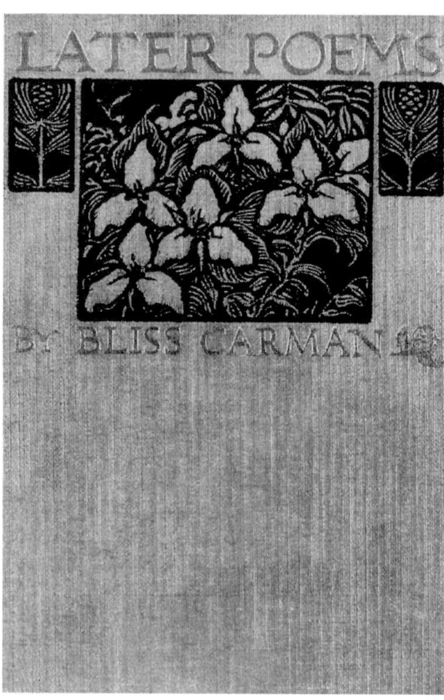

III: 13

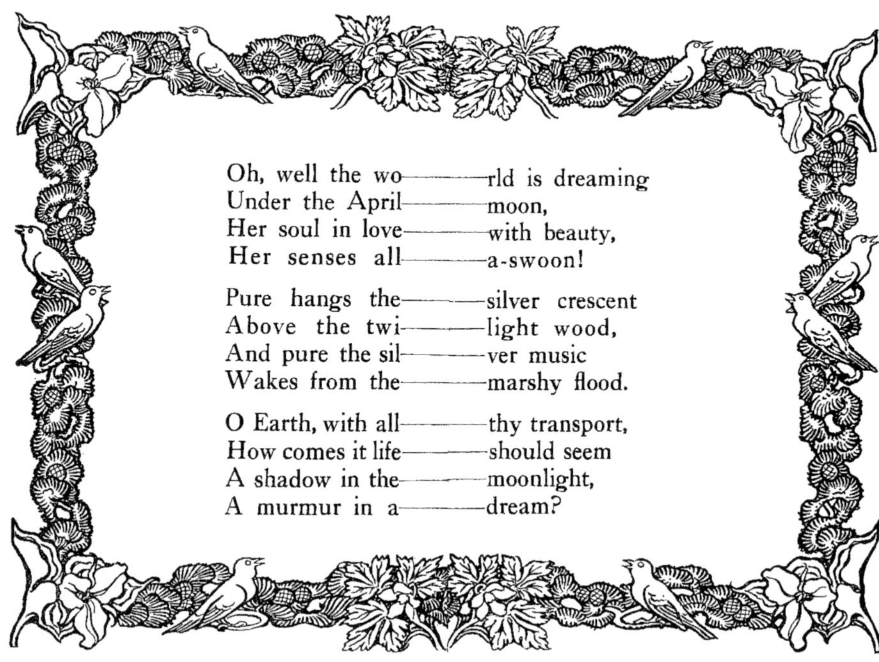

III: 14

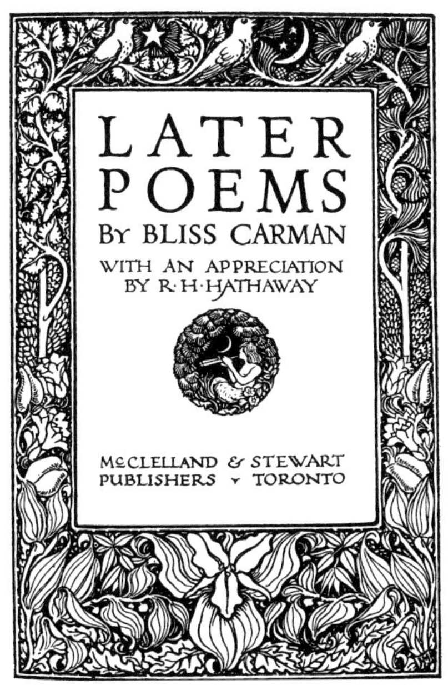

III: 15

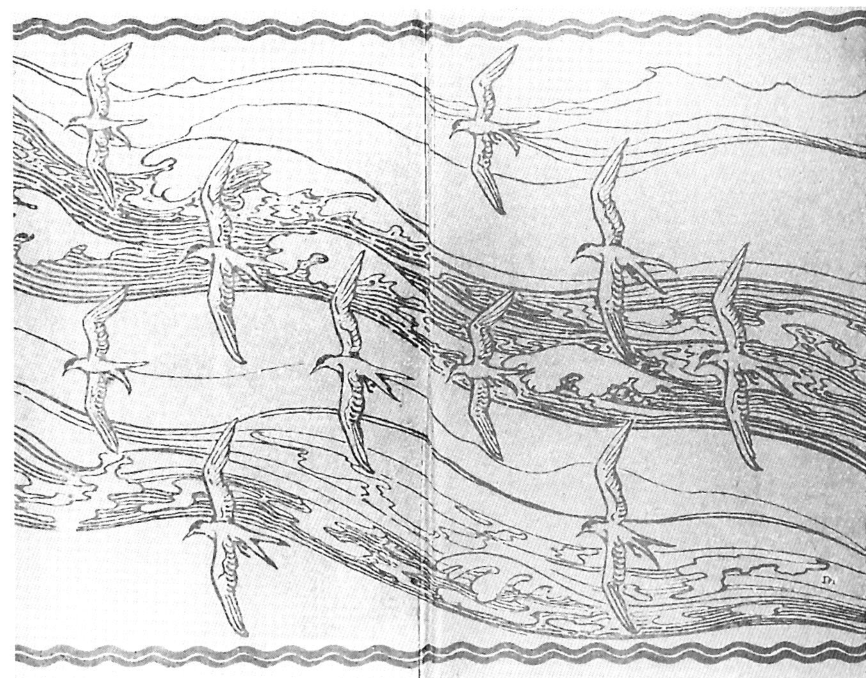

III: 16

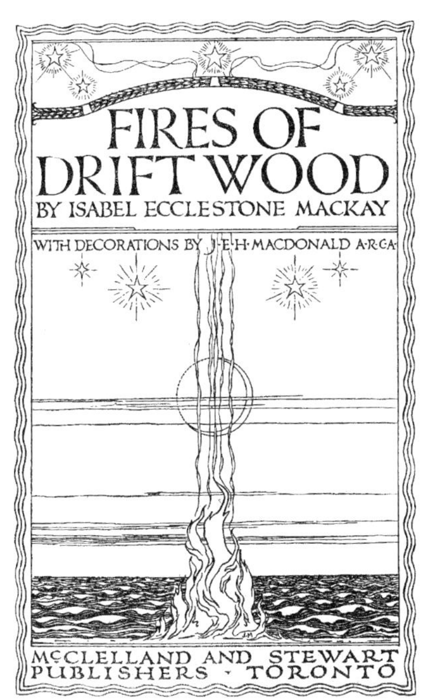

III: 17

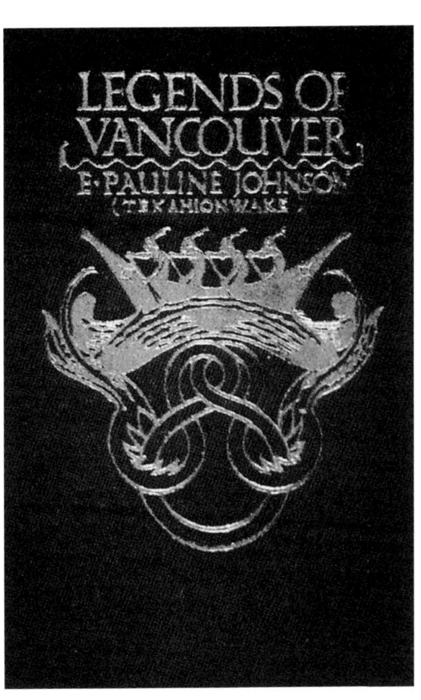

III: 18

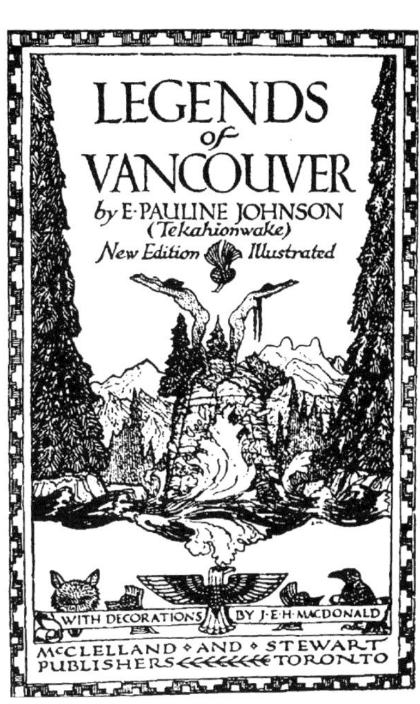

III: 19

III: Illustration

III:20. Sketch for endpapers, *Legends of Vancouver*, c. 1922, red pencil-crayon and graphite on paper (12.5 x 20.0 cm); LKc. *Note*: for printed endpapers, see colour plate **Pl. III:12**.

III:21. Dust jacket, *The Wood Carver's Wife*, by Marjorie Pickthall (Toronto: M&S [1922]). *Note*: large-paper limited edition of 250 copies; trade edition issued in smaller format. Lettering by TM.

III:22. Title page, *The Wood Carver's Wife*. *Note*: lettering by TM. Reprinted as title page decoration in *My Sanctuary Garden*, by Alice E. Wilson (Toronto: M&S, 1937).

III:23. Endpaper detail, *The Wood Carver's Wife*.

III:24. Endpapers, *The Rosary of Pan*, by A.M. Stephen (Toronto: M&S [1923]). *Note*: for dust jacket, see colour plate **Pl. III:10**.

III:25. Title page, *The Rosary of Pan*. *Note*: lettering by TM.

III:26. Dust jacket, *Stories of the Land of Evangeline*, by Grace McLeod Rogers (Toronto: M&S [1923]). *Note*: smaller-format issue; for dust jacket of larger-format issue, see colour plate **Pl. III:14**.

III:27 (a-b). Frontispiece and title page, *Stories of the Land of Evangeline*. *Note*: included in both the larger- and smaller-format issues. Frontispiece figure and lettering by TM.

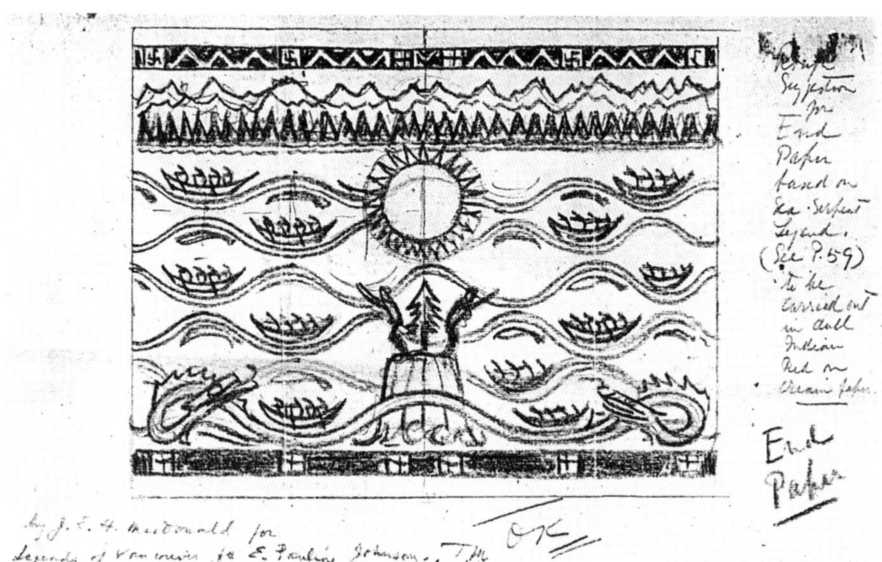

III: 20

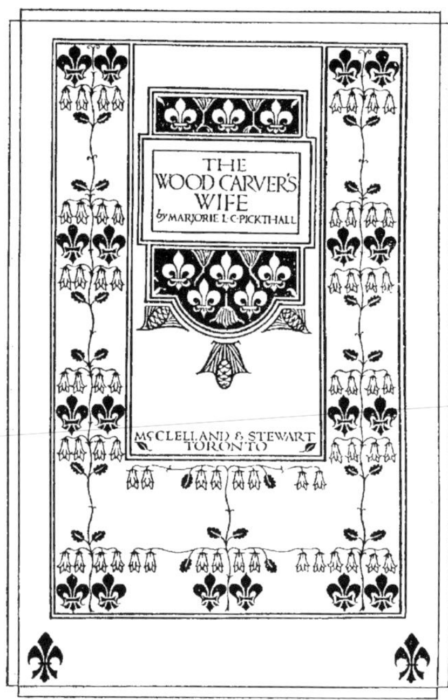

III: 21

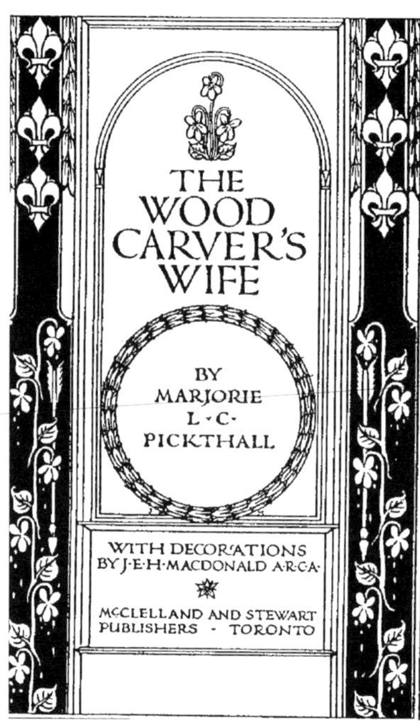

III: 22

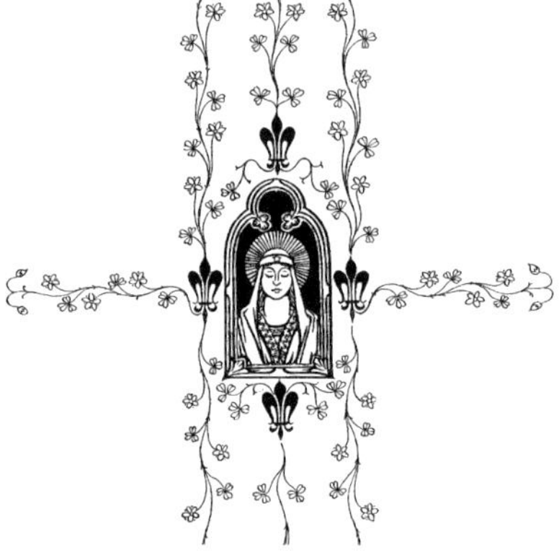

III: 23

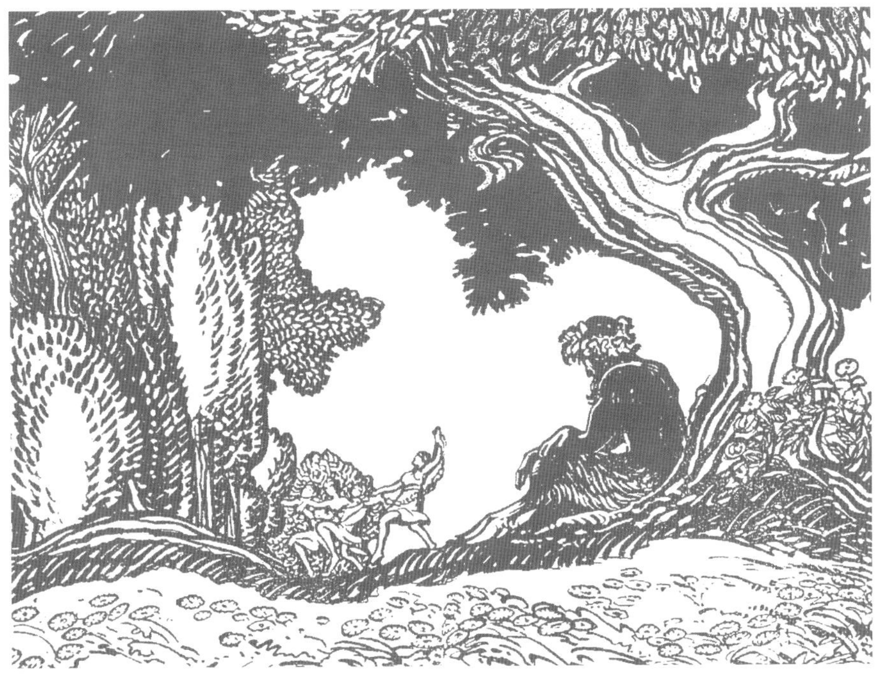
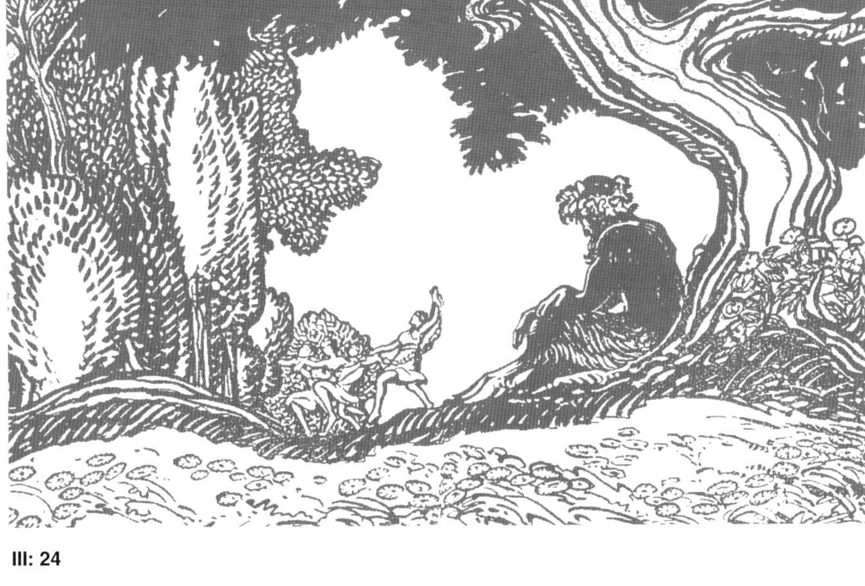

III: 24

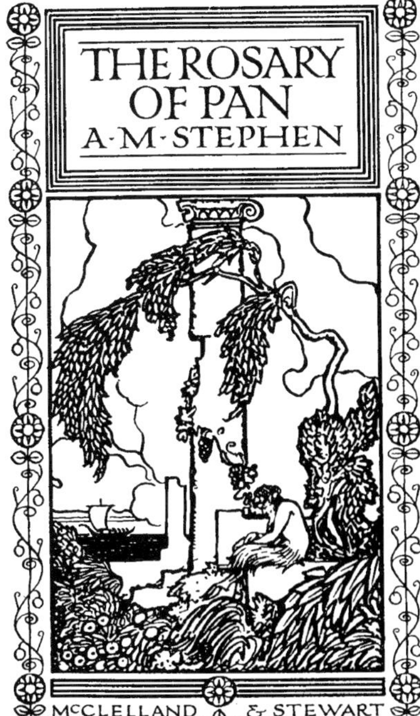

III: 25

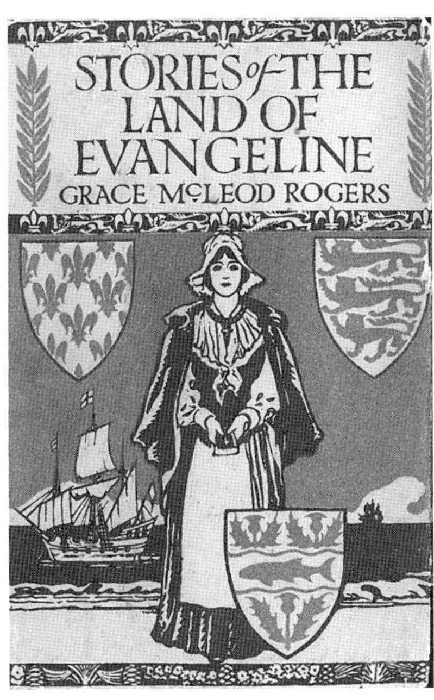

III: 26

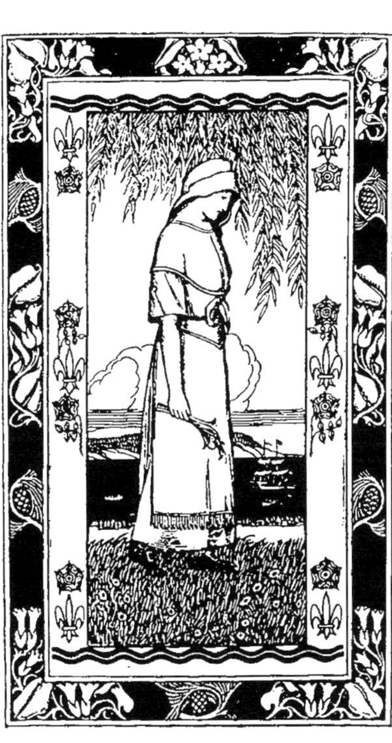

III: 27 (a)

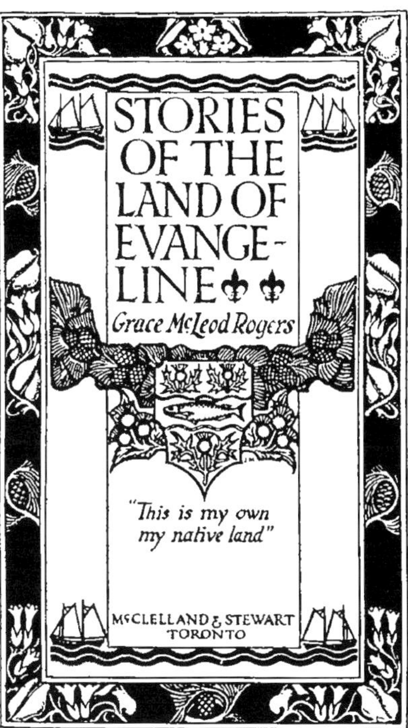

(b)

III: Illustration

III:28. Endpapers, *Stories of the Land of Evangeline. Note*: present only in the larger-format issue.

III:29 (a-x). Illustrations, *Stories of the Land of Evangeline. Note*: several of these illustrations, printed from pen-and-ink drawings, are based on sketch-panels painted by JM during his July-Aug. 1922 sketching trip to Petite Rivière, Nova Scotia. Some of the drawings (not specifically identified by the publisher) are by TM.

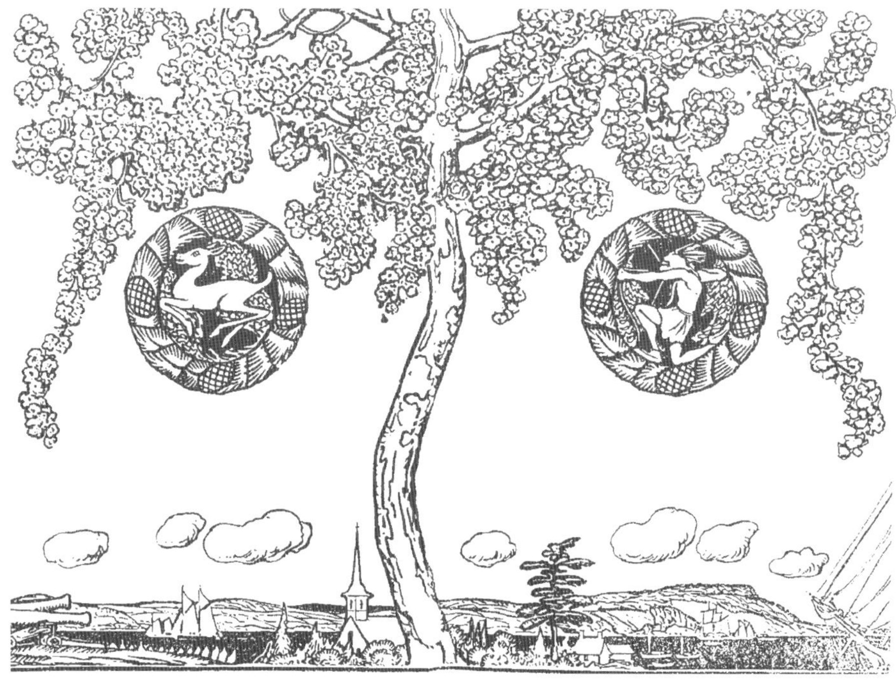

III: 28

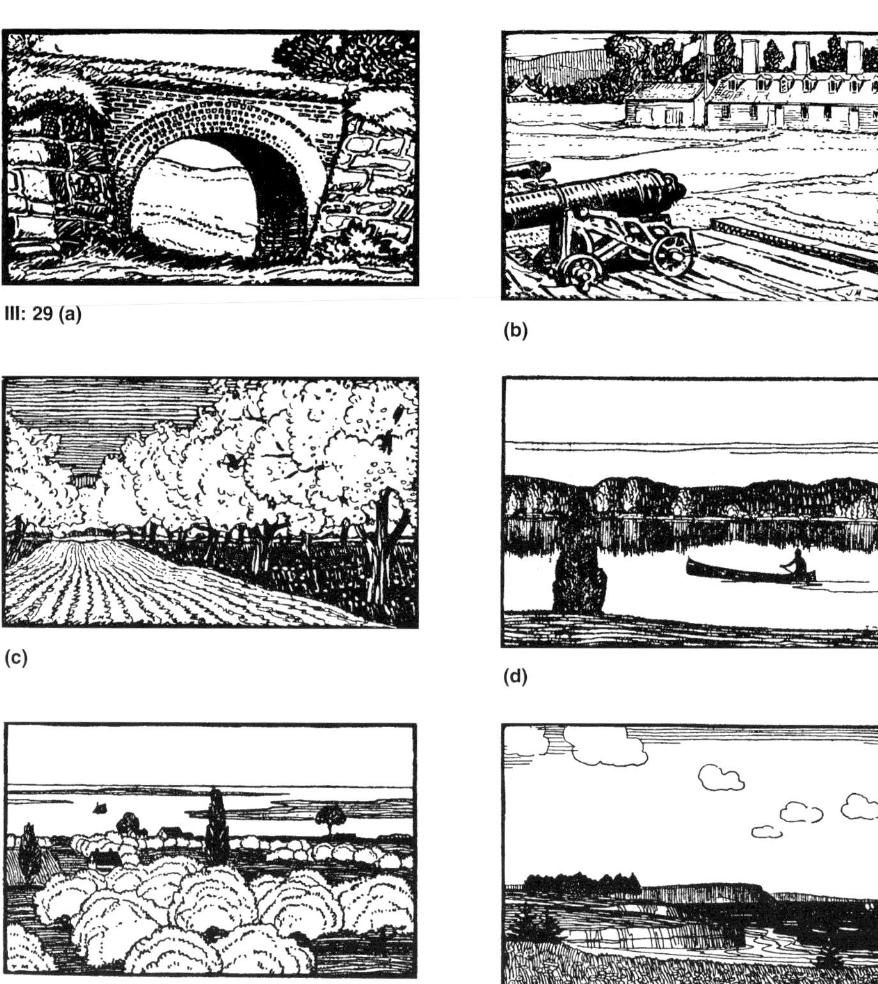

III: 29 (a)

(b)

(c)

(d)

(e)

(f)

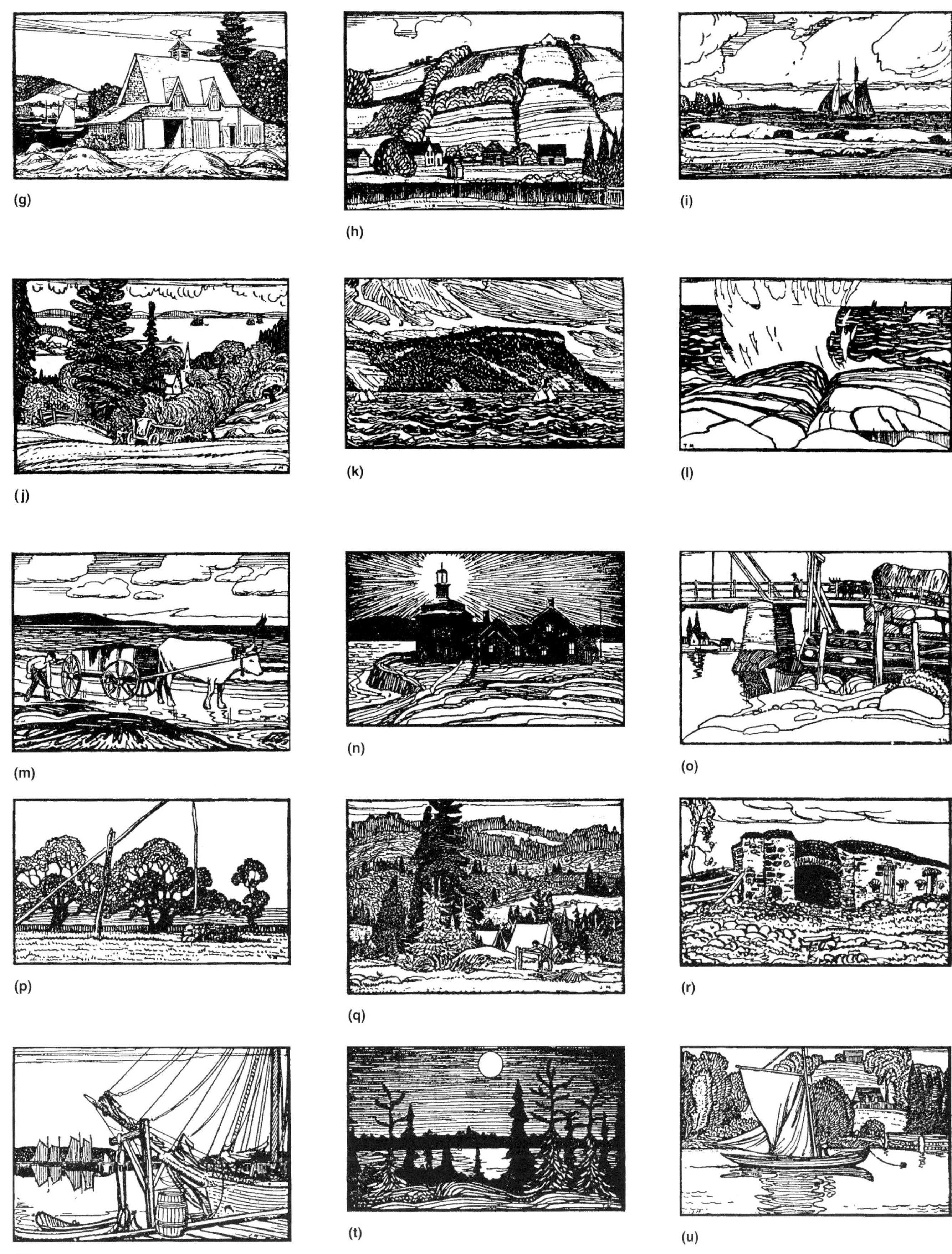

(g) (h) (i) (j) (k) (l) (m) (n) (o) (p) (q) (r) (s) (t) (u)

III: Illustration

III:30. Dust jacket, *The Unheroic North: Four Canadian Plays*, by Merrill Denison (Toronto: M&S [1923]). *Note*: lettering by TM.

III:31. Dust jacket, *White Winds of Dawn*, by Frances Beatrice Taylor (Toronto: M&S, 1924). *Note*: design also printed on endpapers. Some lettering by TM.

III:32 (a-b). Front cover, The Ryerson Poetry Chap-books **(a)**, introduced with *Sweet O' The Year and Other Poems*, by Charles G.D. Roberts (Toronto: Ryerson Press, 1925); design used on 98 Ryerson Poetry Chap-books, then modernized by TM (1942) **(b)**.

III:33. Endpapers, *Lord of the Silver Dragon*, by Laura Salverson (Toronto: M&S, 1927).

III:34 (a-b). Frontispiece and title page, *Lord of the Silver Dragon*. *Note*: lettering on title page and inset illustration in frontispiece by TM.

III:35. Title page vignette, *Hart House Theatre: Toronto* (Toronto: Hart House [1928]).

III:36. Gilt-embossed, cloth-covered cover, *Private Life of Catherine the Great*, by Princess Lucien Murat (New York: Louis Carrier & Co., 1928). *Note*: this design was used on other titles in Carrier's "Love Lives of the Great" series.

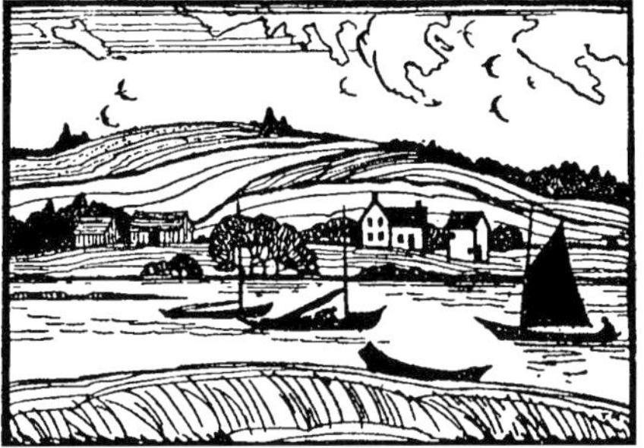

(v)

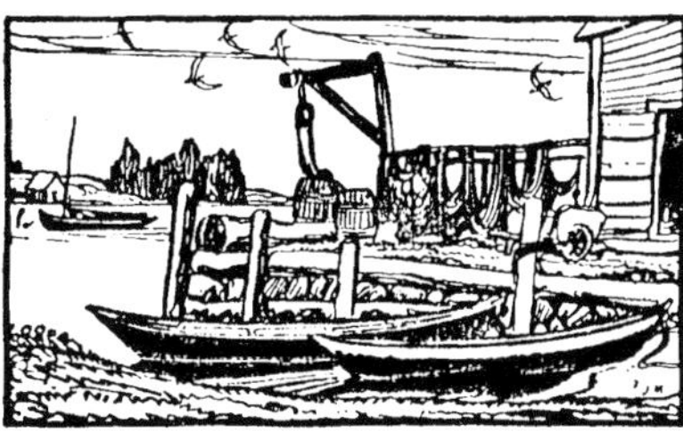

(w)

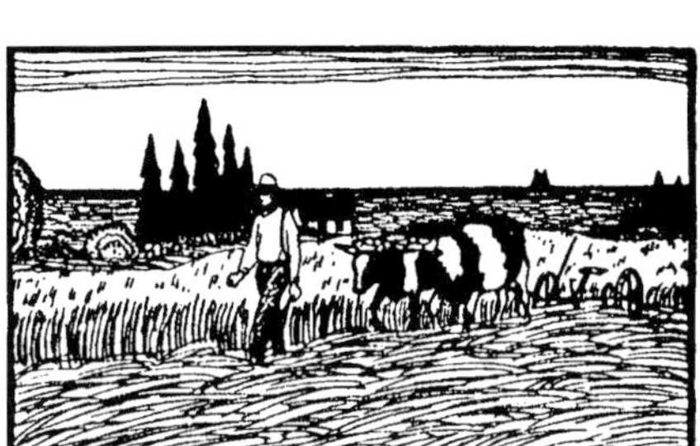

(x)

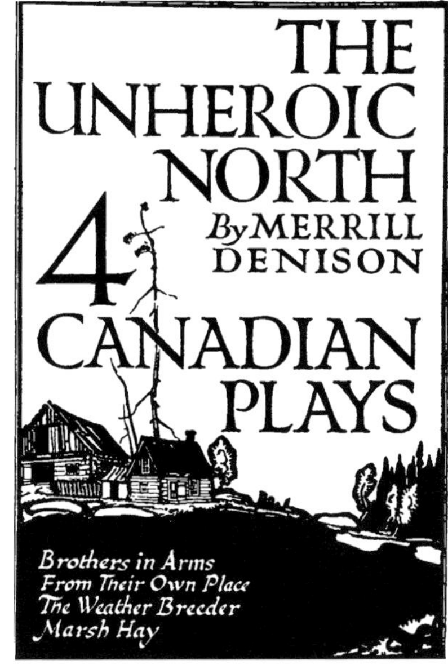

III: 30

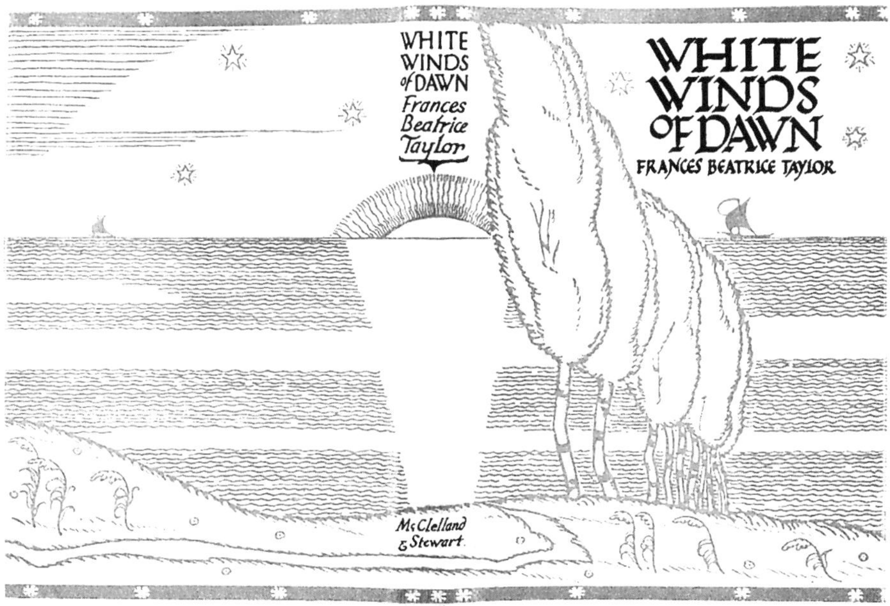

III:31

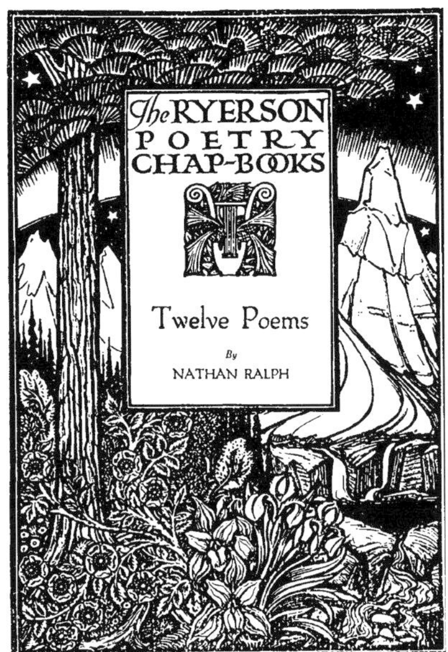

III: 32 (a)

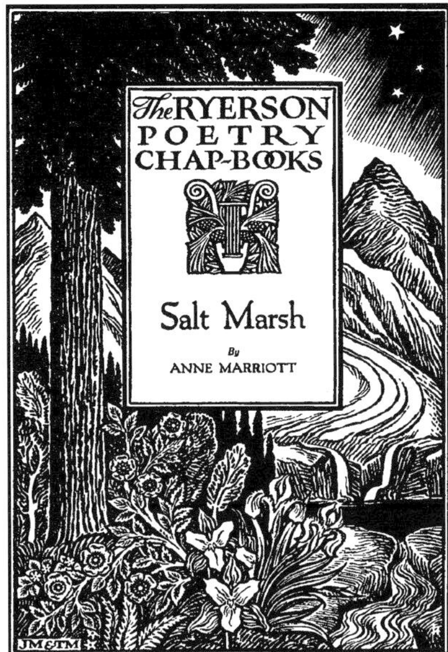

(b)

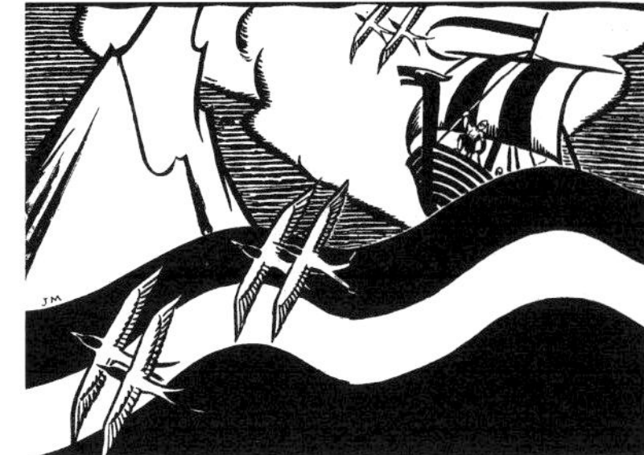

III: 33

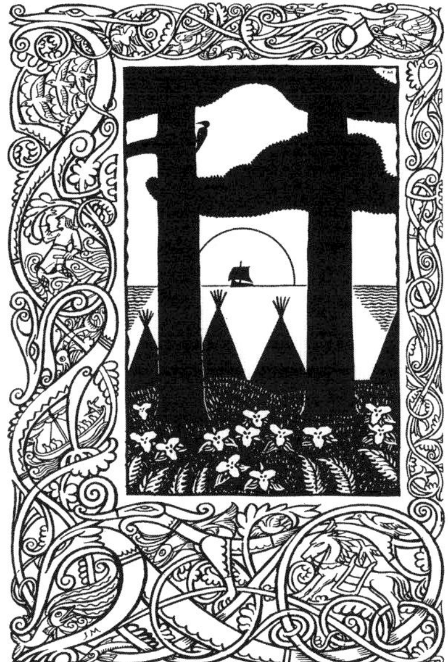

III: 34 (a)

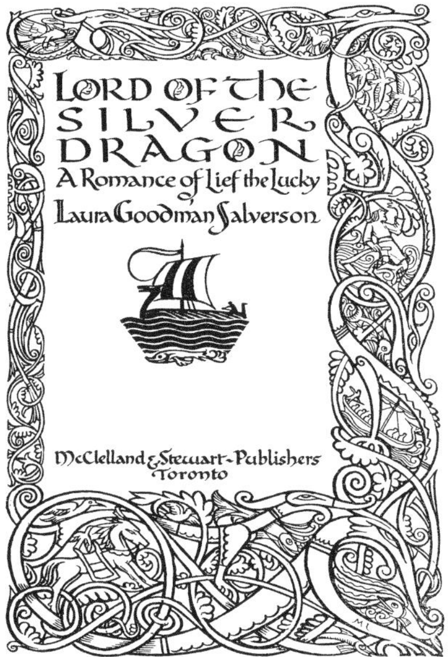

(b)

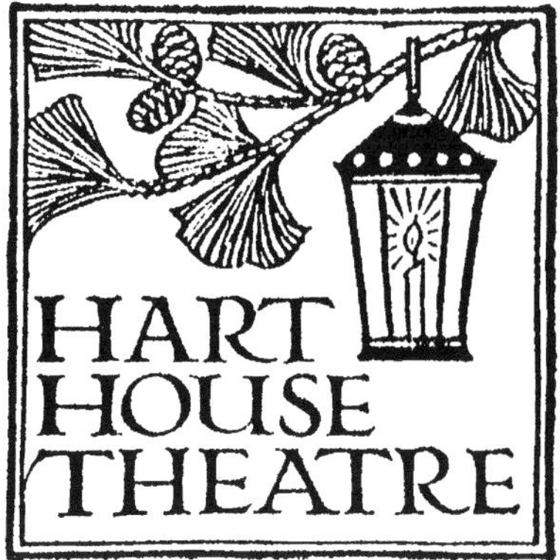

III: 35

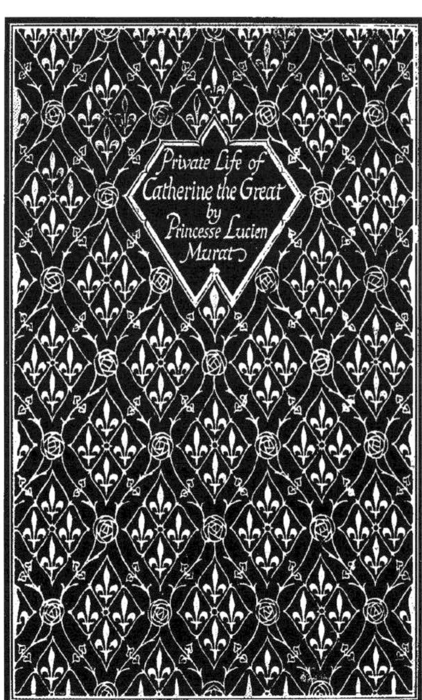

III: 36

III: Illustration

B: Periodicals

Note: dates are for first known appearance of an illustration or decoration; in several instances, the illustration or decoration (especially headpieces and endpieces) was reprinted on subsequent occasions.

III:36. Decorative border for "From my Window," poem by Ethelwyn Wetherald, *The Canadian Magazine* 17 (May 1901). *Note*: JM's first published illustration (?).

III:37. *February*, 1902, pen-and-ink; reproduced in 1904 Toronto Art League calendar; RSc.

III:38. *April*, 1902, pen-and-ink; reproduced in 1904 TAL calendar. RSc.

III:39 (a-c). Headpiece and vignettes, *The Canadian Courier* 1 (8 Dec. 1906).

III:40. Headpiece, *The Canadian Courier* 1 (8 Dec. 1906).

III:41. Headpiece, *The Canadian Courier* 1 (8 Dec. 1906).

III:42. Headpiece, *The Canadian Courier* 1 (12 Jan. 1907).

III:43. Headpiece and illustration, *The Canadian Courier* 1 (12 Jan. 1907).

III:44 (a-c). Decorative borders, *The Canadian Courier* 1; **a)** 12 Jan. 1907; **b)** 19 Jan. 1907; **c)** 5 May 1907.

III:45. Headpiece, *The Canadian Courier* 1 (2 Feb. 1907).

III:46. Masthead, *The Canadian Courier* 1 (13 April 1907).

III:47. Decorative border, *The Canadian Courier* 1 (25 May 1907).

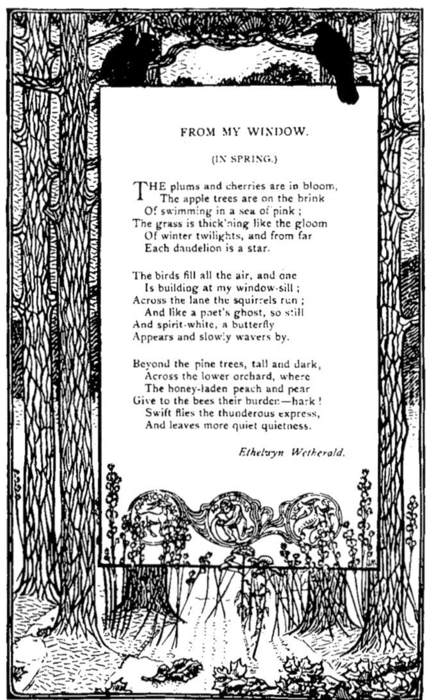

FROM MY WINDOW.

(IN SPRING.)

THE plums and cherries are in bloom,
The apple trees are on the brink
Of swimming in a sea of pink ;
The grass is thick'ning like the gloom
Of winter twilights, and from far
Each dandelion is a star.

The birds fill all the air, and one
Is building at my window-sill ;
Across the lane the squirrels run ;
And like a poet's ghost, so still
And spirit-white, a butterfly
Appears and slowly wavers by.

Beyond the pine trees, tall and dark,
Across the lower orchard, where
The honey-laden peach and pear
Give to the bees their burden—hark !
Swift flies the thunderous express,
And leaves more quiet quietness.

Ethelwyn Wetherald.

III:36

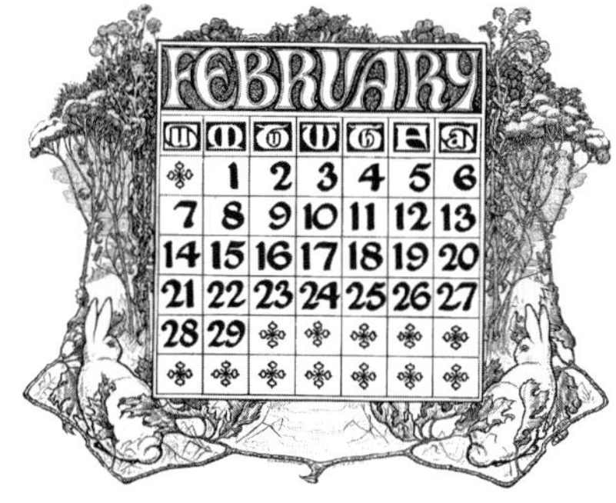

III:37

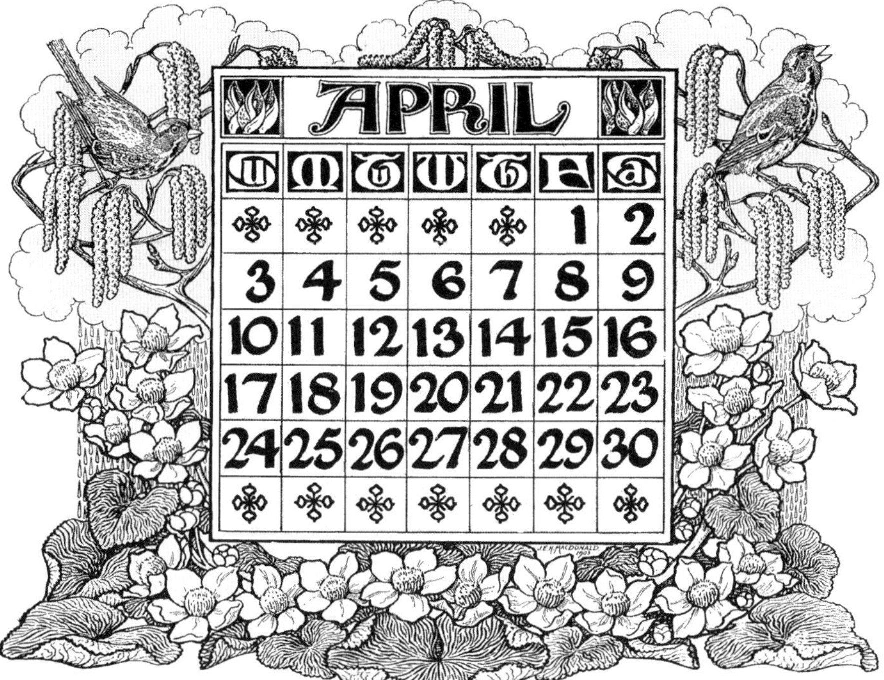

III:38

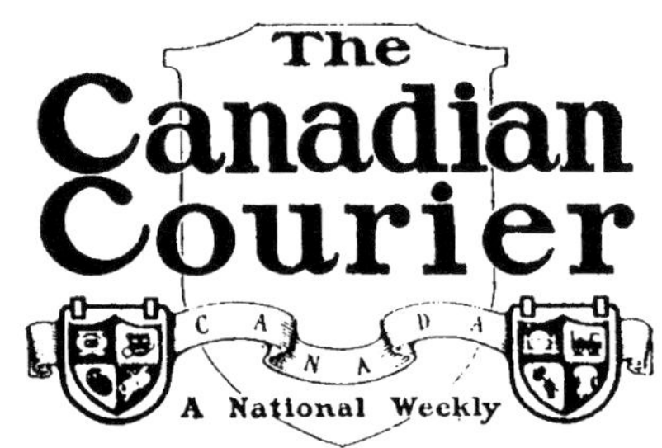

III:39 (a)

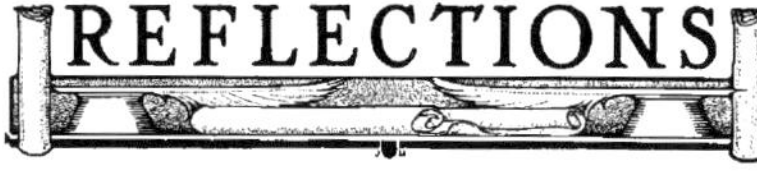

III:40

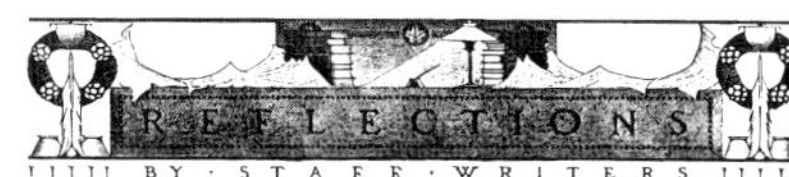

III:42

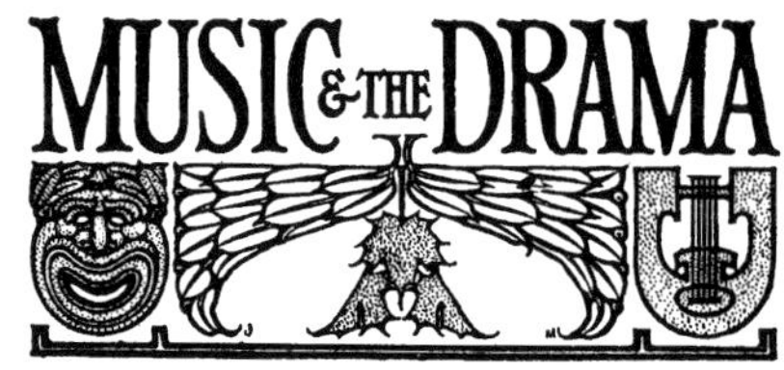

III:41

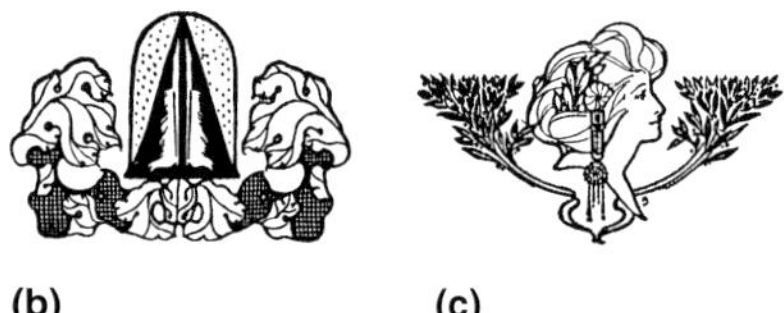

(b)

(c)

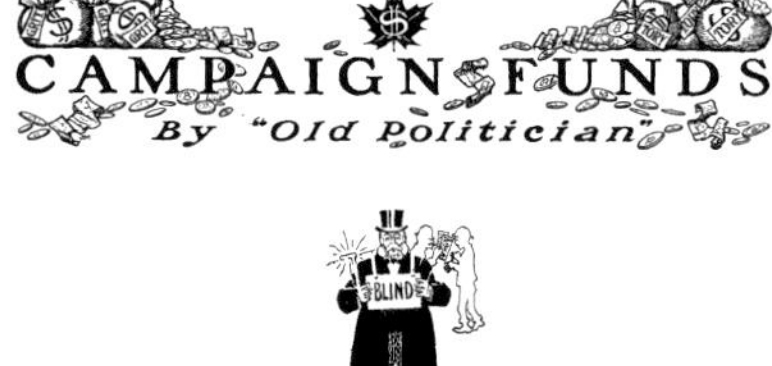

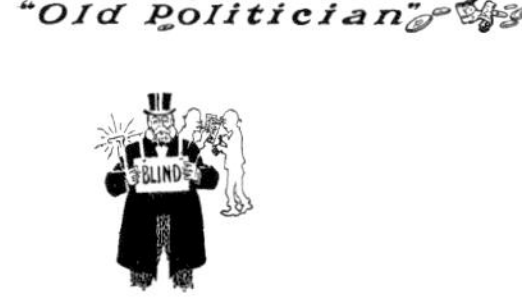

III:43

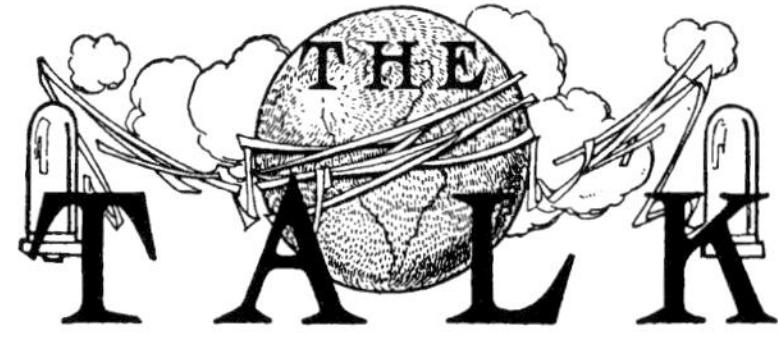

III:45

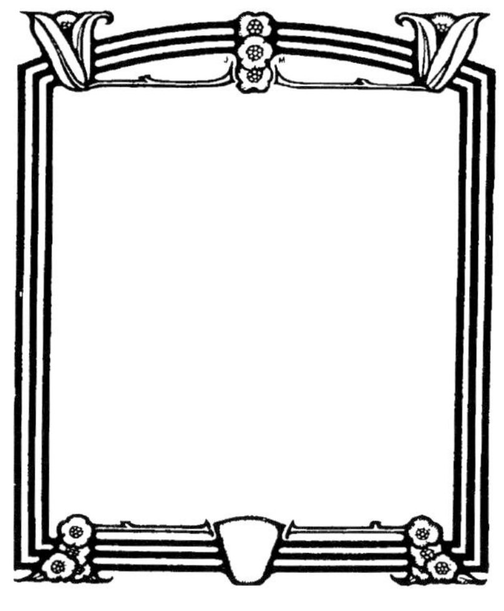

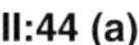

III:44 (a)

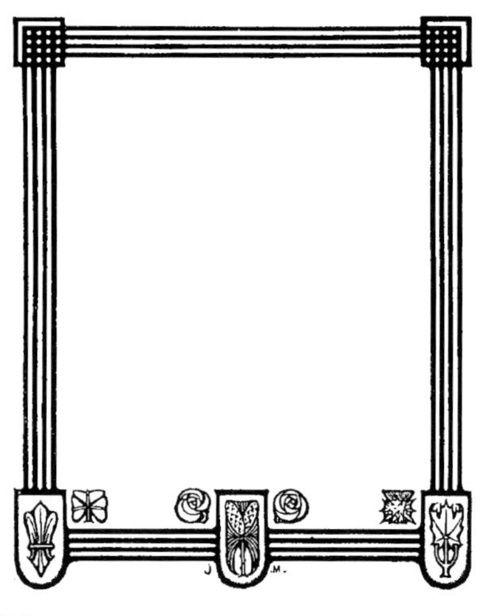

(b)

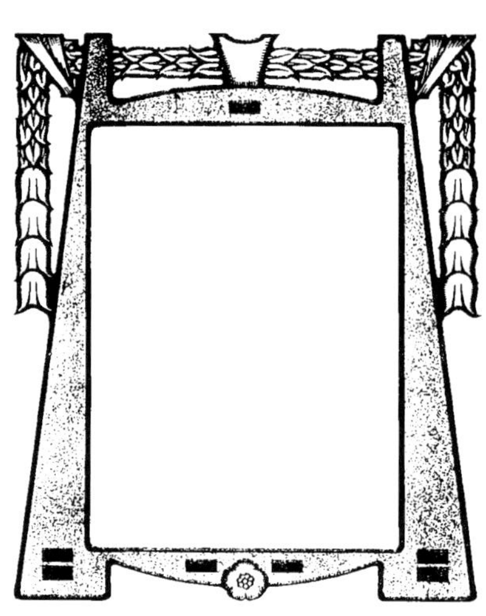

(c)

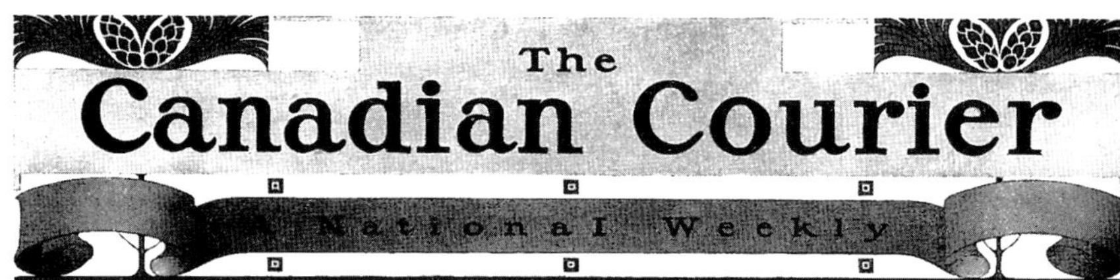

III:46

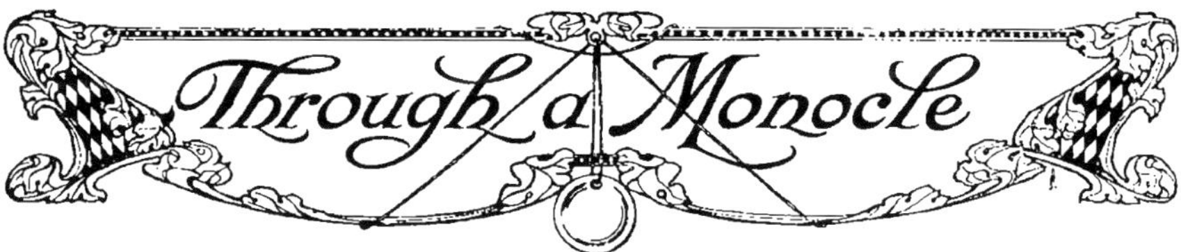

III:47

III: Illustration

III:48. Headpiece, *The Canadian Courier* 2 (9 Nov. 1907).

III:49. Headpiece, *The Canadian Courier* 3 (7 Dec. 1907).

III:50. Headpiece, *The Canadian Courier* 4 (6 June 1908).

III:51. Headpiece, *The Canadian Courier* 4 (6 June 1908).

III:52. Front cover, *The Canadian Courier* 4 (22 Aug. 1908).

III:53. Headpiece and tailpiece, *The Canadian Courier* 5 (12 Dec. 1908).

III:54. Headpiece and tailpiece, *Canadian Courier* 5 (12 Dec. 1908).

III:55. Vignette, *The Canadian Courier* 5 (12 Dec. 1908).

III:56. Headpiece, *Construction* 2 (Dec. 1908).

III:57. Headpiece, *Construction* 2 (Dec. 1908).

III:58. Headpiece, *Construction* 2 (Dec. 1908).

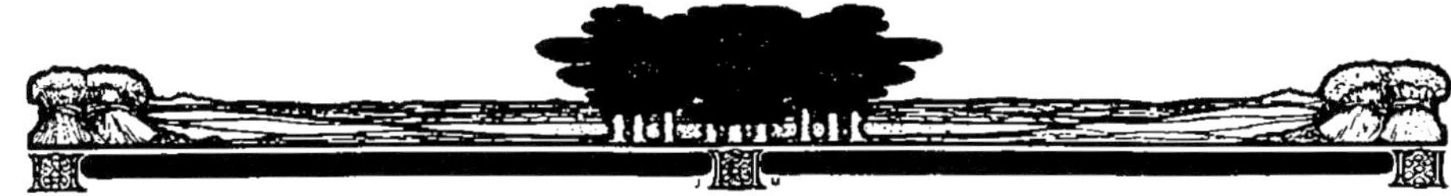

LOST TRAIL

A TALE OF THE NORTHERN WOODS.

By MARJORIE L. C. PICKTHALL

III:48

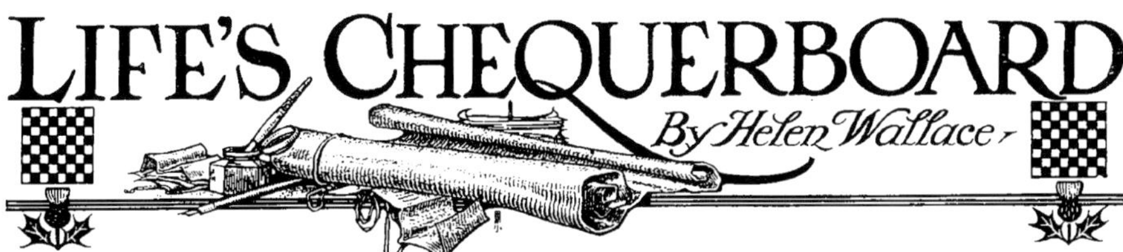

III:49

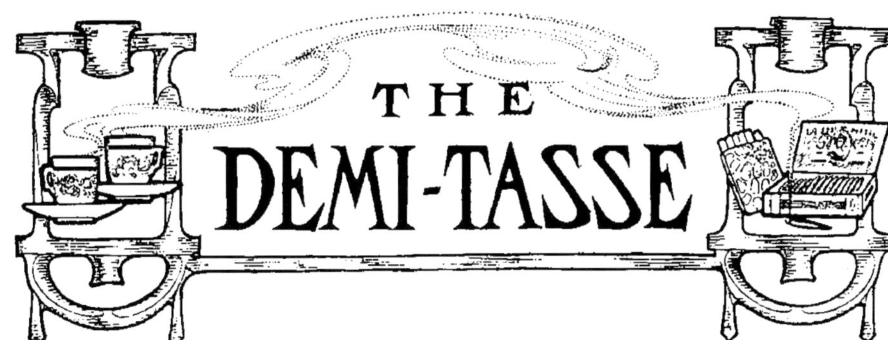

III:50

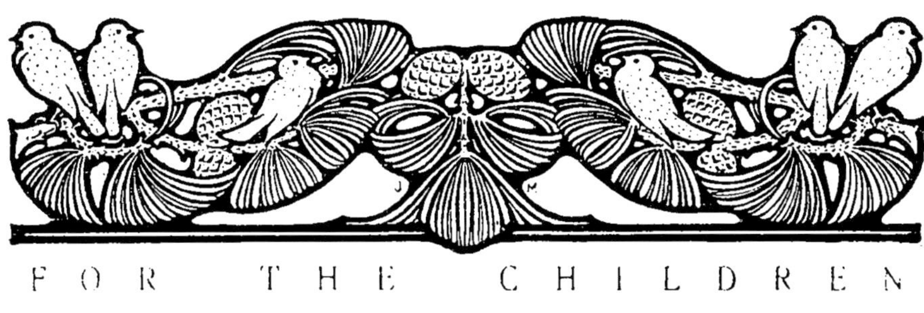

FOR THE CHILDREN

III:51

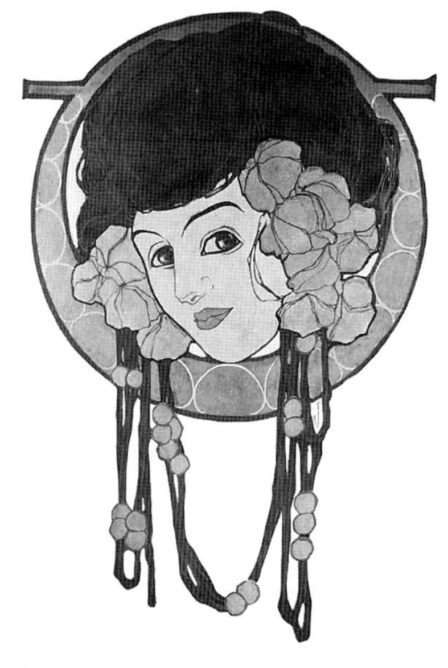

III:52

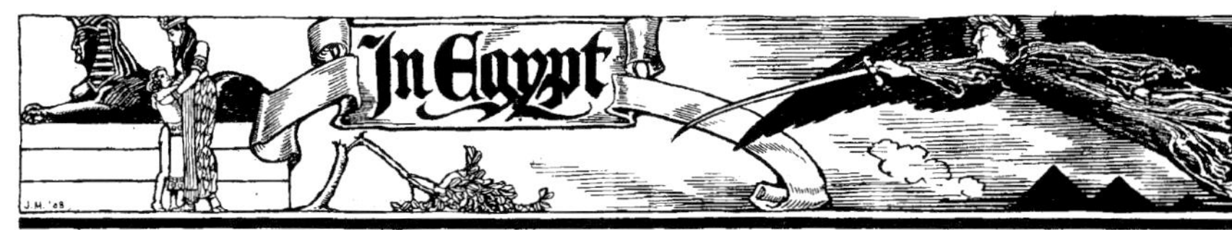

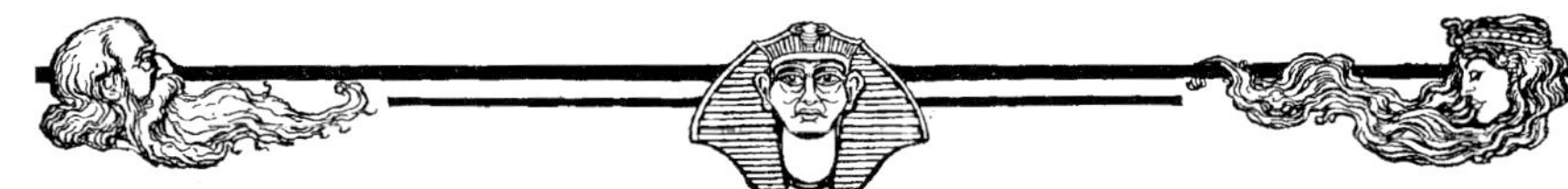

III:53

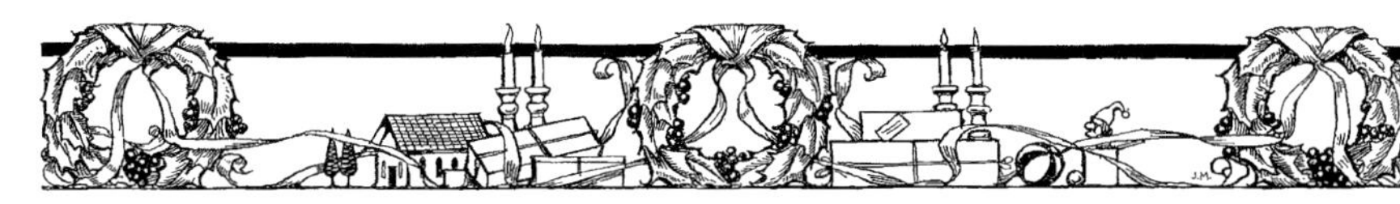

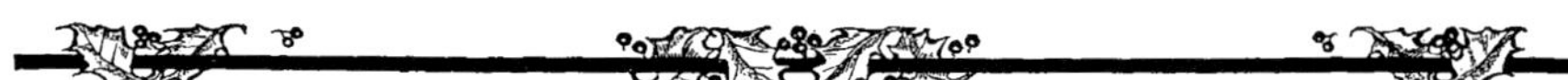

III:54

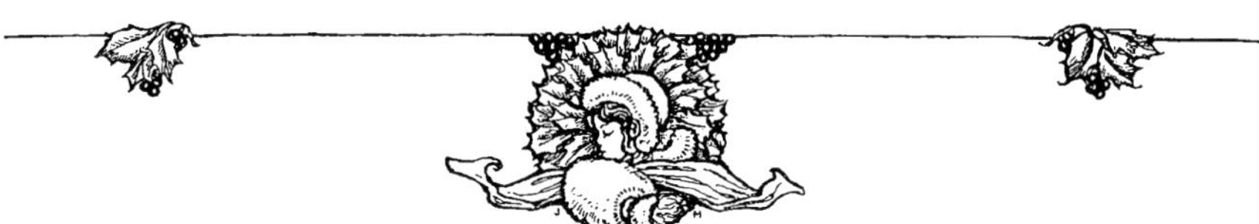

III:55

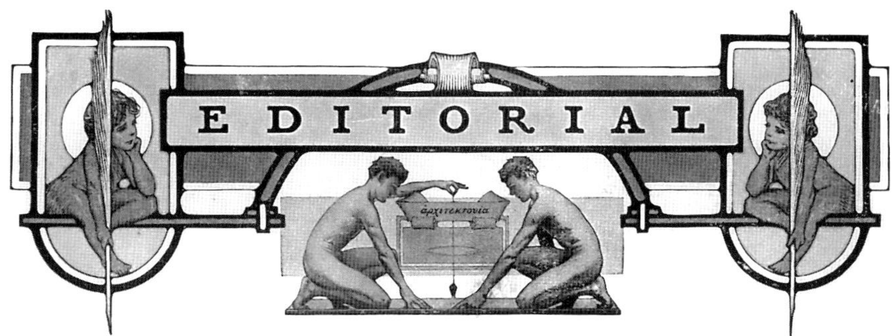

III:56

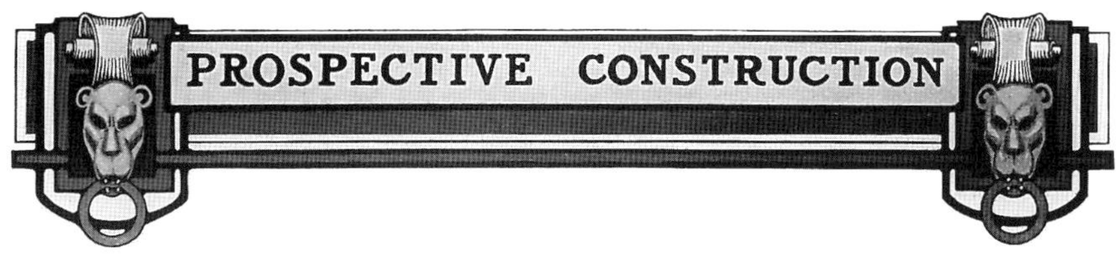

III:57

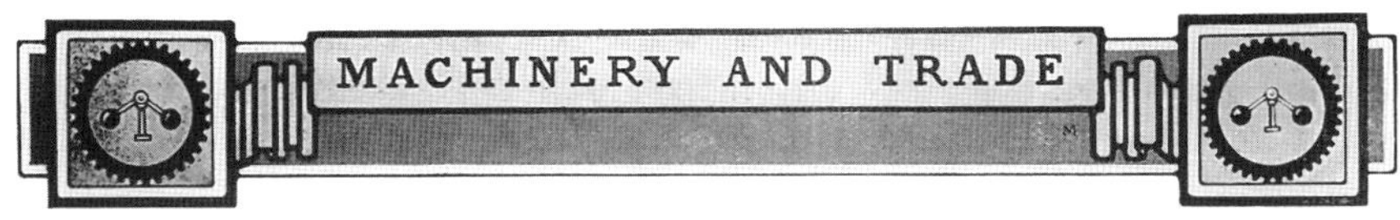

III:58

III: Illustration

III:59. Page layout, *Construction* 2 (Dec. 1908).

III:60. Front cover decoration, *The Canadian Courier* 5 (13 March 1909).

III:61. Tailpiece, *The Canadian Courier* 5 (20 March 1909).

III:62. Front cover, *The Canadian Magazine* 33 (Sept. 1909).

III:63. Front cover, *York Pioneer and Historical Society Annual Report* (1909).

III:64. Decorative border, *The Canadian Courier* 7 (14 May 1910).

III:65. Front cover border, *The Canadian Courier* 7 (28 May 1910).

III:66. *Sunrise in the Old Stone Town*, illustration in *The Canadian Courier* 8 (4 June 1910).

III:67. Front cover, *The Canadian Magazine* 36 (Nov. 1910).

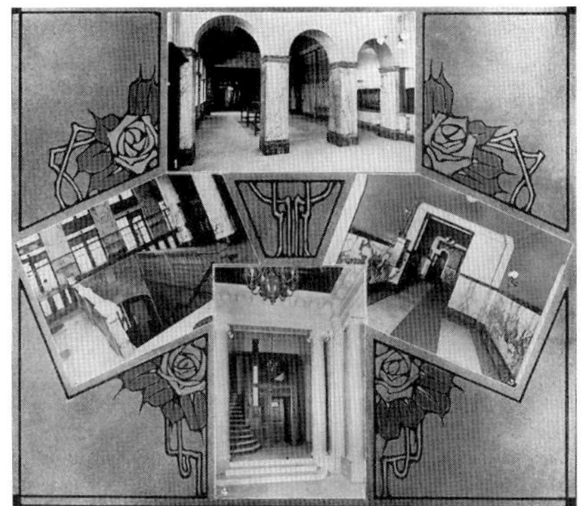

III:59

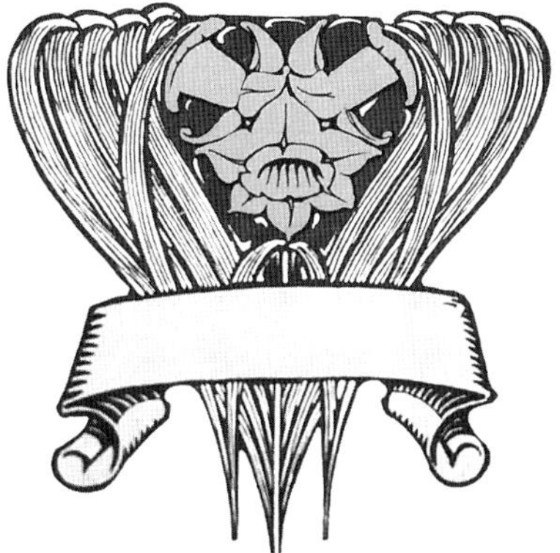

III:61

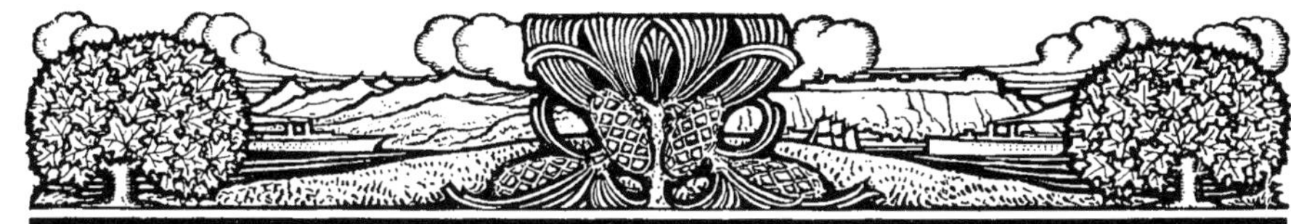

III:60

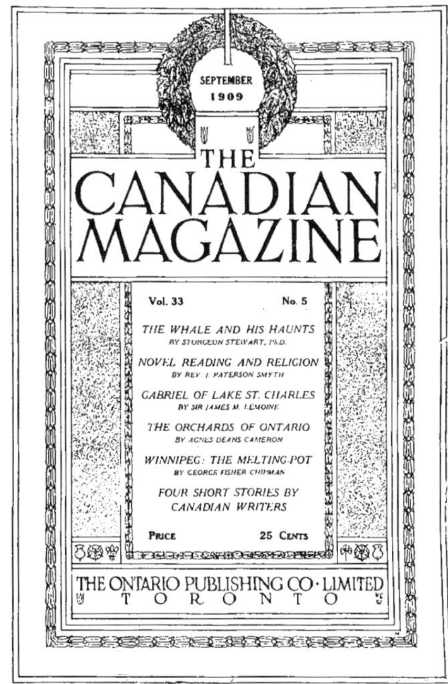

III:62

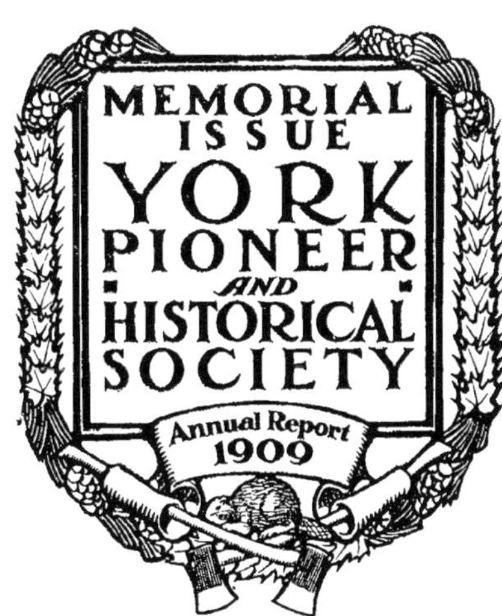

III:63

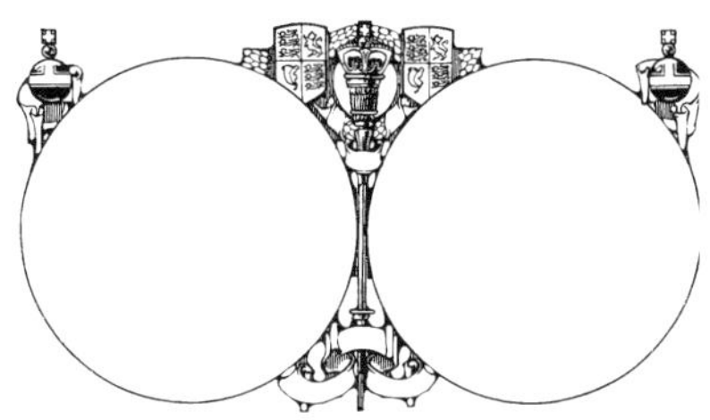

III:64

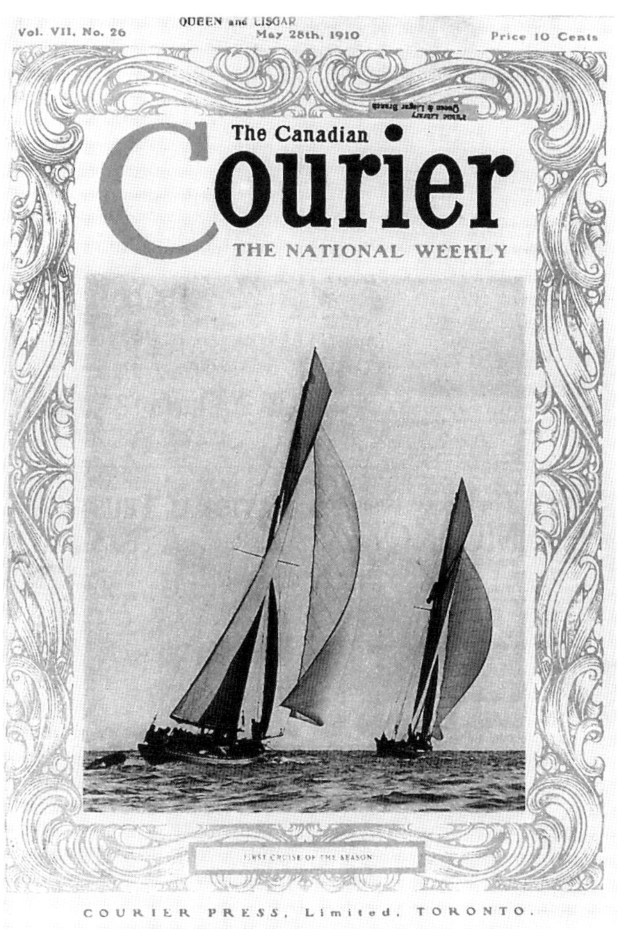

III:65

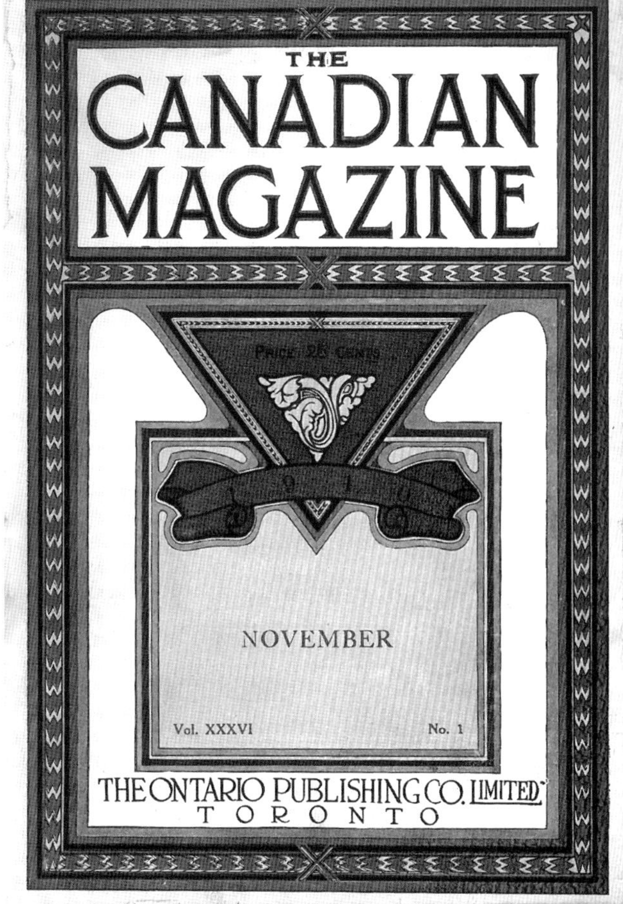

III:67

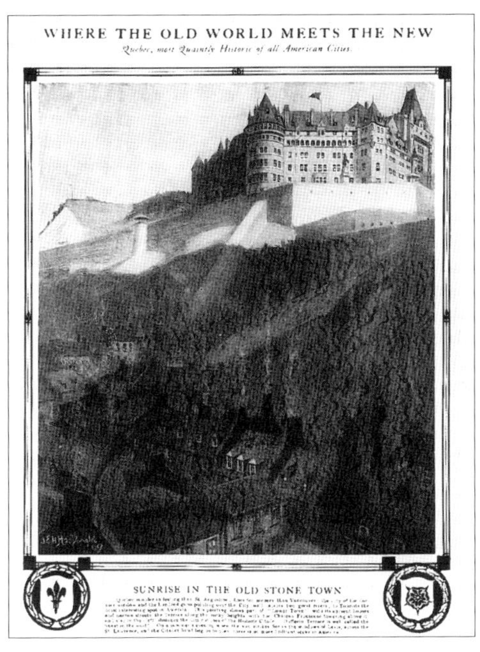

III:66

III: Illustration

III:68. Vignette, *Canadian Courier* 8 (12 Dec. 1910).

III:69. Headpiece, *The Canadian Courier* 10 (22 July 1911).

III:70. Coat of arms, front cover, *The Canadian Magazine* 38 (Sept. 1912).

III:71. *A Night Train in the Northland*, 1913, oil (or gouache?), reproduced as frontispiece, *The Canadian Magazine* 41 (Oct. 1913). *Note*: illustration for "The Spirit of Travel," by Britton B. Cooke; *cf.* **III:72 (j)**.

III:72 (a-q). Illustrations for "The Spirit of Travel," part 1, by B.B. Cooke, *The Canadian Magazine* 41 (Oct. 1913). *Note*: several of these illustrations were reprinted in *Canadian Heroes of Pioneer Days*, by Mabel B. McKinley (Toronto: Longmans, Green & Co., 1930); **III:72 (i)** reprinted on title page of *Clearing in the West*, by Nellie McClung (Toronto: Thomas Allen, 1935).

III:73 (a-o). Illustrations for "The Spirit of Travel," part 2, by B.B. Cooke, *The Canadian Magazine* 41 (Nov. 1913).

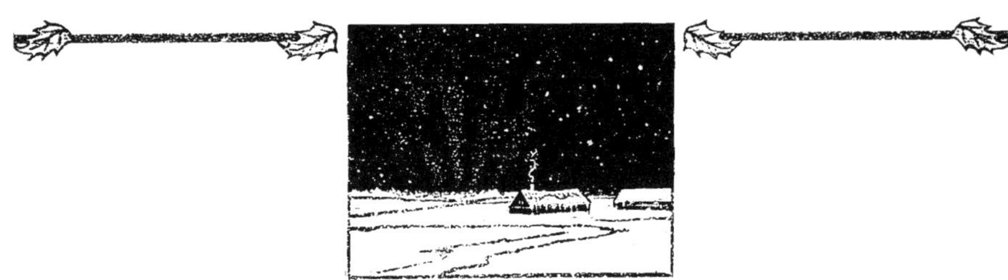

III:68

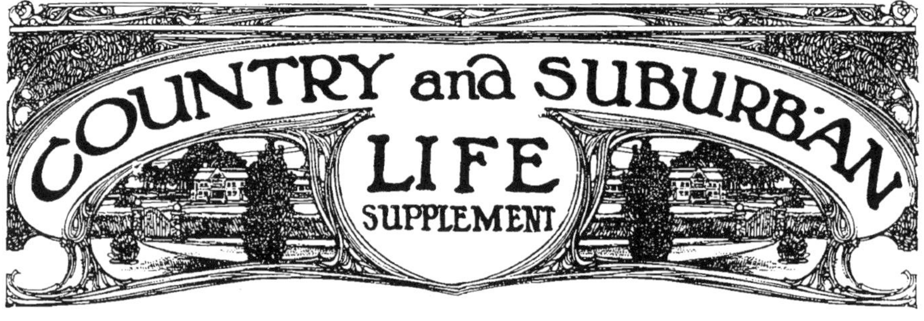

III:69

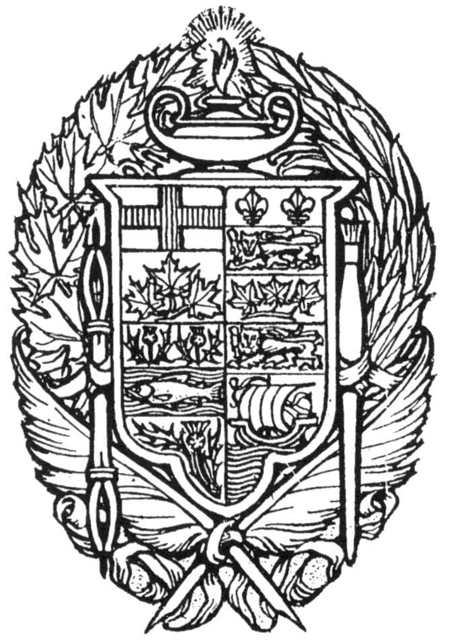

III:70

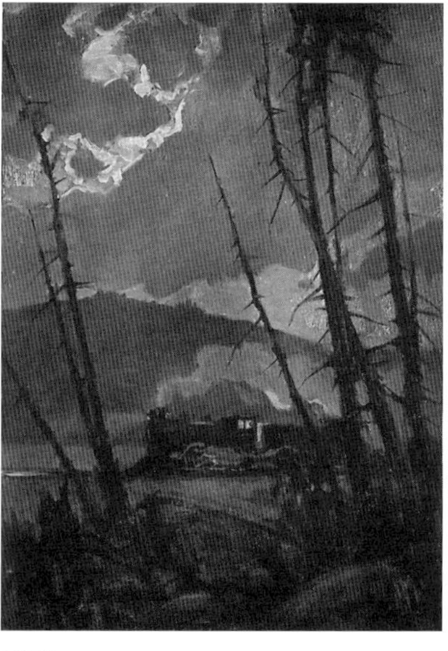

III:71

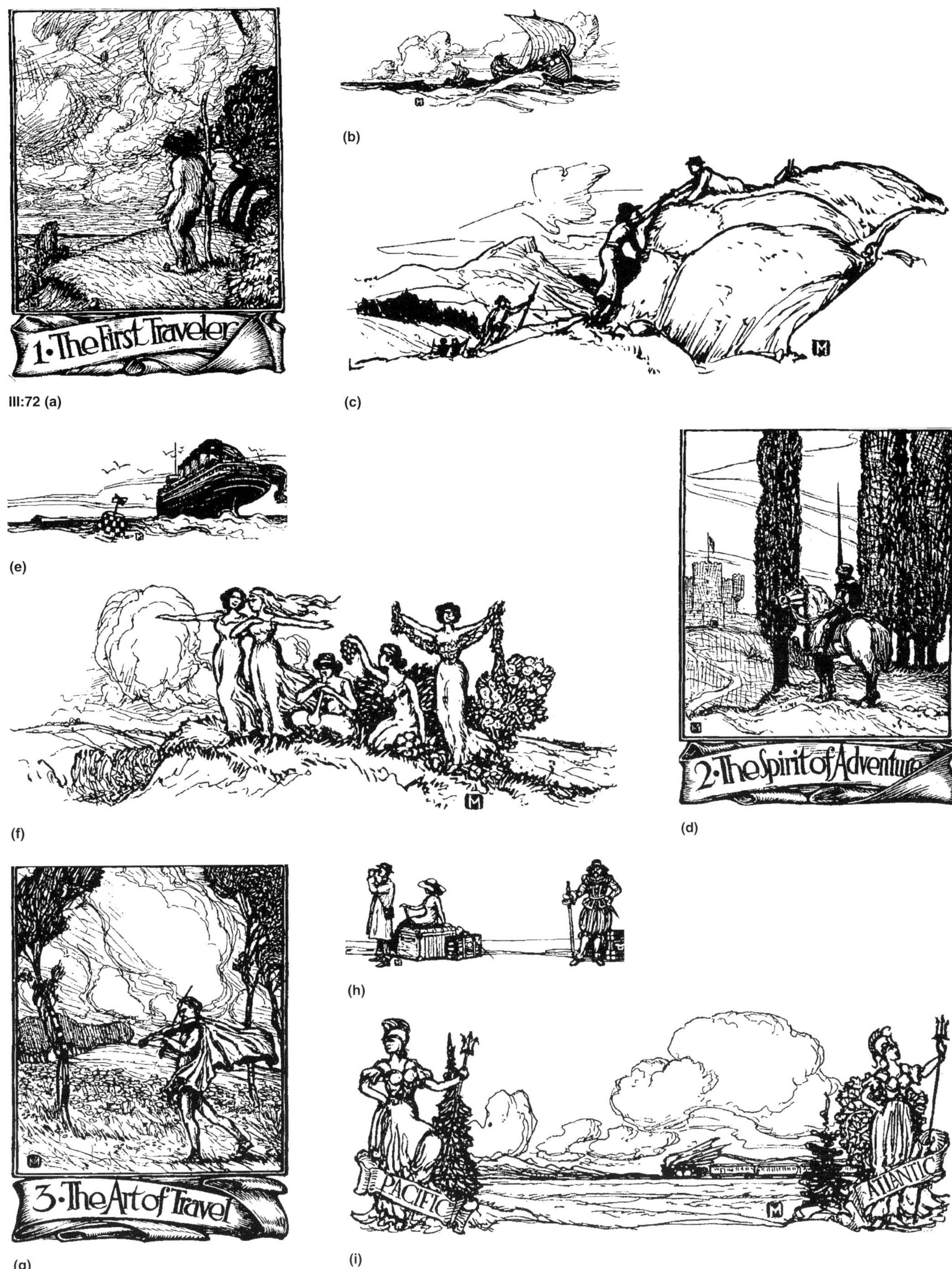

III:72 (a)

(b)

(c)

(d)

(e)

(f)

(g)

(h)

(i)

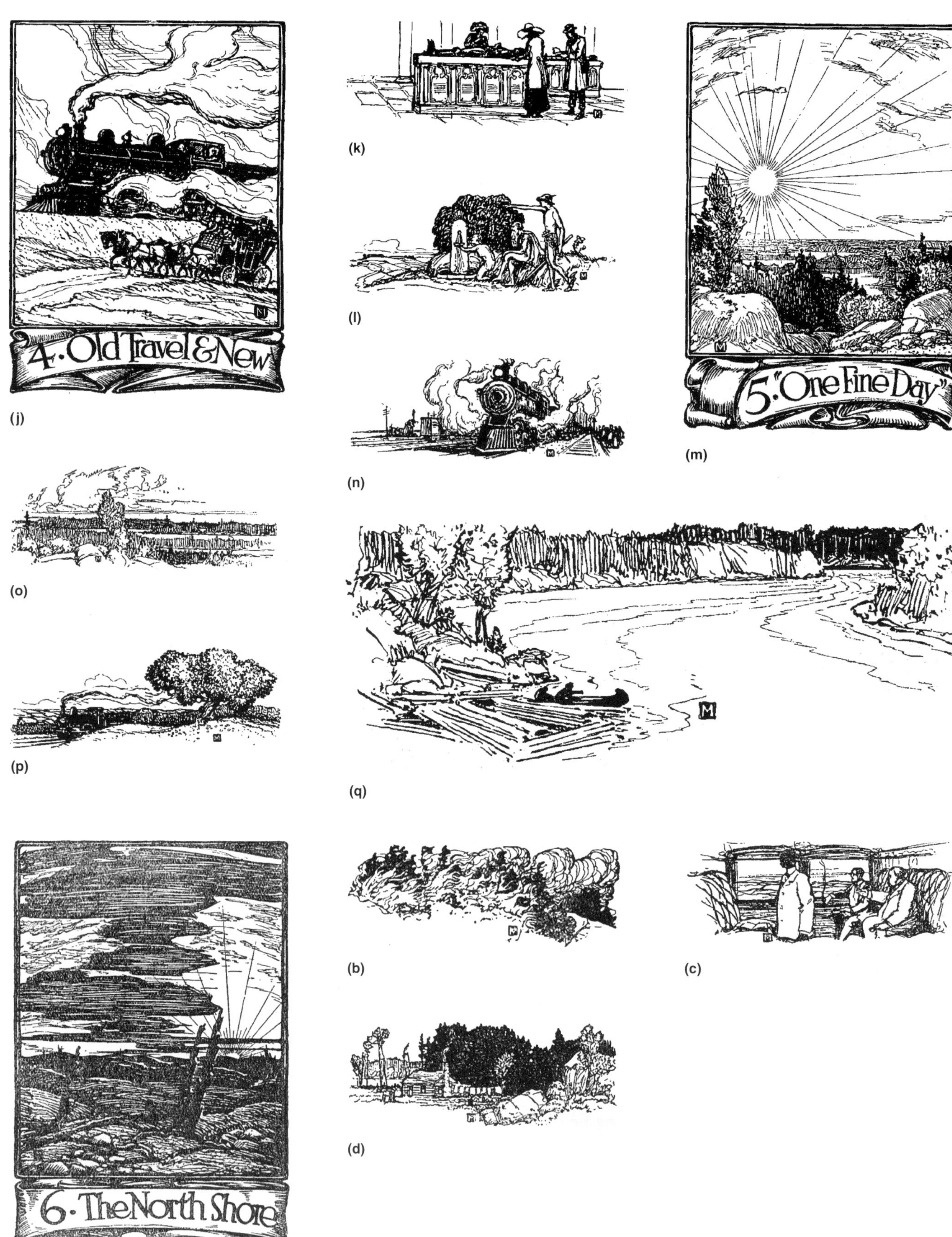

(j)

(k)

(l)

(m)

(n)

(o)

(p)

(q)

(b)

(c)

(d)

III:73 (a)

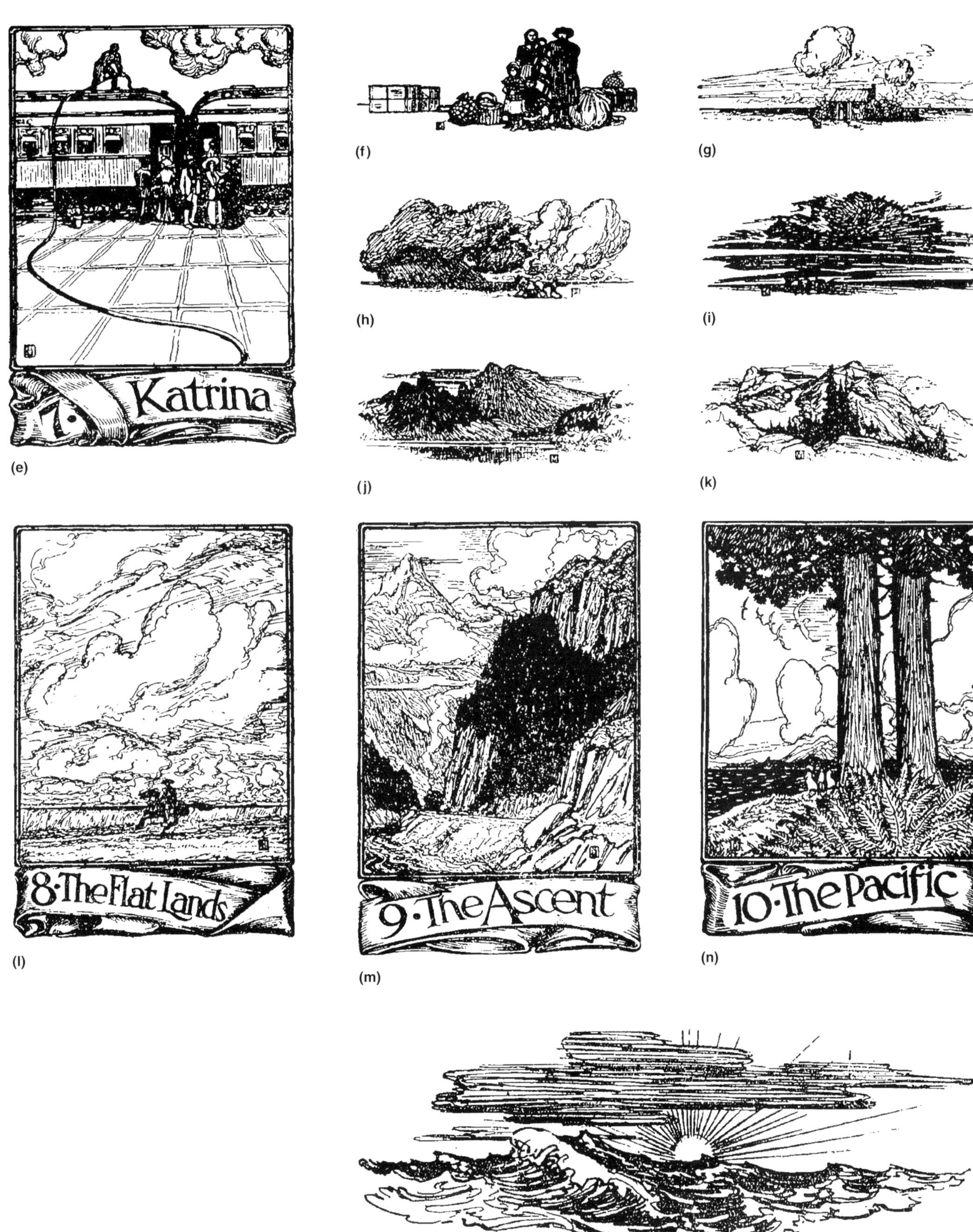

(e)

(f)

(g)

(h)

(i)

(j)

(k)

(l)

(m)

(n)

(o)

IV: *Lettering*

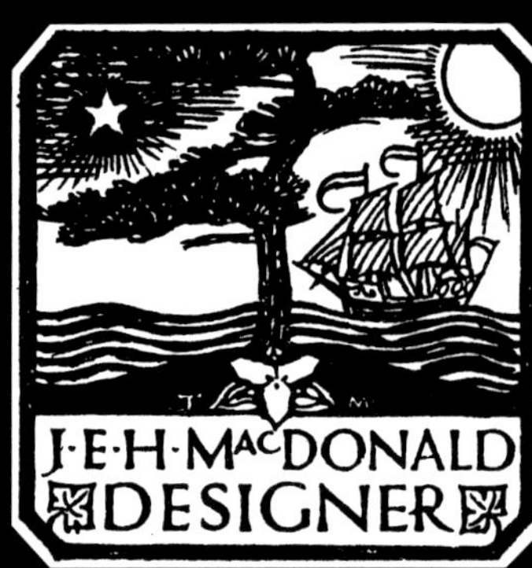

IV: Lettering

Certificates

IV:11. *The Edith Cavell Memorial Prize*, 1918, relief printing on paper, initialled and dated (l.r.): *JEH/ MACD/1918*; reproduced from photostat in HBP.

IV:12. Certificate, The Ontario Association of Architects, 1920, relief printing on paper, initialled and dated (l.r.): *JEH/MACDONALD/DEL 1920*; reproduced from negative in HBP. *Note*: withdrawn by OAA in 1935. *Note*: Eric Arthur's copy, presented January 1929.

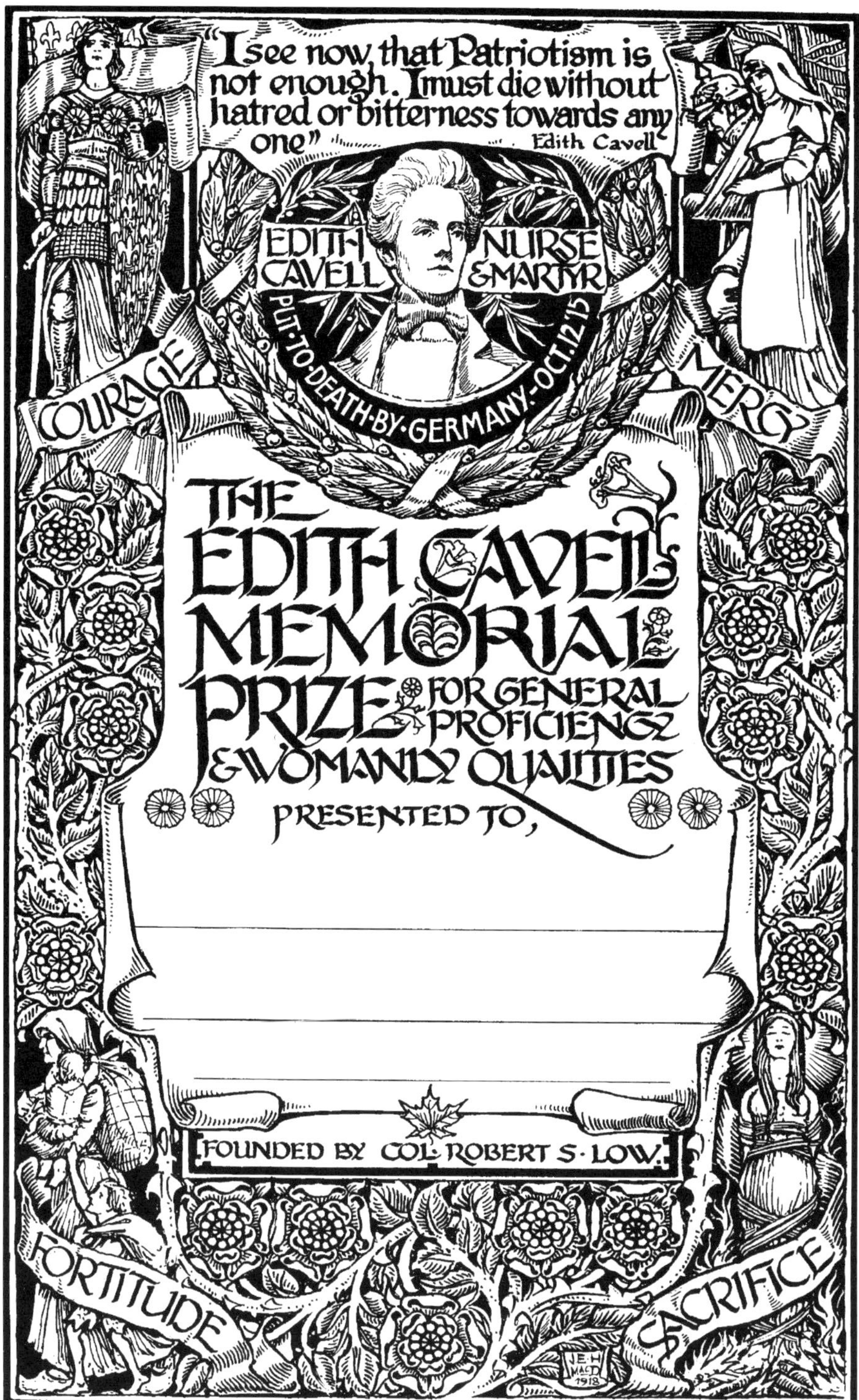

IV:11

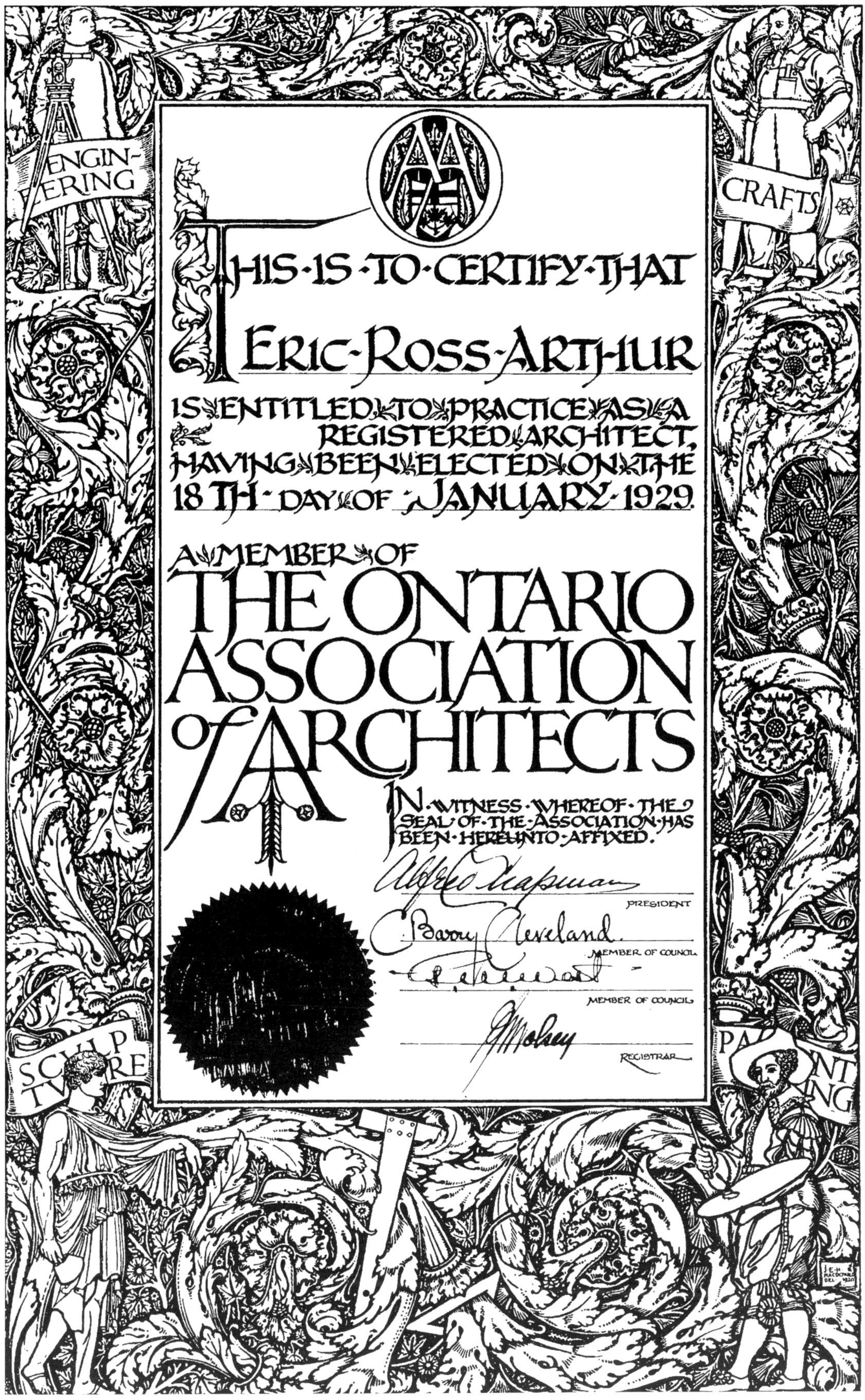
ENGIN-EERING
CRAFTS
THIS·IS·TO·CERTIFY·THAT
ERIC·ROSS·ARTHUR
IS ENTITLED TO PRACTICE AS A
REGISTERED ARCHITECT,
HAVING BEEN ELECTED ON THE
18 TH DAY OF JANUARY 1929.
A MEMBER OF
THE ONTARIO
ASSOCIATION
of ARCHITECTS
IN·WITNESS·WHEREOF·THE
SEAL·OF·THE·ASSOCIATION·HAS
BEEN·HEREUNTO·AFFIXED.
PRESIDENT
MEMBER OF COUNCIL
MEMBER OF COUNCIL
REGISTRAR
SCULP TURE
PAINT ING

IV:12

IV: Lettering

Presentation Addresses

IV:21. Title page, presentation album to Sir John M. Gibson from the Board of Trustees, Toronto General Hospital, 1913, pen-and-ink; Historical Committee, TGH.

IV:22 (a-f). Illustrations in presentation album to Sir John M. Gibson, 1913, pen and black and brown ink-on-paper; Historical Committee, TGH. *Note*: titles of drawings: **a)** *The College Street Front* (12.0 x 15.0 cm); **b)** *The Main Entrance* (16.0 x 11.5 cm); **c)** *The Surgical Wing* (12.0 x 15.0 cm); **d)** *The Out-Patient Building* (12.0 x 15.5 cm); **e)** *The Private Patients' Wing and The Nurses' Home* (16.0 x 11.5 cm); **f)** *The Emergency Building* (12.0 x 15.5 cm).

IV:28. Front cover design, *Private Patients' Building* (Toronto: Toronto General Hospital, [1913]). *Note*: engraved by Grip Ltd., this booklet's pen-and-ink illustrations are by Tom Thomson.

IV:29 (a-c). "Book stamps" for illuminated address cover, "To General Sir Arthur Currie," 1918, pen-and-ink on paper;TMP.

IV:30. Front cover, *In Memoriam Robert Ford Gagen*, 1926, gold-stamped leather (binding by E.J. Hathaway) (23.5 x 15.7 cm); NGC. *Note*: memorial book commissioned by the OSA, 9 March 1926, in honour of the painter Robert F. Gagen (1848-1926), who had taught at COSAD, and who joined the OSA as a foundation member in 1872. He was the author of "Ontario Art Chronicle" (typescript, n.d.). See colour plate **Pl. IV:1** for second leaf of this book.

IV:31. Leaf from *In Memoriam Robert Ford Gagen*, 1926, ink and watercolour on japan imperial paper (22.5 x 14.0 cm); NGC.

IV:32 (a-b). Two leaves from *In Memoriam Robert Ford Gagen*, 1926, ink and watercolour on japan imperial paper (each leaf: 22.5 x 14.0 cm); NGC.

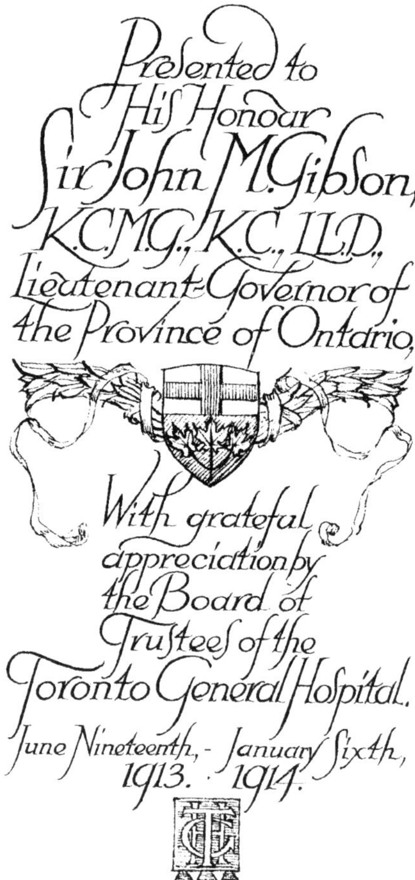

Presented to His Honour Sir John M. Gibson, K.C.M.G., K.C., LL.D., Lieutenant-Governor of the Province of Ontario, With grateful appreciation by the Board of Trustees of the Toronto General Hospital. June Nineteenth, - January Sixth, 1913. · 1914.

IV:21

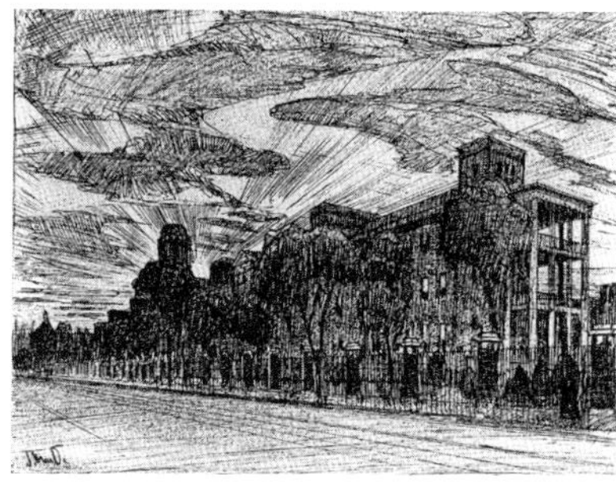

IV:22 (a)

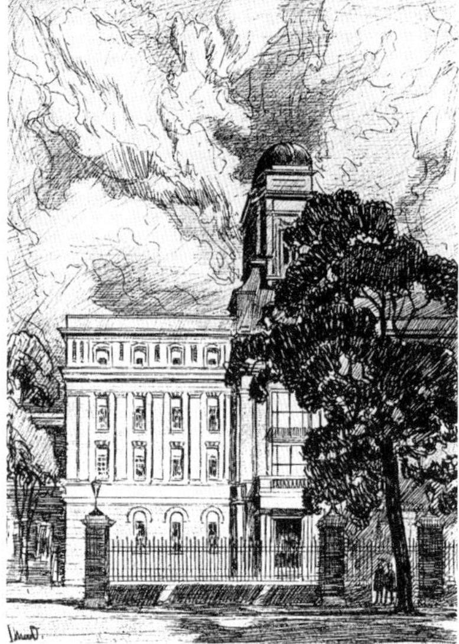

(b)

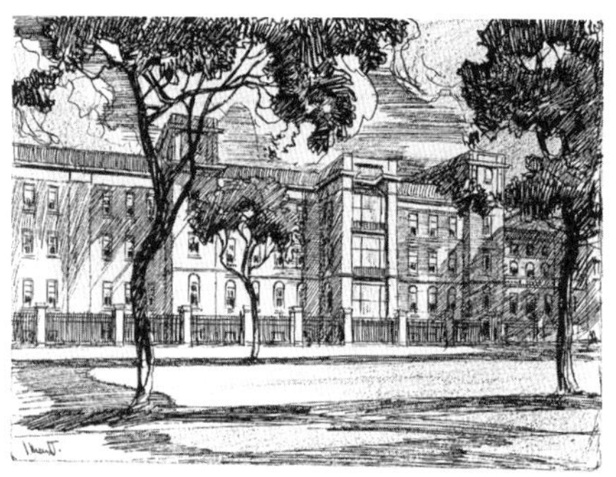

(c)

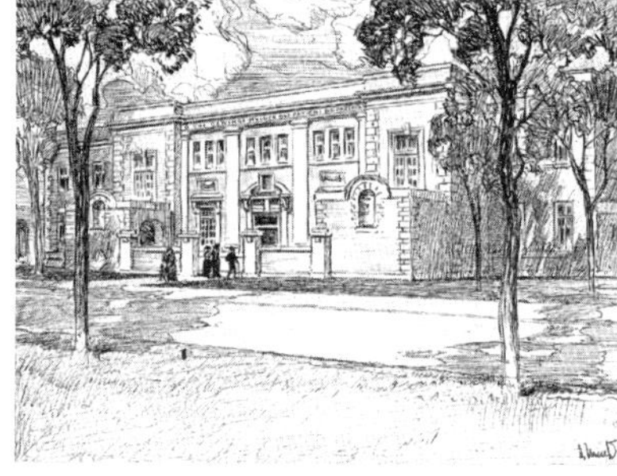

(d)

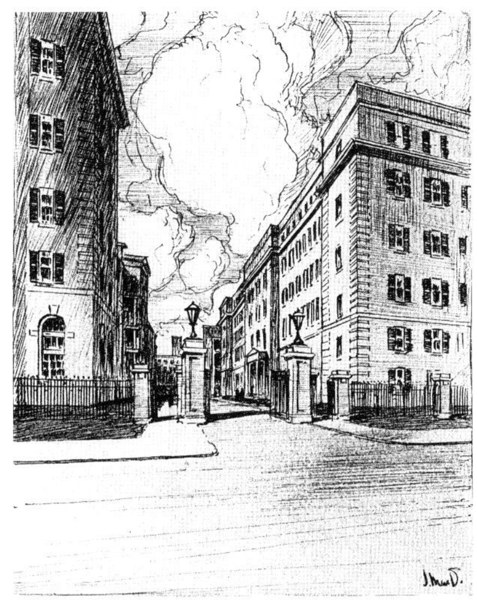

(e)

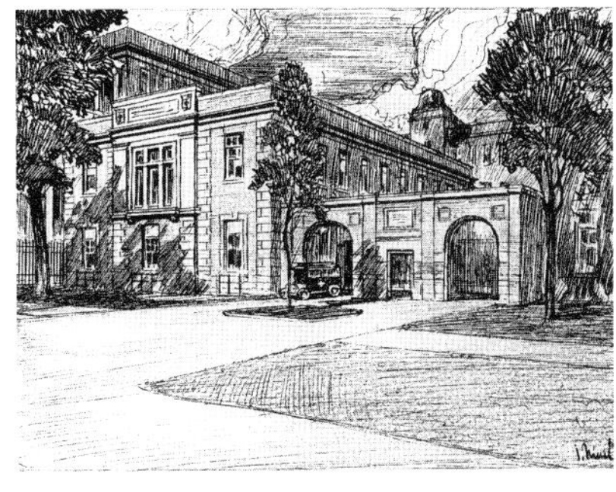

(f)

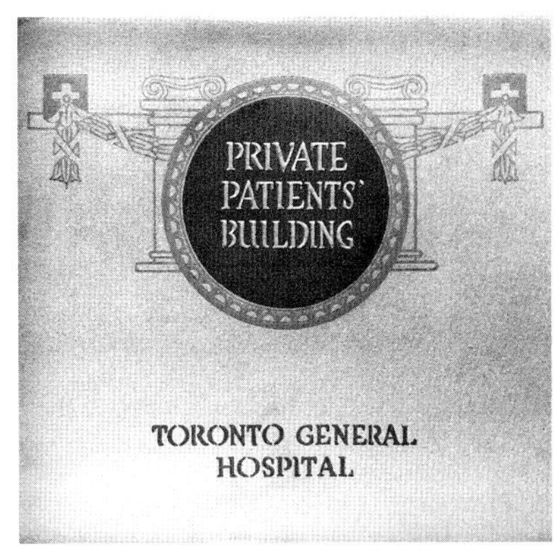

IV:28

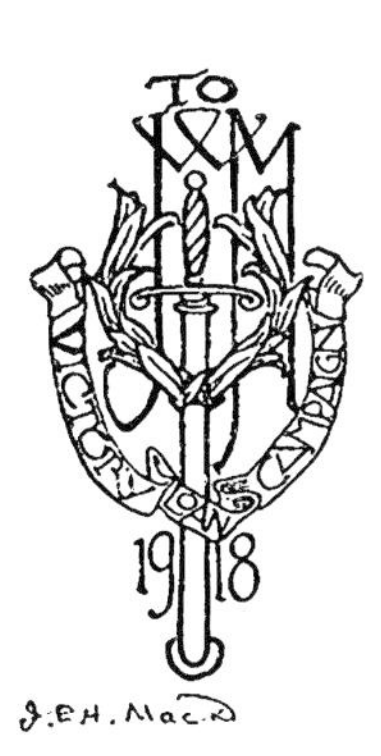

IV:29 (a)

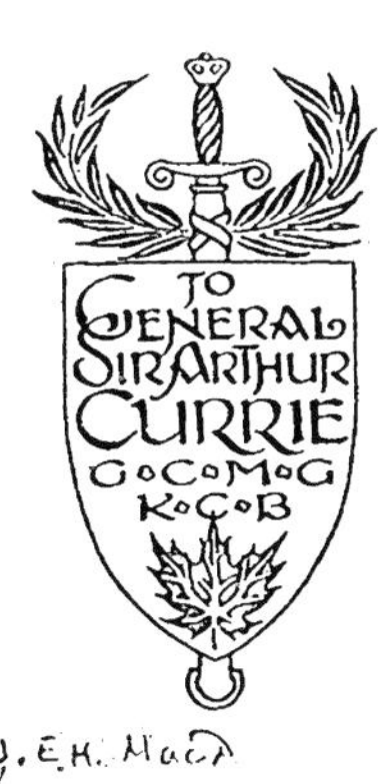

(b)

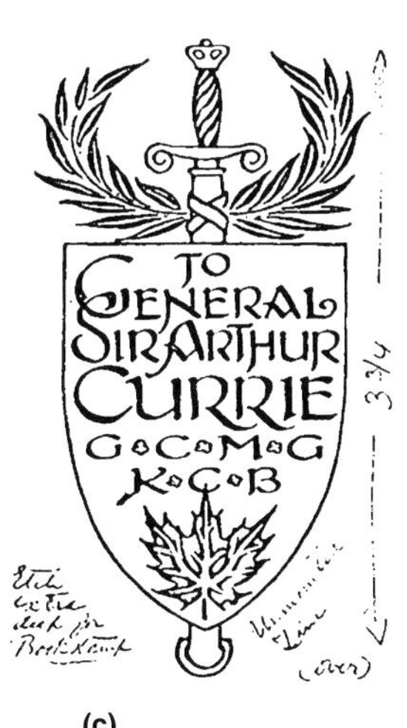

(c)

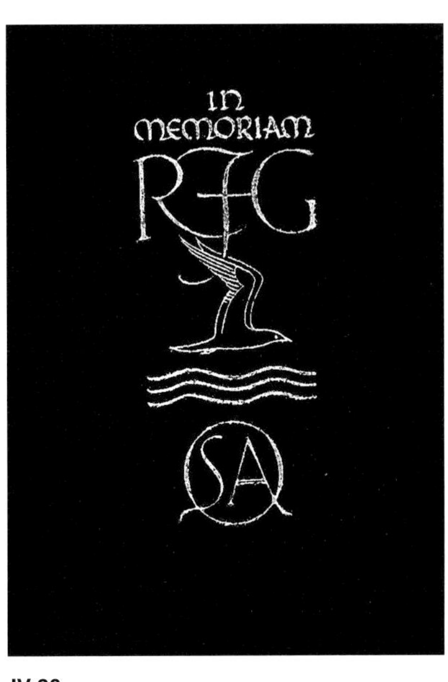

IV:30

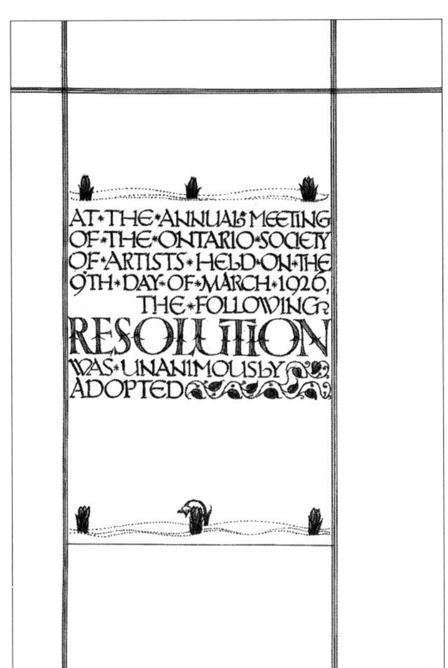

AT·THE·ANNUAL·MEETING OF·THE·ONTARIO·SOCIETY OF·ARTISTS·HELD·ON·THE 9TH·DAY·OF·MARCH·1926, THE·FOLLOWING RESOLUTION WAS·UNANIMOUSLY ADOPTED

IV:31

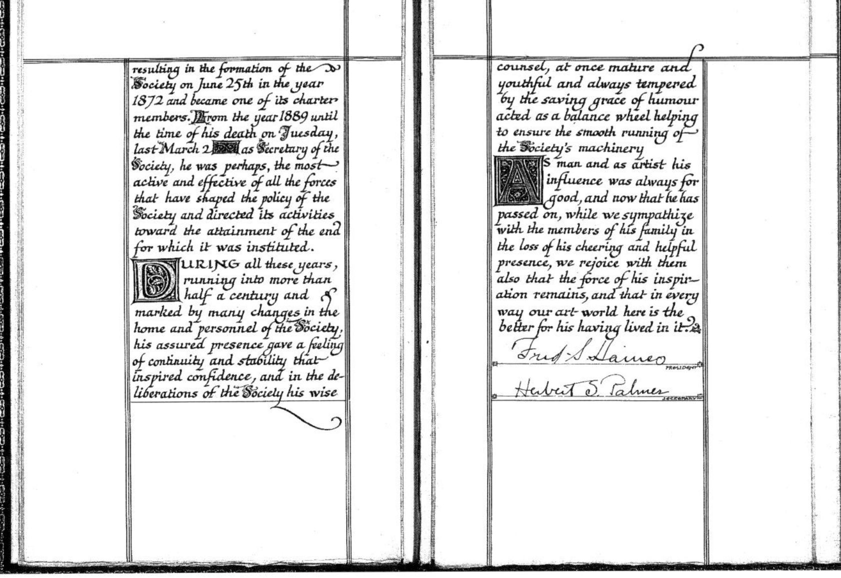

resulting in the formation of the Society on June 25th in the year 1872 and became one of its charter members. From the year 1889 until the time of his death on Tuesday, last March 2[illegible] as Secretary of the Society, he was perhaps, the most active and effective of all the forces that have shaped the policy of the Society and directed its activities toward the attainment of the end for which it was instituted.

DURING all these years, running into more than half a century and marked by many changes in the home and personnel of the Society, his assured presence gave a feeling of continuity and stability that inspired confidence, and in the deliberations of the Society his wise

counsel, at once mature and youthful and always tempered by the saving grace of humour acted as a balance wheel helping to ensure the smooth running of the Society's machinery

AS man and as artist his influence was always for good, and now that he has passed on, while we sympathize with the members of his family in the loss of his cheering and helpful presence, we rejoice with them also that the force of his inspiration remains, and that in every way our art world here is the better for his having lived in it.

Fred S Haines PRESIDENT

Herbert S. Palmer SECRETARY

IV:32 (a) (b)

V: Bookplates

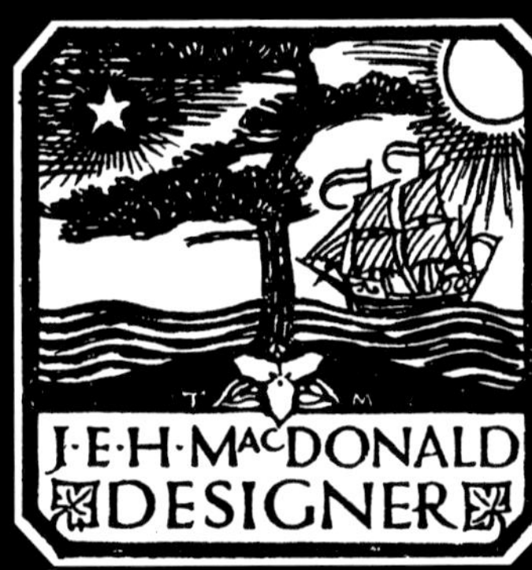

VI: *Designs for the Arts and Letters Club*

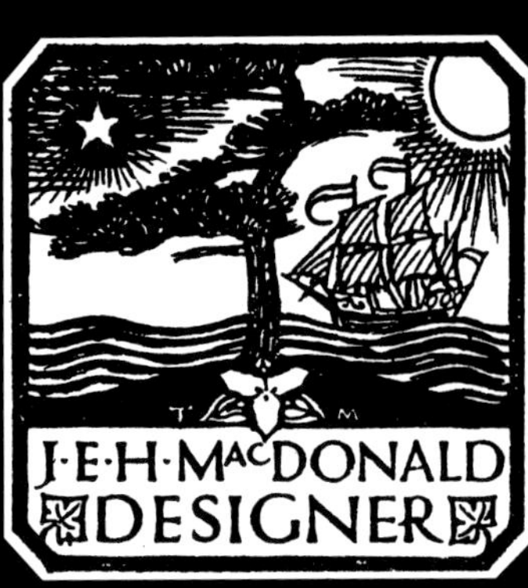

VI: Designs for the Arts and Letters Club

Note: The following items are in chronological order, though dating is sometimes not absolutely certain. For other examples of JM's designs for the ALC, see the colour plate section and section **V: Bookplates**.

VI:1. Front cover, *A Gathering of the Arts* [by Augustus Bridle] (Toronto, 1908), relief printing; RSc.

VI:2. Headpiece, *The Lamps* (Jan. 1910), relief printing; RSc.

VI:3 (a-d). Illustrations for program, *Interior*, by Maurice Maeterlinck, performed at the ALC on 29 April 1911 under direction of Roy Mitchell (Toronto: ALC, 1911), relief printing; RSc.

VI:4. Front cover, *The Lamps* 1, no. 1 (Oct. 1911), relief printing (printed by Acton Publishing Co. Ltd., Toronto); RSc. *Note*: "Toronto, October, 1911" lettered by A.H. Howard.

VI:5. "The Eternal Grouch," illustration for poem by W.A.C., *The Lamps* (Oct. 1911), relief printing; RSc.

VI:6. Front cover, *The Lamps* 1, no. 1 new series (June 1912), relief printing; RSc.

VI:7. "All would be well...," pen-and-ink illustration of stage-set and back-cloth, *The Shadowy Waters*, by W.B. Yeats, performed at the ALC on 28 Dec. 1911, under direction of Roy Mitchell, reproduced in *The Lamps* (June 1912), relief printing; RSc.

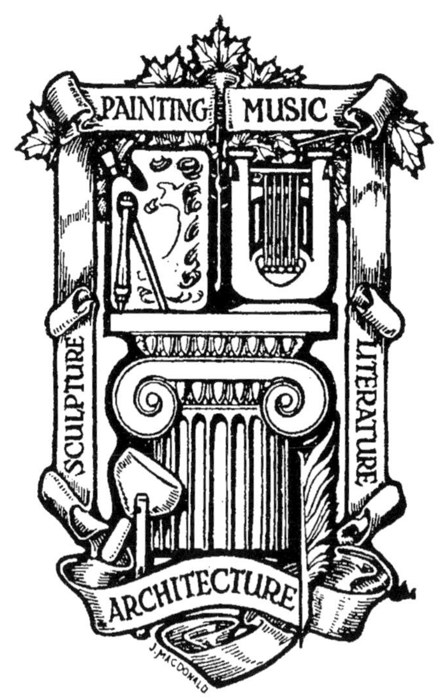

VI:1

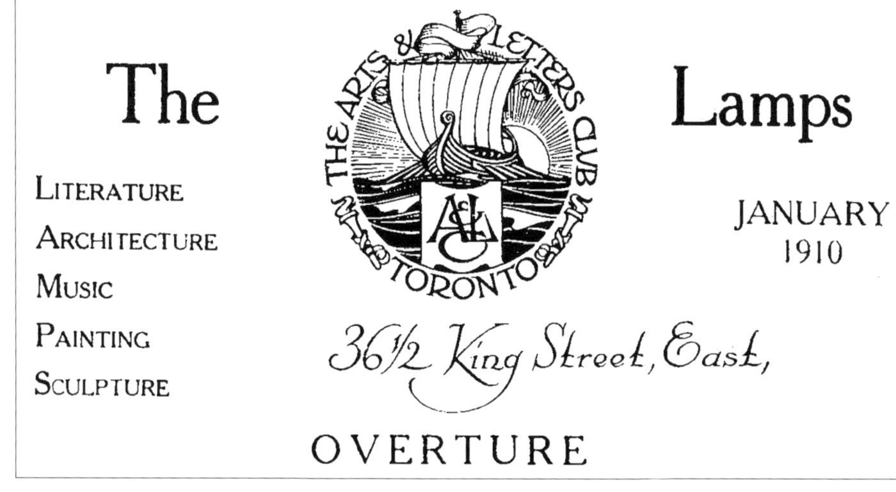

VI:2

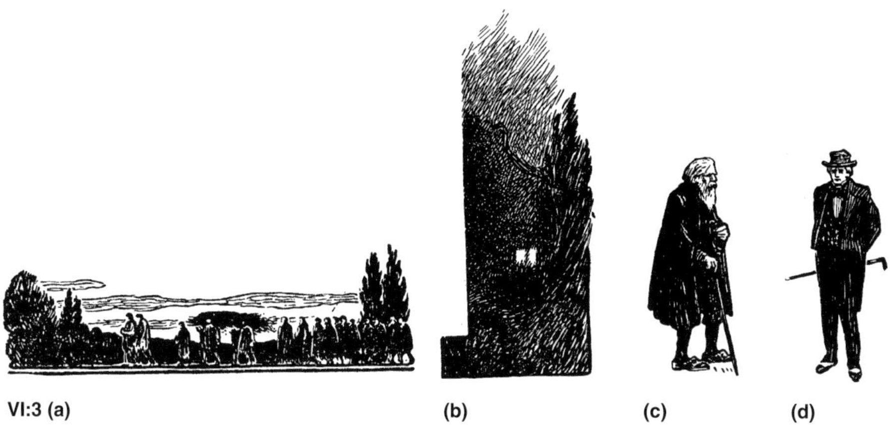

VI:3 (a) (b) (c) (d)

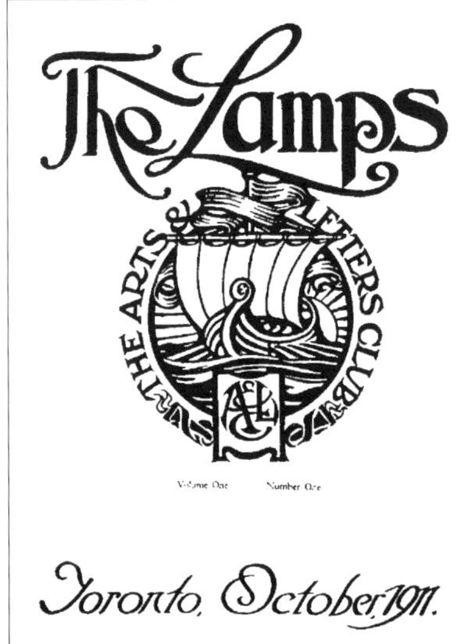

VI:4

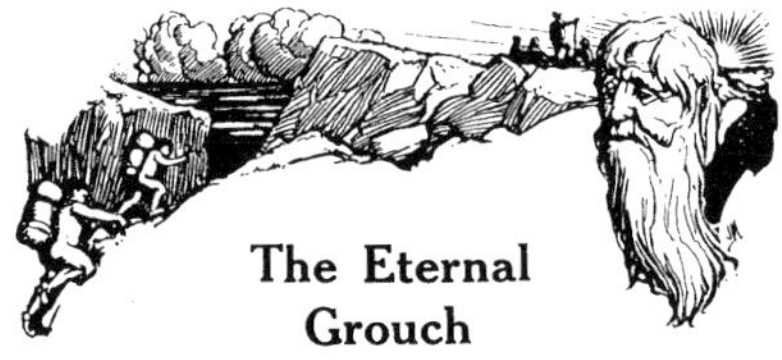

VI:5

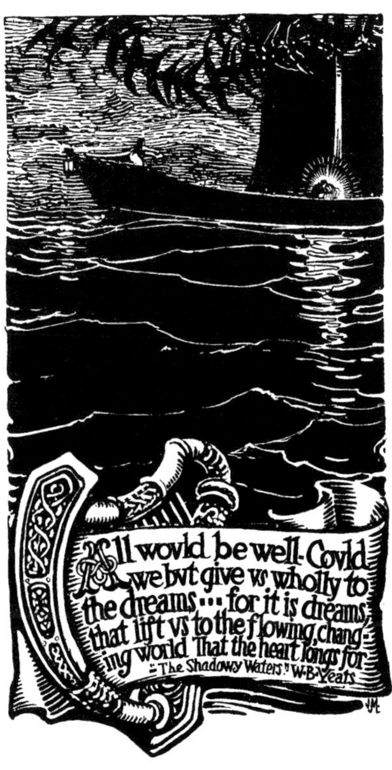

VI:7

VOL. I, No. 1, N.S. JUNE, 1912

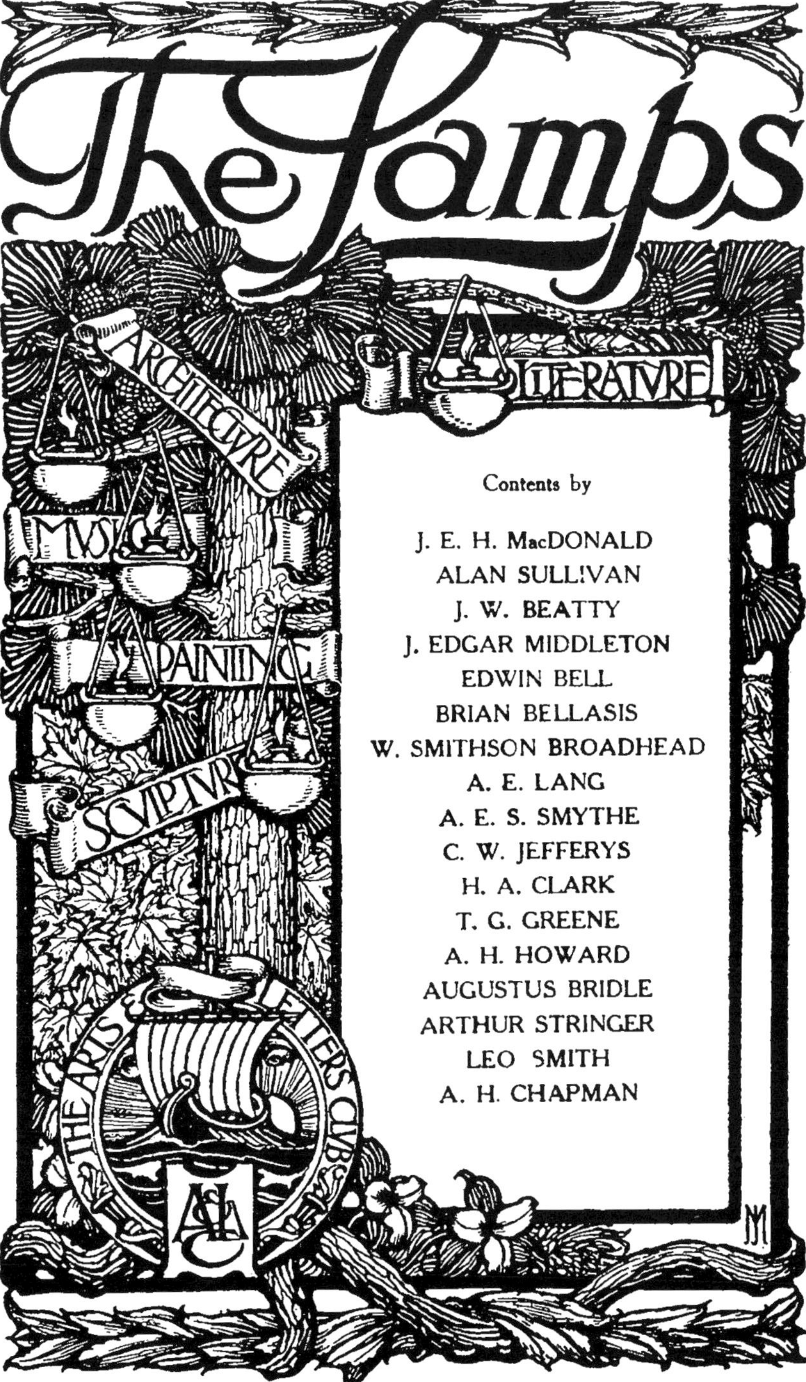

Contents by

J. E. H. MacDONALD
ALAN SULLIVAN
J. W. BEATTY
J. EDGAR MIDDLETON
EDWIN BELL
BRIAN BELLASIS
W. SMITHSON BROADHEAD
A. E. LANG
A. E. S. SMYTHE
C. W. JEFFERYS
H. A. CLARK
T. G. GREENE
A. H. HOWARD
AUGUSTUS BRIDLE
ARTHUR STRINGER
LEO SMITH
A. H. CHAPMAN

Published by the Arts and Letters Club, Toronto.

VI:6

VI: Designs for the ALC

VI:8. Sketch for cover, *The Lamps* (not used), n.d. (c. 1911-12), graphite, in Sketchbook; AGO (acc. no. 50/74).

VI:9. Front cover, presentation address to Percy R. Hollinshead, June 1912, brown and gold ink; ALC. *Note*: Percy Hollinshead was a professional singer and member of the ALC who gave a farewell recital at Forester's Hall, Toronto on 22 April 1912 before sailing for Europe, where he hoped to launch a career as a soloist; JM designed the printed program for this performance (Scrapbook, ALC).

VI:10. List of members of the ALC who enlisted for military service in WWI, 1919, black, red and gold ink on parchment; ALC.

VI:11. Front cover, *The Lamps* (Dec. 1919).

VI:12. Masthead, *The Lamps* (Dec. 1919).

VI:13 (a-d). Illustrations, "A.C.R. 10557," by JM, *The Lamps* (Dec. 1919).

VI:14. Illustration, "Men and Mary," by JM, *The Lamps* (Dec. 1919).

VI:15. "Punning" heraldic shield of J.W. Beatty, 4th president of ALC, for Great Hall, ALC, 14 Elm St.; Toronto, 1920, oil on wood (r.: shield repainted on masonite, c. 1940s, by Robert and Jim Hubbard); ALC; photo: HBP. *Note*: for other shields in this set, see colour plates **Pl: VI:2 (a-h)**.

VI:16. "Punning" heraldic shield of R.F. Gagen, 8th president of ALC, originally painted in 1920, repainted on masonite, c. 1940s, by Robert and Jim Hubbard; ALC, photo: HBP.

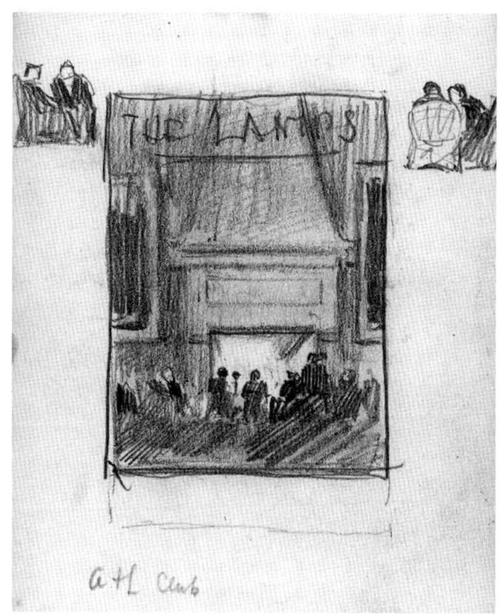

VI:8

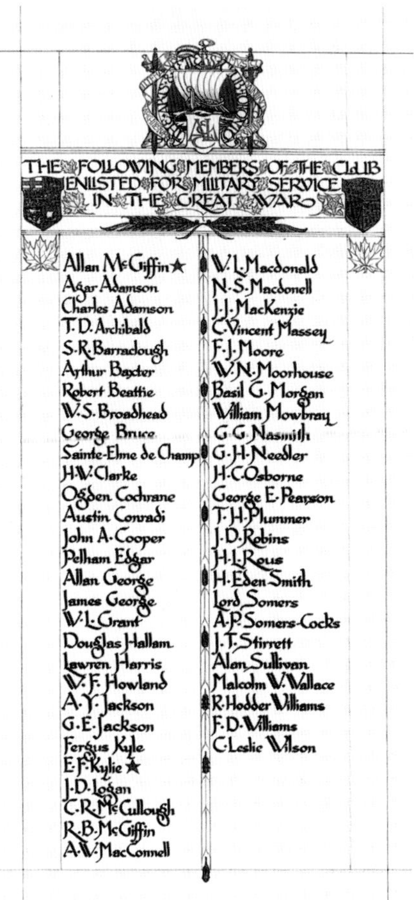
THE FOLLOWING MEMBERS OF THE CLUB ENLISTED FOR MILITARY SERVICE IN THE GREAT WAR

Allan McGiffin ★
Agar Adamson
Charles Adamson
T. D. Archibald
S. R. Barraclough
Arthur Baxter
Robert Beattie
W. S. Broadhead
George Bruce
Sainte-Elme de Champ
H. W. Clarke
Ogden Cochrane
Austin Conradi
John A. Cooper
Pelham Edgar
Allan George
James George
W. L. Grant
Douglas Hallam
Lawren Harris
W. F. Howland
A. Y. Jackson
G. E. Jackson
Fergus Kyle
E. F. Kylie ★
J. D. Logan
C. R. McCullough
R. B. McGiffin
A. W. MacConnell
W. L. Macdonald
N. S. Macdonell
J. J. MacKenzie
C. Vincent Massey
F. J. Moore
W. N. Moorhouse
Basil G. Morgan
William Mowbray
G. G. Nasmith
G. H. Needler
H. C. Osborne
George E. Pearson
T. H. Plummer
J. D. Robins
H. L. Rous
H. Eden Smith
Lord Somers
A. P. Somers-Cocks
J. T. Stirrett
Alan Sullivan
Malcolm W. Wallace
R. Hodder Williams
F. D. Williams
C. Leslie Wilson

VI:10

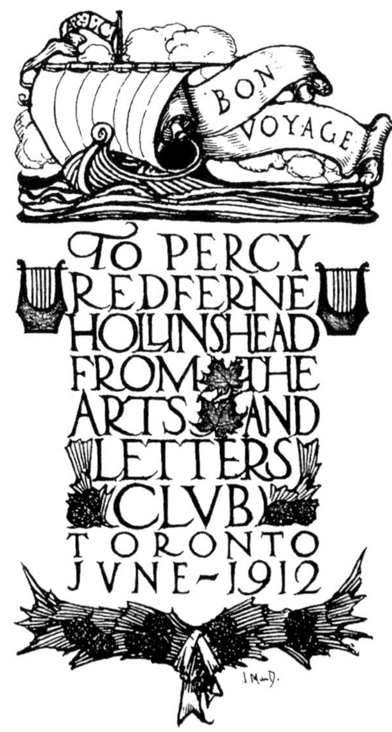

VI:9

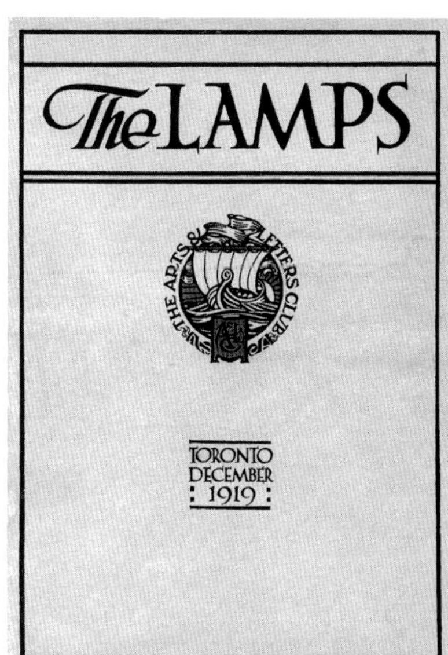

VI:11

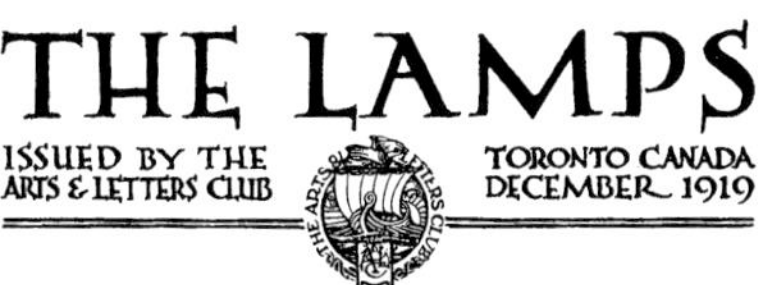

VI:12

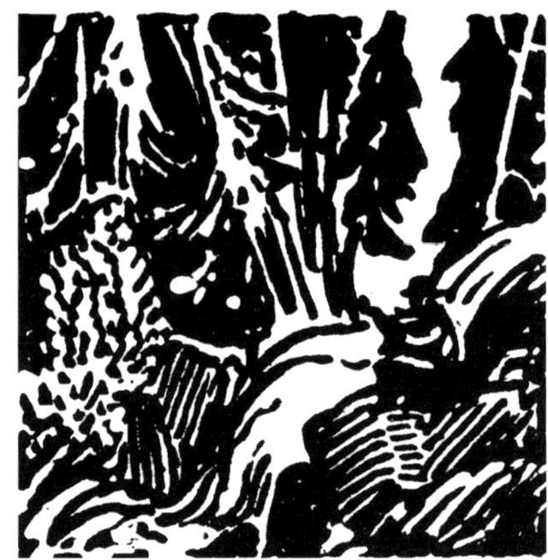

VI:13 (a)

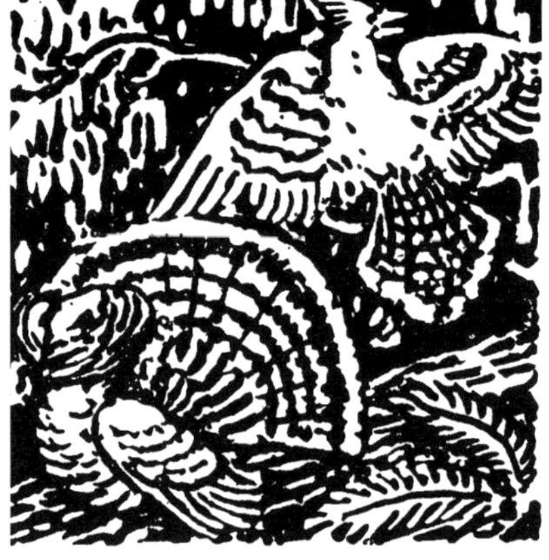

(b)

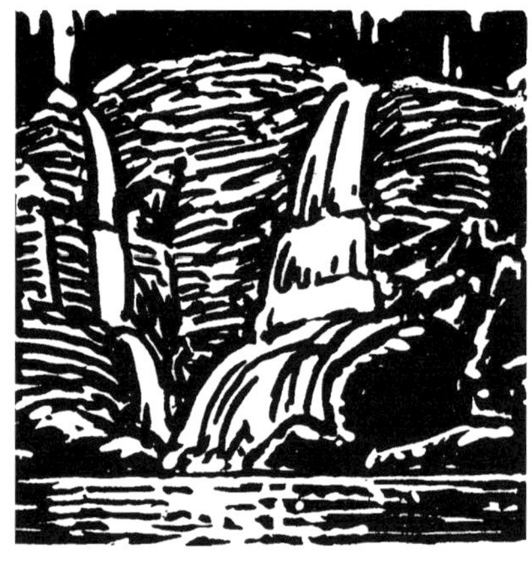

(c)

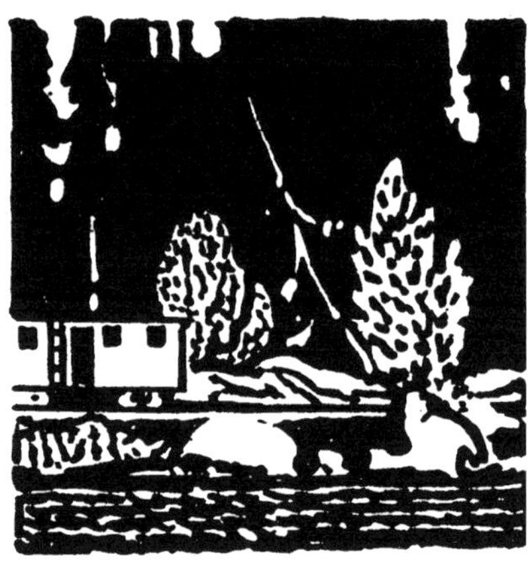

(d)

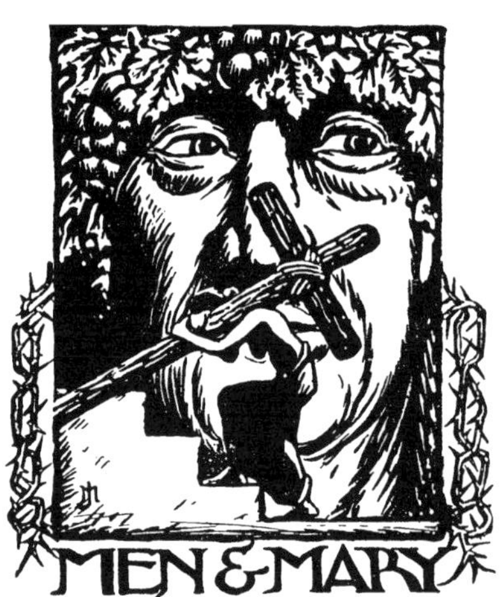

VI:14

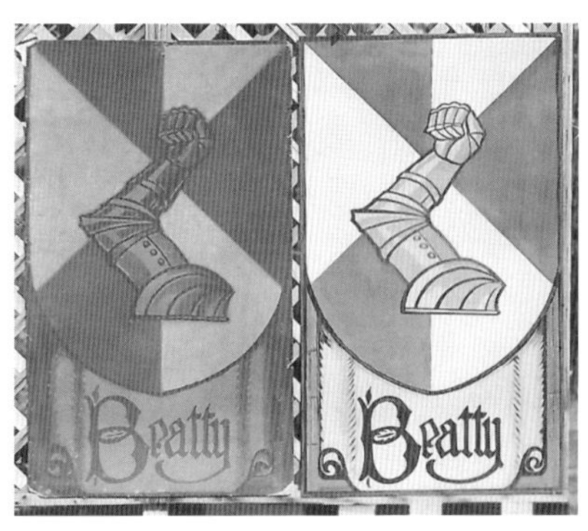

VI:15

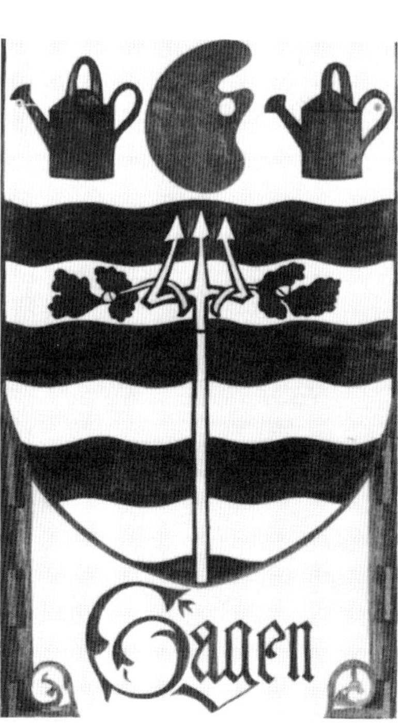

VI:16

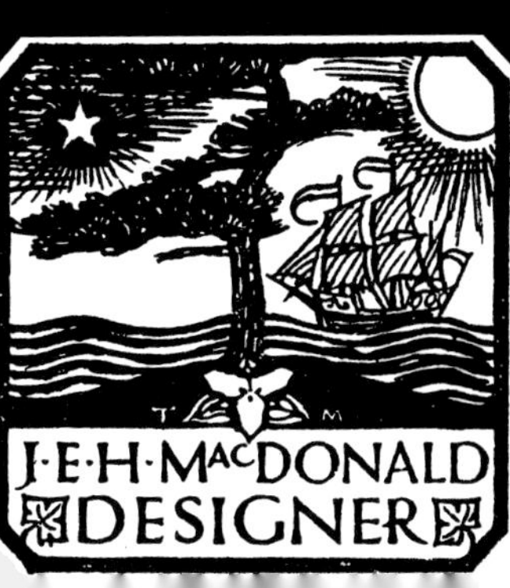
T M
J·E·H·MACDONALD
DESIGNER

CHRONOLOGY

Note: This chronology, based on the "Draft Notes by Year" compiled by Hunter Bishop, augmented by my own researches, does not attempt to be comprehensive. It concentrates on MacDonald's movements and on major events in his life, especially as they pertain to his work as a designer, illustrator, decorative artist, and teacher. It contextualizes these activities by indicating key dates in JM's career as a painter. For a full list of exhibitions in which JM participated, see Charles C. Hill, *The Group of Seven: Art for a Nation* (Ottawa: National Gallery of Canada/McClelland & Stewart Ltd., 1995), pp. 338-41. – RS.

1873
12 May: birth of James Edward Hervey MacDonald at New Elvet, near Durham, Northumberland, England, to William MacDonald, a cabinet-maker, and Margaret Usher.

1886
Founding of Toronto Art Students' League.

1887
28 March: JM receives school-leaving notice, Boy's Model School, Durham, England.

April: MacDonald family emigrates from Durham to Hamilton, Ontario, Canada.

The 14-year-old JM enters 3-year program of night classes at the Hamilton School of Art under John Ireland and Arthur Heming.

1889
MacDonald family moves to 113 Bellwoods Ave., Toronto.

JM begins to read widely.

1890
JM leaves school to work as an apprentice at Toronto Lithographing Co., 13 Jordan St., Toronto.

Ontario School of Art becomes Central Ontario School of Art and Design, G.A. Reid, principal.

1892
W. Henry Shaw founds Central Business College, Forum Building, Yonge and Gerrard Streets, Toronto.

1893
JM begins taking evening and Saturday classes at COSAD, held at the headquarters of the Ontario Society of Artists, 165 King St. W.

1894
TASL opens new studio at 95 Adelaide St. E.

1894 (or 1895?)
Joins design department of Grip Printing and Publishing Co., 201 Yonge St., in the 1st year of its operation following the demise of *Grip*, the satirical paper started by J.W. Bengough in 1873.

1895-97
Residence: 113 Bellwoods Ave., Toronto (with parents).

1896
Father listed in Toronto street directory as MacDonald, Wm. H., 113 Bellwoods, Cabinetmaker.

By this year, JM has begun to carry a small sketchbook with him to record his impressions. Beginnings of his friendship with a young Haligonian named Lewis Smith who had come to work at Grip.

TASL mounts exhibition of modern posters.

July-Aug.: visits L. Smith and his sister, Edith, also an artist, at their summer home town of Kentville, N.S. (?).

Through L. Smith, meets future wife, Harriet Joan Lavis, student of English Literature at McMaster University, Toronto, and a close friend of Lawren Harris's mother.

Leaves Anglican church (influence of Joan Lavis, a Christian Scientist?).

1897
Father listed as MacDonald, Wm. H., 113 Bellwoods, Tor., Furniture Supply Co.

Grip P. & P. located at 26, 28 Adelaide St. W. Here, JM carries out all manner of commercial designs, practises lettering the alphabet as a mirror-image, reads between jobs, and discusses sketches and sketching trips with his fellow workers.

Summer: visits L. Smith, who has moved from Kentville to Rockingham, N.S., where he completes some watercolour sketches (?).

Sept.: begins to write a journal entitled "A Journal of an Ordinary Life" (unlocated).

1898
Summer: Visits L. Smith and E. Smith at Rockingham, N.S.; paints landscapes in watercolours.

Takes Saturday afternoon lessons from G.A. Reid at COSAD.

1899
Father listed as MacDonald, Wm. H., Grocer, 696 Dufferin.

JM listed in Toronto street directory under MacDonald, Jas. E., artist, Grip P. & P. Co., h. 696 Dufferin [St., Toronto]. Salary: $12 per week.

12 May: marries Joan Lavis at an Anglican church in Swansea, a West Toronto village. Guests include A.A. Martin, Norman Price and William Wallace, future founders of Carlton Studio. Honeymoon at Bronte, Ont.; draws *Fish Shanties at Bronte*. Couple moves into a rented cottage on Quebec Ave. (no. 512 or 572), near High Park.

Summer: sketches in Nova Scotia with L. Smith (?).

1900
COSAD supports founding of Art Museum of Toronto (AMT).

T.G. Greene, Arthur Goode, A.A. Martin, Norman Price (and W. Wallace?) join TASL (or 1899?).

JM designs bookplate for Joan MacDonald, showing 1st Quebec Ave. house.

First exhibits with OSA: *Applied Art Exhibition*, Art Gallery, 165 King St. (listed in catalogue as follows: "1. Grip Printing & Publishing Co., 41. Catalogue covers. J.E.R. [sic] MacDonald; 2. MacDonald (James E.H.), 108. Three Designs for Book Plates"). (Other Grip artists listed in catalogue: Carl G. Beal, Fergus Kyle, Edgar McGuire, A. Goode, A.A. Brown, N. Price, T.G. Greene, A.A. Martin – also a design for the constitution and bylaws of the Maulstick [*sic*; i.e. Mahlstick] club.)

Oct.: visits East Aurora, New Yorkto view the Studio of Elbert Hubbard's Roycrofters. (In this same year, Canadian painter-etcher Carl Ahrens moves to East Aurora and founds pottery department at Roycroft Studio.) Nov.: prepares "A Word to us All," a poem on the South African War written and lettered by JM, as a Roycroft submission, but decides not to join this Arts-and-Crafts collective because of suspicions about the motivations of its founder.

1901
Goode, Martin, Price, Wallace take cattle-boat to England to set up commercial art studio in London.

C.W. Jefferys appointed art supervisor of Grip Ltd.

JM designs and helps build, with local carpenter, house at 475 (later 105) Quebec Ave., for total cost of $500.

21 April: birth of son, Thoreau MacDonald, at 475 Quebec Ave.

May: *The Canadian Magazine* publishes JM's illustration for poem "From my Window (In Spring)," by Ethelwyn Wetherald (his 1st magazine illustration?).

8 May: paints small watercolour view of Toronto City Hall, looking east from University Avenue (Baldwin Room, MTRL).

Summer: sketching trip to Bronte, Ont.

1902
Carlton Studio founded in London by Goode, Martin, Price, Wallace as combined commercial art studio and advertising agency.

JM listed under Toronto Junct.[ion], MacDonald, James E.H., artist, h. 512 Quebec Ave.; MacDonald, James E.H., artist, Grip Print. & Pub. Co.

Grip P. & P. Co. name changed to Grip Ltd., rooms 41-50, 26, 28 Adelaide St. W.

JM joins Toronto Art League (formerly, TASL), probably at 3rd location, 75 Adelaide St. W.

1903
Founding of Canadian Society of Applied Art, Toronto.

JM draws two illustrations for 1904 TAL calendar (Feb. and April).

Designs calendar covers for COSAD for school year 1903-04.

Jan.: Travels to London, England to work at Carlton Studio, 180 Fleet St.; lives at Adrian boarding house with N. Price.

Nov.: 1st meeting of Graphic Arts Club, Toronto (C.W. Jefferys, president, 1903-1908).

1904
Father listed under MacDonald, Wm. H., Cabinetmaker, h. 344 Brock.

JEHM listed under Toronto Junct., MacDonald, James E.H., artist, 455 Quebec Ave.; MacDonald, James E.H., wks Grip Ltd.; in fact, working at Carlton Studio, 10 Serjeant's Inn, Fleet St., London (as of 5 March).

Returns to Canada for wife and son; back in England, lives in flat at Loughton, near Epping Forest, northeast of London. Wife and son live at Loughton and Torquay, Devon and Wallington, Surrey, etc.

TM recalls that, between 1904 and 1907, the work done by JM at Carlton Studio amounted to "over 200 pieces," mostly book designs and jackets. Some jackets done at Carlton were framed and hung in JM's studio at 32 Adelaide St. E. (1912-14).

Establishment of Canadian Society of Graphic Art.

1905
Father listed under 344 Brock, MacDonald, Wm. H.

9-23 Dec.: included in 2nd annual exhibition of CSAA, OSA Galleries, 165 King St. W. (as part of 7 submissions from Carlton Studio, London).

1906
Working for Carlton Studio, London.

8 Dec.: publication of second number of *The Canadian Courier*, Toronto, with masthead and column headings by JM (initialled); done in London? Or had JM returned to Toronto by this date?

1907
Returns with family to Toronto, living at 105 Quebec Ave. (?) (i.e., by Nov. 1907?).

Begins to work for Grip Ltd. as head designer, under A.H. Robson, art director.

J.W. Beatty moves from Paris to London, where he studies at the Chelsea Polytechnic; in his spare time he works at Carlton Studio, later that year moving on to Holland.

Tom Thomson hired by Grip Ltd. (or 1908?).

1908
Father listed under MacDonald, Wm. H., Cabinetmaker, J. & J. L. O'Malley, res. Tor. Junc.; O'Malley, J. & J.L., Joseph O'Malley, Furniture, 160 Queen W.

JM listed under Toronto Junct., MacDonald, J.E.H., h. 475 Quebec Ave.; MacDonald, James, artist, Grip.

Begins work for The Shaw Correspondence School, 389-393 Yonge St. (title of 1908-09 prospectus listing JM as and J.W. Beatty as members of "Our Staff": *The Art of Drawing for Profit*).

Grip Ltd. moves from 23, 28 Adelaide St. W. to 48 Temperance St.

Feb.: JM exhibits for the 1st time at OSA Fine Arts Gallery, 165 King St. W..

23 March: formation meeting of Arts and Letters Club, for which JM produces cover for booklet, *A Gathering of Arts*.

Aug.: exhibits for 1st time at CNE.

1909
Father listed under MacDonald, Wm. H., Cabinetmaker, J. & J.L. O'Malley, res. Tor. Junc.

JM listed under West Toronto, MacDonald, James E.H., artist, h. 475 Quebec Ave.; MacDonald, James, artist, Grip.

Designs poster and brochure for *The Atlantic Royals* line of Canadian Steamship Lines.

Designs, illustrates (and writes text of?) 1st of series of booklets for use by students enrolled in Commercial Design course at SCS.

Serves on executive committee, ALC, 1909-10.

2 Feb.: JM proposed for membership in OSA at executive meeting by E. Wyly Grier.

23 Feb.: elected member, OSA.

Spring-summer (?): sketching trip to Burks Falls, Magnetawan River and Lake Cecebe.

Summer: probably 1st visits Georgian Bay (or 1910?), and Algonquin Park.

August: exhibitions sponsored by CSGA begin in Graphic Arts Section at CNE.

November: at 31st annual RCA exhibition, held at Art Gallery, Hamilton Public Library, shows book covers (cat. no. 91).

Dec.: JM's Viking-ship crest for ALC 1st used on stationery, 36 $^1/_2$ King St. E.

1910
Listed under Quebec Av., 105 Quebec, MacDonald, James E.; MacDonald, James E.H., artist, Grip.

Supervisor, Department of Commercial Design, SCS (to 1913, or 1921?); J.W. Beatty is supervisor of Department of Book and Magazine Illustration and Newspaper Illustration.

Designs invoice used by Grip Ltd.

On executive committee, ALC.

Designs cover and 1st page of Augustus Bridle's *A Backwoods Christmas*, published by R.G. McLean.

Writes and illustrates instruction manual no. 2, Commercial Design course, SCS.

March: exhibits at OSA annual show, *Wind, Rain and Sunshine* his 1st painting to be illustrated in an exhibition catalogue.

8 March: attends 1st annual meeting of OSA, elected to executive council.

25 April: OSA, given notice of eviction from Princess Theatre, 165 King St. W., rents studio at 28 College St. for 2 years.

Aug.-Sept.: exhibits at CNE's Applied Art Gallery 2 decorations for CPR hotel brochure covers, illustrations of Chateau Frontenac, etc.

1 Nov.: elected 1 of 3 members of hanging committee of OSA.

1911
Listed under MacDonald, James E., res. 105 Quebec.

JM paints front-cover illustration, and does lettering and bird's eye view of development, for advertising brochure, Lawrence Park Estates, Dovercourt Lands, Buildings and Savings Co. Ltd., printed by Grip Ltd. (other illustrations by C.W. Jefferys).

Jan.: Arthur Lismer emigrates to Canada from Sheffield, England, on advice of W. Smithson Broadhead, settling in Toronto.

A. Lismer and Frank Carmichael hired by Grip Ltd.

Feb.: JM becomes member of ALC.

March: represented by 6 works at annual OSA exhibition, catalogue containing comments by exhibiting artists. Show reviewed in *The Farmer's Magazine* by B.B.C. (i.e., Britton B. Cooke?), "A Departure in Art Criticism."

April (?): moves to 108 Conduit St. (later re-named Glenlake Ave.).

April: at annual meeting of OSA, it is noted that 1 of 2 paintings selected for the Provincial Museum, Queen's Park, is JM's *By the River, Early Spring.*

2 May: JM appointed to CNE hanging committee and for committee *re* abolishing tariffs on artists' supplies.

Summer: takes family to Go Home Bay, Georgian Bay, Lake Huron, accepting offer of cabin owned by Dr. James MacCallum.

Oct.: headpiece for "The Eternal Grouch," poem by W.A.C., published in *The Lamps* (ALC).

1-14 Nov.: 1st 1-man exhibition of little sketches, ALC; reviewed by C.W. Jefferys in *The Lamps* (Dec. 1911).

Nov.: meets Lawren Harris for the 1st time.

Dec.: leaves Grip Ltd., becomes self-employed. (Other Grip employees at this time: T. Thomson, Frank Johnston, A. Lismer, F. Carmichael, F.H. Varley).

Dec.: painting, *The Fireplace as Depicted by J.E.H. MacDonald,* reproduced in *The Lamps.*

Dec.: illustrations for *Saturday Night* published.

20 Dec.: L. Harris arranges for a special CPR train trip for ALC members to see the exhibition of the Société Nouvelle at the Albright Art Gallery, Buffalo; JM probably a member of the party.

28 Dec.: performance at ALC of W.B. Yeats' s poetic drama *The Shadowy Waters*, with stage design by JM.

1912
Listed under Conduit St., 108 Conduit St., MacDonald, James E.H.; MacDonald, James E.H., Grip.

COSAD changes name to OCA, given free premises in the Toronto Normal School Building.

A.H. Robson leaves Grip Ltd. and joins Rous and Mann, taking with him T. Thomson, F. Johnston, A. Lismer and F.H. Varley.

JM begins designing special CNE displays.

Collaborates with C.W. Jefferys on Canadian history chart for *Makers of Canada* series.

Illustration for front cover of brochure, *Strathgowan*, the southern annex of Lawrence Park, Toronto, for DLBSC (printed by Rous and Mann Ltd.); other illustrations by Jefferys.

Designs bookplates for Basil George Morgan and Thoreau MacDonald.

March: takes studio at 32 Adelaide St. E. (Imperial Chambers), Toronto (to Dec. 1913).

March-April: *Tracks and Traffic* (AGO) exhibited at OSA annual exhibition (also at RCA exhibition in Winnipeg, and at CNE); reproduced in *The Studio* (London); *Morning Shadows* purchased.

Spring (?): sketching trip to Burk's Falls and Magnetawan River, Ontario.

Spring: sketching trip with L. Harris to Mattawa and Temiskaming.

June: design for front cover, and illustration of scene from *The Shadowy Waters* reproduced in *The Lamps*.

Summer: to Go Home Bay to visit Dr. James MacCallum, with L. Harris.

Sept.: house in York Mills which belonged to Col. Usher destroyed by fire; JM moves family from Conduit St. to house on Centre St., Thornhill, rented from E. Beaupré; (or 1913-14?).

Aug.-Sept.: NGC purchases 1st JM painting to enter its collection, *In the Pine Shadows, Winter Moonlight.*

29 Nov.: elected Associate, RCA at meeting of General Assembly, Victoria Memorial Museum, Ottawa (together with Ernest Fosbery, Henri Hébert, C.W. Jefferys and Albert Laliberté).

1913
Listed under 108 Conduit St., MacDonald, James E.H.; Bridle, Augustus; Bridle, Augustus, sec. A. & L. Club, h. 108 Conduit.

Member, picture committee, OSA.

Member, picture committee (to 1915?) (L. Harris, chairman), and publication committee, *The Yearbook of Canadian Art*, both ALC.

Member, advisory committee, *First Exhibition of Little Pictures by Canadian Artists.*

Designs text and illustrations for instruction manual no. 4, Commerical Design course, SCS.

Jan.: to Buffalo with L. Harris to see exhibition of Scandinavian art at Albright Art Gallery.

April: sketching-trip to Mattawa with L. Harris.

13 Feb.: receives diploma recognizing him as an associate member, RCA .

6-18 March: exhibition of Canadian paintings at MacDowell Club, New York, JM represented by 8 paintings.

26 Feb.-22 March: *First Exhibition of Little Pictures,* Toronto Reference Library; JM shows 22 sketches.

Commissioned by Toronto General Hospital to produce presentation address for Sir John M. Gibson, lieutenant-governor of Ontario, to mark opening of its new buildings, designed by Darling & Pearson, at 101 College St. (gold-stamped leather binding design, title page inscription, 6 black-and-brown-ink drawings by JM); and book on Private Patients Building and Nurses' Home, TGH (printed by Grip Ltd. for W.G. Macfarlane Ltd.), with decorative borders and cover by JM, line drawings by T. Thomson. (Official opening of TGH: 19 June. Address to Gibson possibly presented 6 January 1914?) (Historical Committee, TGH.)

Aug.: to Burk's Falls, Ont.

Sept.-Oct.: to St. Jovite, then Laurentians, Quebec, with L. Harris, via Montreal.

Oct.: 1st instalment of Britton B. Cooke's 2-part article, "The Spirit of Travel," with total of 33 illustrations by JM, published in *The Canadian Magazine*; 1st headpiece for *The Canadian Magazine*.

Nov.: meets A.Y. Jackson at L. Harris' studio (over Bank of Commerce at Bloor and Yonge sts.).

12 Nov.: receives $15.00 from Dr. J. MacCallum for *Spring Sketch*; publication of H.F. Gadsby's "The Hot Mush School or Peter and I," *Toronto Daily Star.*

Dec.: illustration for W.W. Campbell's poem "Low-Lying Fields" published in *The Canadian Magazine*.

20 Dec.: JM's "The Hot Mush School: In Rebuttal of H.F.G.," published in *Toronto Daily Star*.

1914

Father listed under MacDonald, Wm. H., Cabinetmaker, h. 22 Macauley Ave.

Designs, hand-letters and illuminates quotation from Mary Baker Eddy's *Health and Science* for Joan MacDonald (MSc).

Jan.: JM moves studio from Adelaide St. E. to Studio Building, 25 Severn St., Toronto, occupying no. 6, 3rd floor; devises sign for gate of Studio Building, "25 Severn St. for Canadian Art." Fellow tenants include J.W. Beatty, L. Harris, A. Heming, A.Y. Jackson, T. Thomson, Curtis Williamson. (A. Lismer moves in in the fall.)

7-28 Feb.: included in *Second Exhibition of Little Pictures by Canadian Artists*, Art Galleries of the Public Reference Library, Toronto.

March: 1st visit to Algonquin Park (with J.W. Beatty), to visit A.Y. Jackson.

7 April: elected 1 of 4 members of exhibition committee, OSA.

11 May: 12 named pictures sent to University Club (Toronto) for exhibition (price-range: $140 to $500; total: $2,190).

July (?): moved from E. Beaupré's house on n. side of Centre St., Thornhill, to farmhouse on s. side at Thornhill; pays $600 down, rent standing at 6.5% payable half-yearly. Expects to sell Conduit St. house to pay for purchase of farm, but cannot; appeals to AGT for assistance.

Summer: replaces J.W. Beatty as director of the OSA Summer School (in York Mills, n. of Toronto?).

Aug.-Sept.: to Gatineau and Cascades, Quebec, with L. Harris, sketching at Ottawa and Hull en route.

1 Dec.: at meeting of executive of OSA, it is noted that of 3 best poster designs in competition for *Patriotic Fund* exhibition of OSA, no. 2, by "Bala" (i.e., JM), was the winner: i.e., *Canada and the Call, 1914*. (Judges: A.H. Howard, A.H. Robson, H.M. Tedman, R. Fudger, H. Sproatt, C.M. Manly); award: $500. Poster printed by Rolph & Clark Ltd.; reproduced as frontispiece in *Catalogue of Pictures and Sculpture Given by Artists in Aid of the Patriotic Fund, RCA* (30 Dec. 1914). Original maquette for poster presented to OCA by RCA, May 1953.

Dec.: *The Kaiser's Battle Cry* (illustration for poem, "The Kaiser's Last Ultimatum," by "Van der Tod" [i.e., JM?]) published in *The Canadian Magazine*.

5-19 Dec.: 1-man exhibition of paintings at ALC.

1915

Elected member and picture committee, ALC; executes ALC executive committee lists for 1908-09 in pen lettering on parchment, and for 1915-16 in pen and watercolour.

Begins using sketchbook dated 1915-22 (NGC).

Serves as 1 of 3 members of board of examiners, OCA.

Paints *Belgium, 1914* (AGO), possibly as design for war poster or illustration.

Begins work on *The Tangled Garden* (NGC).

23 January: *Canada and the Call, 1914* reproduced in 4th no. of *The Canadian War* (C.W. Jefferys, art, ed.), p. 16.

16 March: elected vice-president and treasurer, OSA (to 1919); member of hanging and publicity committees.

May: *Snowbound* purchased by NGC.

Spring: A. Lismer, wife and daughter move in with the MacDonalds on a co-operative basis. The two men attempt to make a living by farming. JM earns about $12 per week over the entire year.

Sept.: sketching trip to Cascades, Quebec, and Minden, Ontario, with L. Harris.

15 Sept.: Lismers move to another house in Thornhill.

Oct.: elected member, executive committee and picture committee, ALC.

Oct.: JM and family visit Dr. MacCallum, Go Home Bay, and stay in his houseboat; measures cottage for decorative panels.

Winter: begins work on decorative wall-murals and panels for MacCallum cottage (1915-16).

1916

Listed under MacDonald, Jas. E.H., artist, 6, 25 Severn; Artists, MacDonald, Jas. E.H., 6, 25 Severn; Conduit, 108 Conduit — Augustus Bridle. Fellow artists at the Studio Building: J.W. Beatty, Arthur Heming, Marion Long, Curtis Williamson.

Member, OSA hanging committee (1916-19), with R.F. Gagen and C.W. Jefferys.

Executes hand-carved picture-frames.

Designs dust-jacket design for *In Pastures Green*, by Peter McArthur (Toronto and London: J.M. Dent & Co.).

Introduced by Jefferys to Barker Fairley at English Association, Toronto.

March: *The Tangled Garden* exhibited at OSA, with price of $500, but remains unsold for 20 years.

March: committee struck to arrange for holding of a memorial exhibition of the work of the late A.H. Howard (Robert Holmes, G.A. Reid, C.W. Jefferys, A.H. Robson, JM).

April: to Dr. MacCallum's cottage to help install wall-murals (received $145 for 5 works between Oct. 1915 and June 1916).

22 July: *Belgium, 1914* boxed with poem, "From the Body of this Death," by Sidney Low, in *The Canadian Courier*.

Aug.: sketching trip to Coboconk, Ont..

16 Sept.: publication of full-page political cartoon and illustration, *The Toast Mutual*, and *Midnight at Mt. Royal*, in *The Canadian Courier*.

Sept.-Oct.: sketching trip to Minden with L. Harris (and Frederick Haines?).

Oct.: publication of 1st issue of *The Rebel*, U. of T. student/faculty magazine, ed. Elsinore MacPherson (Haultain); 2nd in Nov..

14 Nov.-16 Dec.: at 38th annual RCA exhibition, held at AAM, shows *Illustration, Belgium, 1914* and *Illustration, War Matters* (cat. nos. 301, 302).

1917

Listed under MacDonald, Jas. E.H., artist, 6, 25 Severn; Artists, MacDonald, Jas. E.H., 6, 25 Severn; Glenlake, 108 Glenlake, — Augustus Bridle. Fellow artists at Studio Building: Beatty, Alex. G. Cumming, Marion Long, Curtis Williamson.

Appointed 1 of 4 instructors for Teachers' Summer Course, OCA.

Member, OSA selection committee for CNE, and committee to find suitable gallery for *Small Picture Exhibition*.

On ALC committee to consider means of raising funds to perpetuate memory of "those who have made notable contributions to Canadian art."

Contributing editor, *The Rebel* (to 1920).

Devises "Northern Lights" headpiece for *The Canadian Magazine*.

Designs hand-carved picture frames.

April: offers Thornhill farm for summer gardening by ALC members as part of war effort.

14 April: drawing for article, "That flag-topped garden of mine," published as cover, *The Canadian Courier*.

17 April: cover-design for *The Farmer's Magazine* published.

22 May: gives 1 of 3 talks *re* "A. & L. C. Night" at OSA exhibition at Central Reference Library; later published in *The Rebel* under title "Art Crushed to Earth" (Jan. 1918).

1 July: publication of special cover design, "Confederation" issue, *Maclean's Magazine*.

30 June: cartoon illustration, *The Second Capture of Quebec*, published in *The Canadian Courier*.

Aug.: cover design for *Maclean's Magazine* (used to March 1919 issue).

17 Aug.: C.W. Jefferys replies to letter from Eric Brown, suggesting that JM be used as one of the artists for the Canadian War Memorials; when artists recruited, JM ill at York Mills. In 1917 rumours are in circulation that commissions are being given to English artists to paint war pictures for hanging in the rebuilt Parliament Buildings at Ottawa. E.W. Grier, J.W. Beatty and Maxwell (architect) form committee to approach Eric Brown and Sir Edmund Walker *re* the use of Canadian artists. Walker, after consulting Jefferys, influenced to send Canadian artists overseas, funding to be aided by Sir Max Aitken (the future Lord Beaverbrook).

Fall: devises wording and design for memorial plaque for Tom Thomson cairn, Canoe Lake, Algonquin Park; reproduction of lettering published in JM article, "A Landmark of Canadian Art," *The Rebel* (Nov. 1918).

Sept.: JM sketching in Minden, then by train to St. Jovite, Quebec.

12 Oct.: to Canoe Lake, Algonquin Park, to assist J.W. Beatty with placement of bronze plaque of JM's design on cairn commemorating Thomson.

Nov.: forced to rent Thornhill house, moves to house of Mrs. Lucille Taylor (Christian Science friend of Joan MacDonald), at the side of the Usher (or Ussher?) farm, York Mills, for approx. 18 months; suffers "severe breakdown" (i.e., stroke?) the day after the move; confined to bed, writes poetry. (ALC rents neighbouring Usher farm from Mrs. Taylor to be cultivated by club members as part of war effort.) TM assists with design and lettering commissions during JM's recovery.

6 Nov.: at monthly meeting of OSA, J.W. Beatty moves that a strong representation to the federal and provincial governments be made re the necessity of sending overseas a competent corps of artists, JM to be one of a 5-man committee to wait on the government concerning this issue.

1918
Listed under MacDonald, Jas. E.H., artist, 6, 25 Severn [studio 2]; Severn, 25 Severn, 7 artists, incl. Jas. E.H.; Glenlake, 108, MacDonald, Jas. A. [sic]. Fellow artists at Studio Building: J.W. Beatty, Alex. G. Cumming, L. Harris, Marion Long, Curtis Williamson.

Moves studio and family from York Mills to Studio Building (from no. 6, 3rd floor, to no. 2, east, ground floor).

Due to health breakdown, declines commission to serve with Canadian War Memorials.

Designs certificate for Edith Cavell Memorial Prize.

Appointed 1 of 4 instructors for teachers' summer course, OCA.

Member, picture committee, ALC; letters ALC executive list for 1916-17.

Illustrations, headpieces, etc., for *Maclean's Magazine*, *The Canadian Courier*, *The Farmer's Magazine*, and *The Canadian Magazine*.

Letters ALC committee list for 1917-18 in pen and watercolour.

Member, with C.W. Jefferys, of OSA committee to study new Copyright Act *re* painters, sculptors, designers and illustrators.

Designs poster and program cover for CNE, *Victory Year 1919*.

7 Jan.: gives talk, "The Spirit of Canadian Art."

8 Jan.: invited (with 5 other artists) to submit design for official seal for AMT. Member, OSA committee *re* joint exhibition of OSA and RCA, for new gallery of AMT.

11 March: elected to executive committee of OSA at annual meeting; member, OSA committee to confer with executive of CNE *re* reorganization of Fine Arts Commission.

1 April: establishment of Ontario Advisory Committee on War Memorials, JM, J.W. Beatty, R. Holmes, G.A. Reid appointed OSA representatives (committee to advise authorities in provincial municipalities *re* the character of War Memorials to be erected).

Summer: replaces J.W. Beatty as director of OCA summer school at York Mills (Beatty in France as official war artist).

23 Aug.-16 Sept.: exhibition of modern Canadian art in Graphic and Applied Art Gallery at CNE; JM represented by *The Little Falls*.

10-30 Sept.: 1st boxcar trip to Algoma, with L. Harris, F. Johnston, Dr. J. MacCallum.

Oct.: group show of work by JM, L. Harris, F. Johnston, ALC.

Nov.: devises stamp for authentication of T. Thomson paintings (used only for oils-on-wood panels). Included in *Exhibition of Paintings by Canadian Artists*, City Art Museum, St. Louis, Mo.; exhibition then travelled to Minneapolis, Chicago and Milwaukee, to June 1919.

Dec.: "A Hash of Art" published in *The Rebel*. 1-man exhibition of paintings at ALC, followed by solo show of JM sketches.

18 Dec.- Jan. 1919: *Algoma Sketches by J.E.H. MacDonald, Lawren Harris and Frank Johnston*, at AGT (made possible by Sir Edmund Walker); JM represented by 16 large paintings.

1919
Member, with F.H. Varley and J.E. Sampson, of Board of Examiners, OCA (1919-20).

Devises bookplate for ALC; letters list of ALC members who enlisted for military service.

The Old Fashioned Executor series of advertisements for National Trust published in newspapers (1919-20), then in booklet format by Rous and Mann.

Designs cover for "War Supplement" no. of *Acta Victoriana* (Victoria University, U. of T.).

Jan.: cover design for *The Rebel* published (used to 1920).

Jan.: entered T. Eaton Co. art competition for catalogue of 50th anniversary of company; placed in c. 4th group, winning 1 of 3 $100 prizes; competition held under SGA (judges: Sir E. Walker, C.W. Jefferys, Eric Brown).

March: "Mentioned in Dispatches" published in *The Rebel*, along with a poem, "The Athletes," the 1st of several to follow in subsequent issues.

11 March: elected to executive committee, OSA; elected member, OSA committee to advise authorities in provincial municipalities re the character of war memorials to be erected; member, with C.W. Jefferys, of OSA committee to study new copyright act re painters, sculptors, designers and illustrators; member, OSA committee to confer with executive of CNE *re* reorganization of Fine Arts Commission.

Sept.-Oct.: to Algoma (Mongoose Lake) with L. Harris, F. Johnston, A.Y. Jackson.

Dec.: 1-man exhibition of paintings at ALC, followed by sketches.

Dec.: cover design, illustrations and advertisement drawings for *The Lamps* published.

22-24 Dec.: *The Chester Mysteries*, with stage set by JM, performed at Hart House Theatre; 1-man exhibition of JM's sketches held in lobby of theatre.

1920
Founding of *The Canadian Forum* (formerly, *The Rebel*), Barker Fairley, editor.

Paints punning personal shields of past ALC presidents and executtive committee members for new ALC quarters, 14 Elm St., Toronto.

Member, library and archives committee, ALC.

Member, OSA publicity committee, *re* exhibition of small pictures.

Designs certificate of membership, Ontario Association of Architects (also inserts names and years for about next ten years) (certificate withdrawn, 1935).

Illuminates address for Sir Auckland Geddes, British Ambassador to Washington, for presentation at opening of CNE, Aug.

Designs corporate seal for Frontier College, Toronto.

March: formation of Group of Seven at L. Harris's house, Queen's Park Circle, Toronto; present: Harris, JM, F. Johnston, F.H. Varley, F. Carmichael.

Spring: 2nd boxcar trip to Algoma, with L. Harris, A.Y. Jackson, A. Lismer.

25 March: gives talk on "The Decorative Element of Art," ALC.

April: cover design, title page and 2 illustrations by JM published in *The Sailor*.

7-27 May: included in *Group of Seven* (inaugural exhibition), AGT; JM represented by 10 canvases, 10 sketches).

July: sketching at Fenelon Falls and Cuckoo Lake, Ontario.

Sept.: 3rd boxcar trip to Algoma, with L. Harris, A.Y. Jackson, F. Johnston; rented cottage on Mongoose Lake (late Sept. or early Oct.).

Oct.: a photograph of JM's *Chester Mysteries* set published in article on "The Players Club" in *University of Toronto Monthly*.

7-28 Nov.: included in *Exhibition of Paintings by the Group of Seven Canadian Artists*, Worcester Art Gallery, Worcester, Mass.; then travels to Rochester, N.Y., Toledo, Indianapolis, Detroit, Cleveland, Buffalo, Columbus, Minneapolis, and Muskegon, Mich., to Jan. 1922.

27 Nov.: "A Pageant of the Guild of Arts and Letters," presented, with dinner program designed by JM.

30 Nov.: *Small Pictures Exhibition*, OSA, opens at AGT; JM represented by 6 sketches, priced at $30 each.

11 Dec.: auction sale of art at ALC to aid in cost of renovating 14 Elm St.; JM contributes 2 oils and original artwork for his design for ALC bookplate.

1921

Member, OSA committee *re* publications relating to 50th anniversary of the society.

Appointed instructor in decorative art and commercial design, Department of Design and Applied Art, OCA (appointment arranged by A. Lismer, vice-principal); OCA opens own building on Grange Park, Toronto on 30 Nov. 1921.

Designs title page, *University of Toronto Roll of Service, 1914-1918*.

Designs bronze war memorial plaque for National Trust Co., cast by Alexander and Cable Co.

Designs bookplates for Dalhousie College Library (lettering by TM), Edward Everett Norwood, library of Hart House.

Supervises painting of mural for Christie, Brown, Ltd. display for CNE, carried out by A.J. Casson and Arthur Keelor (or 1923?).

7-29 May: included in *Exhibition of Paintings by Group of 7* (2nd), AGT.

July: TM's linocut after JM's ink drawing *In the Bush* reproduced in *The Canadian Forum*.

July-Sept.: sketching at Coboconk and Gull River, Ontario.

Oct.: included in *Exhibition of Small Paintings and Sculpture by Members of the Ontario Society of Artists*, AGT.

26 Nov.: JM's large painted caricature of Vincent Massey presented at ALC dinner (at which time Massey was standing as candidate for MP for Durham).

1922

Member, with R. Holmes (president), of OSA committee to devise new design for OSA seal (design executed by TM).

Produces executive committee list (1920-21), ALC.

Wins award for design of cover of catalogue of *Retrospective Loan Exhibition of the Works of Members of the Ontario Society of Artists Covering the First Half-Century of the Society's History*.

Contributes designs for books published by McClelland & Stewart Ltd.: *Fires of Driftwood*, by J.E. McLay; *Legends of Vancouver*, by E. Pauleen Johnson; *The Wood-Carrier's Wife*, by M.C.L. Pickthall (lettering assistant: TM).

G7 receives backing from NGC for a year-long travelling exhibition; paintings sent to the *International Art Exhibition*, Pittsburgh.

6 Jan.: gives lecture, "Lettering: Origins and Historic Styles," before students, OCA (1st of 4). These lectures formed the basis for an annual series.

13 Jan.: gives lecture, "Lettering: Examples in Early Books," before students, OCA (2nd of 4).

20 Jan.: gives lecture, "Lettering: The Technique of the Early Books, and Some Books on Lettering," before students, OCA (3rd of 4).

27 Jan.: gives lecture, "Lettering: Modern Developments and Uses of Lettering," before students, OCA (4th of 4).

7 Feb.: appointed by OSA to "Jury of Award" of OAA *re* choosing architect student at U. of T. for scholarship medal.

11 Feb.-12 March: included in *Retrospective Loan Exhibition of the Works of Members of the Ontario Society of Artists*, AGT.

22 Feb.: 3 linocuts by TM appear in *The Canadian Forum*: his 1st published artworks under his own name.

March: appointed chairman, archives committee, ALC.

5-29 May: included in *Group of 7 Exhibition of Paintings* (3rd), AGT; JM shows *Decoration for Christmas Party* (cat. no. 19) among, other works.

20 June: gives lecture, "Lettering and Design," OCA.

July: JM drawing, *A Breezy Shore*, published in *The Canadian Forum*.

24 July: gives slide-lecture on "Design" to highschool teachers at summer course, OCA.

July-Aug.: sketching trip to Petite Rivière, Nova Scotia, with L. Smith, E. Smith and Robert Strath.

6-30 Oct.: memorial exhibition of work by Mary Hiester Reid, AGT, with invitation and catalogue design by JM.

15 Dec.: gives lecture on "Lettering: Origins and Historic Styles," location unknown.

20-21 Dec.: "A King for a Night": festival of carols organized by A. Bridle as part of *Toronto Daily Star* series of "Community Programmes"; JM and A. Scott Carter design stage sets, JM one of 5 designers who devise costumes.

1923

Sketches at Coboconk, Ontario with F. Haines.

Sketches at Georgian Bay.

Member, hanging committee, OSA.

Contributes designs and illustrations to books published by M&S: *Ballads and Lyrics*, by Bliss Carman; *Bliss Carman*, by Odell Shepherd; *The Rosary of Pan*, by A.M. Stephen; *Stories of the Land of Evangeline*, by Grace McLeod Rogers; *The Unheroic North: Four Canadian Plays*, by Merrill Denison.

Elected vice-president, ALC (to 1925).

Jan.: JM drawing, *Church by the Sea, Nova Scotia*, reproduced in *The Canadian Forum*.

Feb.: appointed art editor, and member, board of editors, *The Canadian Forum*.

Feb.: JM drawing, *In the Sugar Bush*, published in *The Canadian Forum*.

10 Feb.: at council meeting of RCA, A.Y. Jackson proposes a mural competition for a decorative panel on the theme of "settlement of Canada."

April: begins research on designs for interior decoration of St. Anne's Church, Gladstone Ave., Toronto; borrows books from U. of T. Library, researches Byzantine mosaics at library of Pontifical Institute of Medieval Studies, U. of T. Drafts designs for 21 panels. Commissions 10 artists and 2 sculptors to contribute to the scheme. Paints *The Crucifixion* (pendentive), *The Transfiguration* (apse), *The Stilling of the Tempest* (apse).

July: JM drawing, *Northern Pine*, reproduced in *The Canadian Forum*.

25 July: JM one of 7 signators of a letter released to several newspapers requesting that RCA members ignore the RCA Committee's recommendation for a boycott of submissions to the *Canadian Section of Fine Arts*, British Empire Exhibition, to be held in Wembley Park, London, England, in 1924.

Oct.: exhibition of paintings by JM, A. Lismer and L. Harris held at Victoria School of Art and Design, Halifax (organized by L. Smith).

Oct.: designs program for *The Beggar's Opera or An Executive Year*, performed at annual meeting, ALC (completed 1925).

1-31 Nov.: included in *An Exhibition of Modern Canadian Paintings*, Minneapolis Institute of Arts; exhibition then travels to Kansas City, Omaha, Milwaukee, Providence, R.I., Worcester, Mass., Brooklyn, to 15 Sept.

Nov.: linocut by TM after JM drawing, *Fisherman's Dory, Nova Scotia*, reproduced in *The Canadian Forum* (reprinted April 1927).

Nov.(?): *A Friendly Meeting* wins $500 1st prize in RCA competition for large decorative mural painting; F.H. Varley wins second prize ($300). Sixty entries received in competition, 6 finalists chosen. (Winning entry was supposed to have hung in the Parliament Buildings, Ottawa.)

22 Nov.-2 Jan. 1924: *A Friendly Meeting*, along with 5 other finalists in mural competition, shown at 45th annual RCA exhibition, AGT (cat. no. 239).

1924

JM and family move back into Studio Building for approximately 1 year; rents Four Elms, Thornhill to F. Johnston and family (or 1925-26?).

All work on St. Anne's Church completed.

Designs layout and catalogue cover of NGC-organized *Canadian Section of Fine Arts*, British Empire Exhibition, London (most work carried out by TM), also used on cover of catalogue, 2nd exhibition, 1925, and on cover of catalogue of *Exhibition of Canadian Art*, NGC, 1932.

Designs layout, catalogue cover and vignettes, *A Portfolio of Pictures from the Canadian Section of Fine Arts*, British Empire Exhibition, London (most work carried out by TM).

Contributes designs to books published by M&S: *Old Province Tales*, by Archibald MacMechan; *The White Winds of Dawn*, by F.B. Taylor.

Jan: represents OSA on 3-man selection committee appointed to choose Toronto Cenotaph Memorial (Vaux Chadwick and Alan George both represent RAIC); winning design by Messrs. Pomphrey and Ferguson. Design sent for tenders, Jan. 1925. Text submitted by JM not used.

Jan.: included in *Exhibition of Canadian Graphic Art* (1st exhibition of CSGA, held in connection with 6th annual exhibition of the SCP-E), AGT (shows 3 decorations for St. Anne's Church and 4 titled brush drawings).

11 Jan.: gives lecture, "Lettering: Origins and Historic Styles," at OCA.

25 Jan.: gives lecture, "The Workmanship of the Manuscript Book," before students, OCA (also given Jan. 1925, Feb. 1926).

23 April-31 Oct.: included in *Canadian Section of Fine Arts*, British Empire Exhibition, Wembley Park, London; exhibition then travels to Leicester, Glasgow, Birmingham, to 31 March 1925.

July: hangs exhibition of drawings by David Milne at ALC.

July: cover design for *The Canadian Forum* published.

10 July: gives talk on "Lettering," before students, OCA (also given June 1925, February 1926).

August: sketching for 19 days around Lake O'Hara, in Rocky Mountains, staying at Lake O'Hara Camp, Hector, B.C. (1st of 6 successive annual trips to Rockies).

Aug.-Sept.: *A Friendly Meeting* shown at CNE.

October: presentation of "On Account of Defries," with lettering, page decorations, and 2 miniature paintings by JM, to R.L. Defries on his retirement as treasurer, ALC, at Club dinner; work on book finished 5 July 1926 (NGC).

Oct.: at suggestion of Vincent Massey, JM. commissioned to paint decorative wall panels, and heraldic shields, and 2 cartoon portraits (Principal Maurice Hutton and Prof. W.J. Alexander) for Junior Common Room, University College, U. of T. Submits 3 proposals, 1 chosen (cost: approx. $185).

20 Nov.-20 Dec.: *A Friendly Meeting* shown at 46th annual RCA exhibition, held at NGC (cat. no. 137).

1925

Moves self and family back to Thornhill house, having changed his mind about renting to F. Johnston (or 1926?).

Commissioned by M&S to design *Lyrics of Earth*, by Archibald Lampman, but work carried out by TM.

Sweet O'The Year and Other Poems, by Charles G.D. Roberts, with cover design by JM, published by Ryerson Press; design used on 98 Ryerson Poetry Chapbooks, then modernized by TM, 1942.

Canadian Drawings by Members of the Group of Seven published by Rous and Mann Press; 4 drawings by JM included (*Church by the Sea*, *Autumn Sunset*, *A Glacial Lake, Rocky Mountains*, *Lake O'Hara, Rocky Mountains*); label and title page of portfolio by TM.

Produces large working drawings for wall-medallions for exterior of AGT (1. Province of Ontario; 2. City of Toronto; 3. AGT) (Archives, AGO); finished bronze medallions may have been completed by Toronto sculptors Frances Loring and Florence Wyle (?).

Doris Huestis Mills holds 1st solo exhibition at JM's studio, Studio Building, Toronto.

Sekido Yoshida, visiting Japanese artists, lives in JM's studio, c. 1925 to 1927.

Jan.: JM drawing, *A Glacial Lake, Rocky Mountains*, reproduced in *The Canadian Forum*.

Jan.: gives talk on Dynamic Symmetry and other topics at opening dinner, Ontario Architects' Club, Ottawa, in company with F. Johnston and John Pearson.

9 Jan.-2 Feb.: included in *Group of Seven Exhibition of Paintings* (4th), AGT.

7 Feb.: gives talk, "Main Principles that Should Govern Architectural Design," at Architects' Dinner, ALC; at same dinner, F. Johnston gives talk on Dynamic Symmetry.

5 May: appointed to Publicity Committee, OSA *Small Picture Exhibition*, opening 22 May at Simpson's Art Gallery, Toronto.

9 May-October: included in *Canadian Section of Fine Arts*, British Empire Exhibition, Wembley Park, London; exhibition then travels to Whitechapel Art Gallery, London, York, Bury, Blackpool, Rochdale, Oldham, Bradford, Manchester, Sheffield, Plymouth, to 12 February 1927.

10 July: gives talk on "Some Origins and Historic Examples of Lettering," as highschool art teachers' summer course, OCA.

30 July: gives talk on "Lettering," before students, OCA.

Aug.: 2nd sketching trip to Rocky Mountains; stops at Winnipeg to see Manitoba Legislature.

Aug.-Sept.: shows *Design for Mural Painting, R.C.A. Competition* (i.e., *A Friendly Meeting*), in International Graphic Art Section, CNE.

Oct.: designs cover, *Canadian Homes and Gardens* (also used on November 1925 issue).

25 Oct.: opening of exhibition of paintings by JM at Hart House, U. of T.

12 Nov.: opening of exhibition of JM's Rocky Mountain sketches, ALC; gives brief artist's talk.

27 Nov.-28 Feb. 1926: included in *First Pan-American Exhibition of Oil Paintings*, Los Angeles Museum.

Dec.: decorates ALC dining hall for Christmas.

30 Dec.: commissioned by Eric Brown of NGC to select 50 Canadian posters for display at international exhibition of posters to be held in 1926 in connection with 3rd International Motor Show, Zagreb, Croatia, organized by British Institute of Industrial Art at invitation of Department of Overseas Trade, London.

1926

Buys 40 Duggan Ave., Toronto, for residence during summer months.

Designs ironwork sign for Boys and Girls House, Toronto Central Reference Library, St. George St., Toronto.

Letters and illuminates memorial address to Charles Lewis of T. Eaton Co. (private collection, Montreal).

Jan.: begins to select c. 50 Canadian posters and show-cards for international exhibition of poster art, 3rd International Motor Show, Zagreb, Croatia. Artists included: A.Y. Jackson, W. Langdon Kihn, James McKell, J.E. Sampson, A.J. Casson, Ricvhard Baker, F. Carmichael, Elsie Lynch, J.S. Hallam. Shipment received by BIIA, Feb. 1926.

Spring: letters and illuminates "Robert Gagen Memorial Booklet" for OSA (NGC).

Spring: designs decorations for *Spring Festival* sponsored by *Toronto Daily Star*.

6 Feb.: dedication of Walker Court and Gallery, AGT, to "Humanities in Art"; JM designs heraldic banners representing local societies: OSA, SCP-E, CSPWC, ALC.

19 Feb.: gives talk on "Lettering," before students, OCA.

10 March-3 April: included in *Canadian Painters: The Ontario Society of Artists*, Boston Arts Club, Boston.

24 April: paints 2 panels spoofing "Great Events in Canadian History" for Hotairian Dinner, ALC: *Discovery of Toronto by Sir Tommy Church* and *Lief Erickson Discovers First Arts and Letters Club*.

7-31 May: included in *Exhibition of the Group of 7* (5th), AGT.

Aug.-Sept.: 3rd sketching trip to Rocky Mountains, accompanied this time by Joan MacDonald.

30 Oct.: gives talk, "An Artist's View of Whitman," to English Association at Toronto Central Reference Library.

1927

Hand-letters and illuminates a souvenir book from the membership of the ALC for Vincent Massey on his moving to Washington, DC to assume the office of Canadian High Commissioner; presented at dinner at ALC, 5 Feb. (Archives, ALC).

Designs cover for catalogue of NGC-organized *Exposition d'Art Canadien*, Musée du Jeu du Paume, Paris; TM designs poster (and catalogue cover: rejected).

Designs cover of CNR "Diamond Jubilee" dining-car menu ("*A mare…*" lettering by TM).

Contributes 7 ink drawings to CNR booklet, *Jasper National Park*; other illustrations by A.Y. Jackson, F. Carmichael and A.J. Casson.

Contributes designs and illustrations to books published by M&S: *The Book of Ultima Thule*, by Archibald MacMechan; *Lord of the Silver Dragon*, by Laura G. Salverson.

Appointed head of Department of Graphic and Commercial Art, OCA.

Entering, respectively, as "St. Lawrence" and "Go Home Bay," wins Royal Canadian Mint-sponsored competition for reverse-side designs for .25- and .5-cent pieces to commemorate Canada's Diamond Jubilee; awards bring $500 each. (Assessors: Dr. A.G. Doughty, G.H. Campbell, C.W. Jefferys). (Emmanuel Hahn wins one-cent coin design; no winner for ten-cent coin.) Coins not struck.

Jan.: illustration, *Paul Bunyan Takes an Evening Stroll in Algoma*, accompanying article by J.D. Robins, published in *The Canadian Forum*.

28 Jan.: gives talk on exhibition of "metaphysical pictures" by Bertram Brooker at ALC.

30 Jan.-Feb.: included in *Exhibition of … Canadian Paintings…*, Memorial Art Gallery, Rochester, N.Y.; exhibition then travels to Toledo and Syracuse, to 8 May 1927.

1 Feb.: elected to annual Hanging and Selection Committee, OSA.

March: gives talk, "An Artist's View of Whitman," Toronto.

8 March: elected to Executive Committee of OSA at annual meeting.

April-May: included in *Exposition d'Art Canadien*, Musée du Jeu du Paume, Paris.

22 April: A. Lismer resigns as vice-principal of OCA.

Summer: fourth sketching trip to Rocky Mountains.

August: brush drawing, *Georgian Bay Pines*, reproduced in *The Canadian Forum*.

Oct.: elected chairman of Picture Committee, ALC.

Oct.: designs symbolic standards, backdrops and scenery for representatives of groups of nations to carry in "Heart of the World Pageant," CNE Coliseum, in connection with the Second Biennial Conference of the World Federation of Education Associations, U. of T.

1928

With TM, designs gold-stamped cloth book cover and dust jacket design for *The Private Life of Catherine the Great*, by Princesse Lucien Murat (New York: Louis Carrier & Co., 1928); design also used on other Carrier titles in the "Love Lives of the Great" series.

Commissioned to design ceiling decorations for lobby of Claridge Apartments, Clarendon Ave., Toronto.

Commissioned to prepare designs for decoration of lobby, entranceway frieze and parapet, Concourse Building, 100 Adelaide St. W.; assisted by TM.

Prepares design for ceiling of reception room, studio of photographer Charles Aylett, 96 Yonge St., Toronto; work carried out by Carl Schaefer.

Designs device for use on front cover of booklet, *Hart House Theatre: Toronto*.

Canadian Forum Reproductions: A Series of Drawings, Series No. 1 published by Rous and Mann Press.

Visits Boston, Mass. (on OCA business?).

OCA student body threatens to go on strike if JM not chosen to succeed G.A. Reid as principal.

Appointed acting principal OCA; continues as head of Dept. of Graphic and Commercial Art.

Delivers lecture, "From the Golden Age Onward, Decline and Revival, Some Great Printers and their Work," at OCA, as part of series sponsored by the Toronto Typothetae; published under that title in *Art as Applied to*

Typography (Toronto: Toronto Typothetae/ Rous and Mann Press Ltd., 1931). (Also delivered 9 Jan. 1931.)

11-26 Feb.: included in *Exhibition of Canadian Paintings by the Group of Seven* (6th), AGT.

6 March: elected to executive committee of OSA.

28 March: gives slide-lecture on "Lettering," to teachers, "College Teachers Course, First Lecture" (OCA?).

2 April-30 June: included in *Exhibition of Paintings, Drawings, Engravings and Sculpture by Artists Resident in Great Britain and the Dominions*, Imperial Institute, London, England.

July: visits New York City with Martin Baldwin *re* ceiling design for lobby of Claridge Apts., Toronto; takes notes on Congo Room, Almanack Hotel. On their return, Carl Schaefer begins work realizing JM's design scheme, consisting of series of banded patterns for ceiling beams.

12 July: in attendance at meeting at ALC with the Hon. William Finlayson, Minister of Lands and Forests (also present: F.H. Brigden, G.A. Reid, F. Haines, A. Heming, H.S. Palmer), to discuss measures for the protection of natural beauty of Northern Ontario.

Aug.-Sept.: fifth annual sketching trip to the Rocky Mountains.

Oct.: elected president, ALC; gives acceptance speech, 13 Oct.; chairs 1st executive committee meeting, 19 Oct..

Nov.: designs 2 modernist screens for Arcade windows, T. Eaton Co.

Nov.: contributes stage and room decorations for *Musical Evening* (program of modern French and English music), ALC, held 24 Nov.

Nov.-1 Dec.: exhibition of sketches by JM at ALC.

Dec.: designs wall panels for Christmas dinner, ALC.

7 Dec.: gives illustrated talk on "The Art of the Book," AGT (also delivered Jan. 1931).

1929

One of 3 judges (with J.D. Robins and Merrill Denison) of *Art of the Theatre*, Canadian play competition conducted by Central High School, Toronto, under supervision of Herman Voaden. Entries had to have an "exterior northern setting."

Designs and letters illuminated presentation address marking retirement of M.W. German as federal MP for Niagara riding.

Gives talk, "The Making of the Book," AGT.

28 Jan.: gives talk on Walt Whitman (i.e., "An Artist's View of Whitman"?), ALC.

5 Feb.: elected to Hanging Committee, OSA.

13 Feb.: trip to Ottawa to serve on selection committee *re* exhibition at NGC.

18-20 Feb.: JM's "A Prologue to the Players' Revue" read as part of a performance by associates and friends of the late Bertram Forsythe, sometime director of HHT; published in *The Canadian Forum* (April 1929).

23 Feb.: gives talk (as Club president) at Architects' Dinner, ALC.

March: "The Claridge Apartments" published in *Construction*.

April: drawing, *Coboconk Village*, reproduced in *The Canadian Forum*.

May: "The Concourse Building" published in *Construction*.

May: designs broadside-format program for complimentary dinner for G.A. Reid on his retirement from OCA, ALC, 13 May.

Oct.: trip to Washington, D.C.

18 Oct.: spoke to OCA students on "the mountains."

Nov.: drawing, *Mountain Snowfall*, reproduced in *The Canadian Forum*.
11 Nov.: gives talk on "The Relation of Poetry to Painting, with Special Reference to Canadian Painting," at ALC.

21-27 Dec.: *Pageant of Carols*, organized by A. Bridle for *Toronto Daily Star*, performed at Massey Hall, with standards and banners designed by JM.

1930

Canadian Heroes of Pioneer Days, by Mabel Burns McKinley, with pen-and-ink endpieces by JM (reprinted from *The Canadian Magazine*), published by Longmans, Green and Co.

Gives talk entitled "Occupational Guide — Painting and Sculpture," to graduating class, OCA (or 1931?).

21 Jan.: gives talk, "The Group of Seven: The Modern Movement in Art," to "Women's Arts and Letters" (?), location unknown (ALC?).

Feb.-March (?): gives talk, "Constable," at AGT (one of 6 lectures in series on "Great Artists"); and at NCG (17 March?).

9-30 March: included in *Exhibition of Paintings by Contemporary Canadian Artists under the Auspices of the American Federation of Arts*, Corcoran Gallery of Art, Washington, D.C.; exhibition then travels to Providence, R.I., Baltimore, New York City, Minneapolis, St. Louis, Mo., to Aug.

April: drawing, *Fish Shanties at Bronte* (1900), reproduced in *The Canadian Forum*.

5-27 April: included in *Exhibition of Group of Seven*... (7th), AGT; exhibition then shown at AAM, 3-18 May.

5 April-27 June: included in *Exhibition of Paintings, Drawings, Engravings and Sculpture by Artists Resident in Great Britain and the Dominions*, Imperial Institute, London.

May (or later): designs bronze plaque for tombstone of R. Holmes (d. May 1930), Cannington cemetery, Cannington, Ontario.

June: train trip to Buffalo, Cleveland, Chicago, to visit art schools.

Summer: visits OCA summer school at Port Hope.

Aug.-Sept.: 6th and last sketching trip to Rocky Mountains (Lake O'Hara Bungalow Camp, Hector, B.C.).

Nov.: included in *Exhibition of Paintings by Contemporary Canadian Artists under the Auspices of the American Federation of Arts*, University of Wisconsin, Madison; exhibition then travels to Davenport, Iowa, Memphis, Tenn., Montclair, N.J., and Amherst, Mass., to March 1931.

8 Nov.: delivers lecture, "From the Golden Age Onward. Decline and Revival. Some Great Printers and their Work," at OCA, as part of series on "Art as Applied to Typography"; published under that title in *Art as Applied to Typography*. JM's text, "The Wise Printer" ("From that very rare work, 'The Erratica of Gasolinus'/ Translated by J.E.H. MACDONALD"), typeset by Cooper & Beatty, Ltd., for printing by Brigden's Ltd. as a broadside for distribution as a souvenir at Toronto Typothetae lectures, OCA, 1931-32. Talk reported in *Toronto Globe*, 11 Nov.

14 Nov.: gives talk, "Educators after Art," location unknown.

Dec.: supervises Christmas decorations, ALC.

1931

9 Jan.: delivers lecture, "From the Golden Age Onward, Decline and Revival, Some Great Printers and their Work," at OCA, as part of Toronto Typothetae series; published under that title in *Art as Applied to Typography*. (Also delivered in 1928.)

21 or 22 Jan.: gives talk, "Art of the Book," U. of T. Extension class, AGT.

Feb. 2: designs and letters program for dinner in honour of Lieut.-Col. A.D. LePan, Great Hall, HH, given by his friends upon completion of 10 years of service as superintendent of buildings and grounds of U. of T.
17 April: delivers slide-illustrated lecture, "Scandinavian Art," AGT, *re* trip to Albright Art Gallery, Buffalo, Jan. 1913, with L. Harris.

Summer: sketching at Pointe au Baril, Georgian Bay, Ontario.
Summer: completes 3 canvases for 1932 RCA annual exhibition.

Sept.: sketching trip to Sturgeon Bay; sketching at McGregor Bay. (Last trip to "north country.")

9 Oct.: delivers lecture, "The Harmony of Means and Purpose" at OCA, as part of Toronto Typothetae series; published under that title in *Art as Applied to Typography*.

Nov.: suffers stroke; bedridden. Obtains year's leave of absence from OCA; J.W. Beatty appointed acting principal.

Nov.: elected to full membership, RCA, at annual meeting.

Dec.: A. Scott Carter assumes JM's duties as archivist of ALC while he recuperates from illness.

4-24 Dec.: included in *Exhibition of the Group of Seven* (8th and last), AGT.

5 Dec.: at meeting held at L. Harris's Toronto residence, A.Y. Jackson announces that the Group of Seven is disbanding.

1932
Designs cover for *Exhibition of Canadian Art*, held at the NGC in conjunction with the Imperial Economic Conference, Ottawa, using design for *Canadian Section of Fine Arts* (1925) catalogue cover design.

Jan.: JM and wife sail on Canadian Steamship Line RMS *Drake* from Boston., Mass., for Barbados, BWI, *via* Nevis and Dominica.

11 Feb.: MacDonalds disembark at Bridgetown, Barbados; Feb.-March: stays at Welshes, Bridgetown, and at Bathsheba; JM sketches in oils and keeps diary for Doris Mills.

5 March-5 April: included in *Exhibition of Paintings by Contemporary Canadian Artists*, International Art Center of Roerich Museum, New York City; exhibition travels to Boston and Kalamazoo, Mich., to May.

April: MacDonalds return from Barbados by CSL RMS *Lady Hawkins* to Boston; by train to Toronto.

7 May: back in Toronto.

Nov.: Eric Brown of NGC meets with JM and fellow RCA members E.W. Grier, E. Hahn to choose works for exhibition at NGC.

22 Nov.: suffers second stroke at OCA, taken home to 40 Duggan Ave. on advice of Dr. Frederick Banting.

26 Nov.: death of J.E.H. MacDonald.

29 Nov.: burial at Prospect Cemetery, West Toronto; Lorne Pierce reads at address at the funeral.

12 Dec.: F. Haines, curator of AGT, writes to Eric Brown announcing intention of mounting a memorial exhibition of JM's work; asks for loan of *The Solemn Land* and *Falling Leaf*.

Presidential portrait of JM drawn at ALC by Charles Comfort (from small photo).

1933
Publication by Woodchuck Press, Thornhill, of *Village and Fields: A Few Country Poems*, by JM, designed and illus. by TM.

Publication by Ryerson Press of *West by East and Other Poems by J.E.H. MacDonald*, designed and illustrated by TM.

OCA student body raises funds to purchase a collection of JM's work for presentation to AGT.

Jan.: drawing, *Autumn Sunset*, reproduced in *The Canadian Forum* (also in July 1935 issue).

6 Jan.: *Memorial Exhibition of the Work of J.E.H. MacDonald, R.C.A.* opens at AGT (40 canvases, 80 sketch panels), then shown at NGC, 7. Feb.-6 March.; part of exhibition travels to Winnipeg Art Gallery, April-8 May 1933; Vancouver Art Gallery, from c. 20 May 1933; Calgary Exhibition and Stampede, 10-15 July 1933.

19 Jan.: special evening gathering held at AGT to which members of OSA, council and staff of OCA, members of ALC, faculty of U. of T., and friends invited to honour JM's memory.

1934
Publication by Woodchuck Press (Thornhill) of *My High Horse: A Mountain Memory*, by JM, designed and illus. by TM.

1935
Work by JM included in *A Century of Canadian Art*, Tate Gallery, London.

1936
20 Feb.-15 April: included in *Retrospective Exhibition of Painting by Members of the Group of Seven: 1919-1933*, NGC; travelled to Montreal and Toronto, to 15 June 1936.

1937
Publication by Ryerson Press of *J.E.H. MacDonald, R.C.A.*, by A.H. Robson.

My Sanctuary Garden, by Alice E. Wilson, with endpapers, title page and cover by JM (from *Fires of Driftwood*, 1922), published by M&S.

The Tangled Garden sent to Germany in order to have colour prints made from it; Aug.-Sept.: 1st 2 prints displayed at CNE and at J. Merritt Malloney Galleries, Toronto.

20 Oct.-13 Nov.: *A Loan Exhibition of the Work of J.E.H. MacDonald* held at Mellors Fine Art Galleries, Toronto.

1938
18 Nov.-18 Dec.: *Legends of Vancouver* and *Stories of the Land of Evangeline*, both designed and illustrated by JM, A. Robson's *J.E.H. MacDonald, R.C.A.*, and JM's *West by East and Other Poems*, representing, respectively, M&S, Rous and Mann Press Ltd., and Ryerson Press, included in *Canadian Industrial Arts Exhibition*, mounted at AGT under auspices of the RCA (cat. nos. 184, 186, 257, 267).

1939
1-18 Feb. 1939. *Exhibition of the Work of Tom Thomson and J.E.H. MacDonald* held at Mellors Fine Art Galleries, Toronto.

1940
Publication by Ryerson Press *J.E.H. MacDonald: A Biography and Catalogue of His Work*, by E.R. Hunter.

1945
Lorne Pierce publishes JM's "A Word to Us All" (1900) in reduced facsimile format as Christmas keepsake for Ryerson Press.

1947
20 Nov. to 3 Dec.: *J.E.H. MacDonald: Memorial Exhibition* held at Dominion Gallery, Montreal.

1957
9 March: *J.E.H. MacDonald: 1873-1932*, organized by T.R. MacDonald (no relation) with assistance from TM, opens at Art Gallery of Hamilton, Hamilton, Ontario.

1965
13 Nov.-12 Dec.: *J.E.H. MacDonald, R.C.A., 1873-1932*, organized by Nancy Robertson, held at AGO; also shown at NGC, 7 Jan.-6 Feb. 1966.

1966
J.E.H. MacDonald: Designs for Bookplates, published by TM (Woodchuck Press).

1973
Canada Post issues special .15-cent stamp commemorating death of JM, reproducing *Mist Fantasy* (AGO).
Publication of by U. of T. Press of Margaret E. Edison's *Thoreau MacDonald: A Catalogue of Design and Illustration*.

3 Nov.: unveiling of Archaeolgical and Historic Site Board Ministry of Colleges and Universities commemorative plaque to JM at Oakbank

Pond, Thornhill; speeches given by TM and John W. MacDonald.

1979
Publication by Penumbra Press of *J.E.H. MacDonald: Sketchbook*, ed. Hunter Bishop.

1989
Publication by Penumbra Press of *J.E.H. MacDonald: The Barbados Journal*, ed. John Sabean.

30 May: death of TM at Thornhill.

1990
12 Jan.-25 Feb.: *J.E.H. MacDonald, Lewis Smith, Edith Smith,* held at Dalhousie University Art Gallery, Halifax; exhibition travels to Edmonton Art Gallery, 24 March-May 1990, and Beaverbrook Art Gallery, Fredericton, N.B., 1 June-15 July 1990.

1995
Publication by Quarry Press (Kingston) of *J.E.H. MacDonald* by Bruce Whiteman.

Canada Post issues Group of Seven 75th-anniversary commemorative stamps; JM represented by *Falls, Montreal River* (AGO).

1996
100th anniversary of the death of William Morris.

Publication by Archives of Canadian Art/Carleton University Press of *J.E.H. MacDonald: Designer.*

SELECTED REFERENCES

Note: This selected bibliography concentrates on basic Canadian art references, and on published monographs, articles and exhibition catalogues on J.E.H. MacDonald. For fuller listings of publications by and about MacDonald and the Group of Seven and their exhibitions, see Dennis Reid, *The Group of Seven: A Bibliography* (Ottawa: National Gallery of Canada, 1970), and Charles C. Hill, "Bibliography," *The Group of Seven: Art for a Nation* (Ottawa: National Gallery of Canada, 1995), pp. 342-67. For miscellaneous unpublished writings (correspondence, diaries, notebooks, loose notes, poems, etc.) in the J.E.H. MacDonald *fonds*, National Archives of Canada, see "J.E.H. MacDonald Papers," MG30, D111, Finding Aid No. 30, NAC. Hill's bibliography also lists other manuscript collections in Canadian libraries, museums and archives where MacDonald papers can be found. Starred items (*) are exhibition catalogues. An extensive bibliography will append the projected companion volume to the present book.

Bishop, Hunter. "Introduction." *J.E.H. MacDonald: Sketchbook, 1915-1922*. Moonbeam, Ont.: Penumbra Press, 1979.

Colgate, William. *Canadian Art: Its Origin and Development*. Foreword by C.W. Jefferys. Toronto: Ryerson Press, 1943.

——. *The Toronto Art Students' League: 1886-1904*. Toronto: Ryerson Press, 1954.

Cronin, Fergus, Jack A. Carr and Franklin Arbuckle. *The Group of Seven: Why not EIGHT or nine or ten? With rare illustrations from the Club's Archives*. Toronto: The Arts and Letters Club of Toronto, 1995.

Duval, Paul. *The Tangled Garden: The Art of J.E.H. MacDonald*. Scarborough, Ont.: Cerberus Publishing Co. Ltd./ Prentice-Hall of Canada Ltd., 1978.

Edison, Margaret E. *Thoreau MacDonald: A Catalogue of Design and Illustration*. Toronto: University of Toronto Press, 1973.

Exhibition of the Work of Tom Thomson and J.E.H. MacDonald. Introduction by Thoreau MacDonald. Toronto: Mellors Gallery, 1939.*

Harper, J. Russell. *Dictionary of Canadian Painters and Engravers*. Toronto: University of Toronto Press, 1970.

——. *Painting in Canada: A History*. Toronto: University of Toronto Press, 1966; 2nd ed. 1977.

Hill, Charles C. *The Group of Seven: Art for a Nation*. Ottawa: National Gallery of Canada, in collaboration with McClelland & Stewart Ltd., 1995.*

Housser, Frederick Broughton. *A Canadian Art Movement: The Story of the Group of Seven*. Toronto: Macmillan, 1926; repr. 1974.

Hubbard, Robert. *An Anthology of Canadian Art*. Toronto: Oxford University Press, 1960.

——. *The Development of Canadian Art*. Ottawa: National Gallery of Canada, 1963.

Hunkin, Harry. *There is No Finality*. Toronto: Burns and MacEachern, 1971.

Hunter, E.R. "J.E.H. MacDonald." *The Educational Record of the Province of*

Quebec 70 (July-Sept. 1954): 157-62.

——. *J.E.H. MacDonald: A Biography and Catalogue of His Work.* Toronto: Ryerson Press, 1940.

J.E.H. MacDonald: 1873-1932. Foreword by Thoreau MacDonald. Hamilton: Art Gallery of Hamilton, 1957.*

J.E.H. MacDonald: Memorial Exhibition. Montreal: Dominion Gallery, 1957.*

Kelley, Gemey. *J.E.H. MacDonald, Lewis Smith, Edith Smith: Nova Scotia.* Halifax: Dalhousie Art Gallery, Dalhousie University, 1990.*

Landry, Pierre B. *The MacCallum-Jackman Cottage Mural Paintings.* Ottawa: National Gallery of Canada, 1990.

Lord, Barry. *The History of Painting in Canada: Toward a people's art.* Toronto: NC Press, 1974.

A Loan Exhibition of the Work of J.E.H. MacDonald, R.C.A. Introduction by Barker Fairley. Toronto: Mellors Gallery, 1937.*

MacDonald, Colin S. *Dictionary of Canadian Artists*, vols. 1-7 (Ottawa: Canadian Paperbacks, 1968-90).

MacDonald, Thoreau. *J.E.H. MacDonald: Designs for Bookplates.* Thornhill: Woodchuck Press, 1966.

——. *The Group of Seven.* Toronto: Ryerson Press, 1944; repr. McGraw-Hill, Ryerson, 1972.

McInnes, Graham. *A Short History of Canadian Art.* Toronto: Macmillan Co., 1939.

MacTavish, Newton. *The Fine Arts in Canada.* Toronto: Macmillan, 1925; repr. Toronto: Coles Canadiana Reprints, 1974.

Mellen, Peter. *The Group of Seven.* Toronto: McClelland & Stewart, 1970.

Middleton, J.E.: "J.E.H. MacDonald: An Appreciation, Nov. 29th, 1932." *The Lamps* (Toronto), 28 Nov. 1932.

Modern French Paintings from Manet to Matisse; Water Colours by Contemporary American Painters; Memorial Exhibition of the Work of J.E.H. MacDonald, R.C.A. Toronto: Art Gallery of Toronto, 1933.*

Murray, Joan. *The Best of the Group of Seven.* Edmonton: Hurtig, 1984; repr. Toronto: McClelland & Stewart, 1993.

——. *Northern Lights: Masterpieces of Tom Thomson and the Group of Seven.* Toronto: Key Porter, 1994.

Pierce, Lorne. *A Postscript on J.E.H. MacDonald.* Toronto: Ryerson Press, 1940.

Reid, Dennis. *A Bibliography of the Group of Seven.* Ottawa: National Gallery of Canada, 1970.

——. *A Concise History of Canadian Painting.* Toronto: Oxford University Press, 1973.

——. *The Group of Seven.* Ottawa: National Gallery of Canada, 1970.*

——. *The Group of Seven: Selected Watercolours, Drawings and Prints from the Collection of the Art Gallery of Ontario.* Toronto: Art Gallery of Ontario, 1989.*

——. *The MacCallum Bequest of paintings by Tom Thomson and other Canadian painters & The Mr and Mrs H.R. Jackman Gift of the murals from the late Dr MacCallum's cottage painted by some of the member of the Group of Seven.* Ottawa: National Gallery of Canada, 1969.*

Robertson, Nancy E. *J.E.H. MacDonald, R.C.A, 1873-1932.* Toronto: The Art Gallery of Toronto, 1965.*

Robson, Albert H. *Canadian Landscape Painters.* Toronto: Ryerson Press, 1932.

——. *J.E.H. MacDonald, R.C.A.* Canadian Artists Series. Toronto: Ryerson Press, 1937.

Stacey, Robert. *The Canadian Poster Book. 100 Years of the Poster in Canada.* Toronto and New York: Methuen, 1979.

——. "The Nautical Motif in Bookplates by Canadian Artists." *Canadian Notes and Queries*, No. 44 (Spring 1991): 8-18.

——. "Visions of Canada: From Carlton Studio to the 'Grip' of Seven." *Graphics International* (London), Fall 1996. In "Special Report: Canada" section.

Torell, Rosemarie L. *A New Class of Art: The Artist's Print in Canadian Art 1877-1920.* Ottawa: National Gallery of Canada, 1991

Whiteman, Bruce. *J.E.H. MacDonald.* Kingston: Quarry Press, 1995.

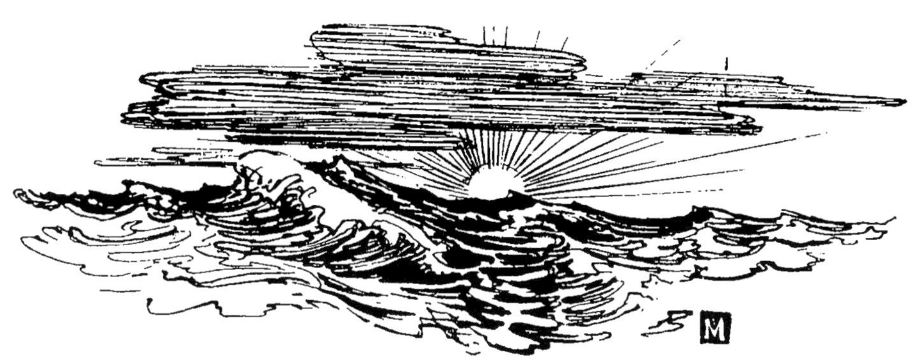

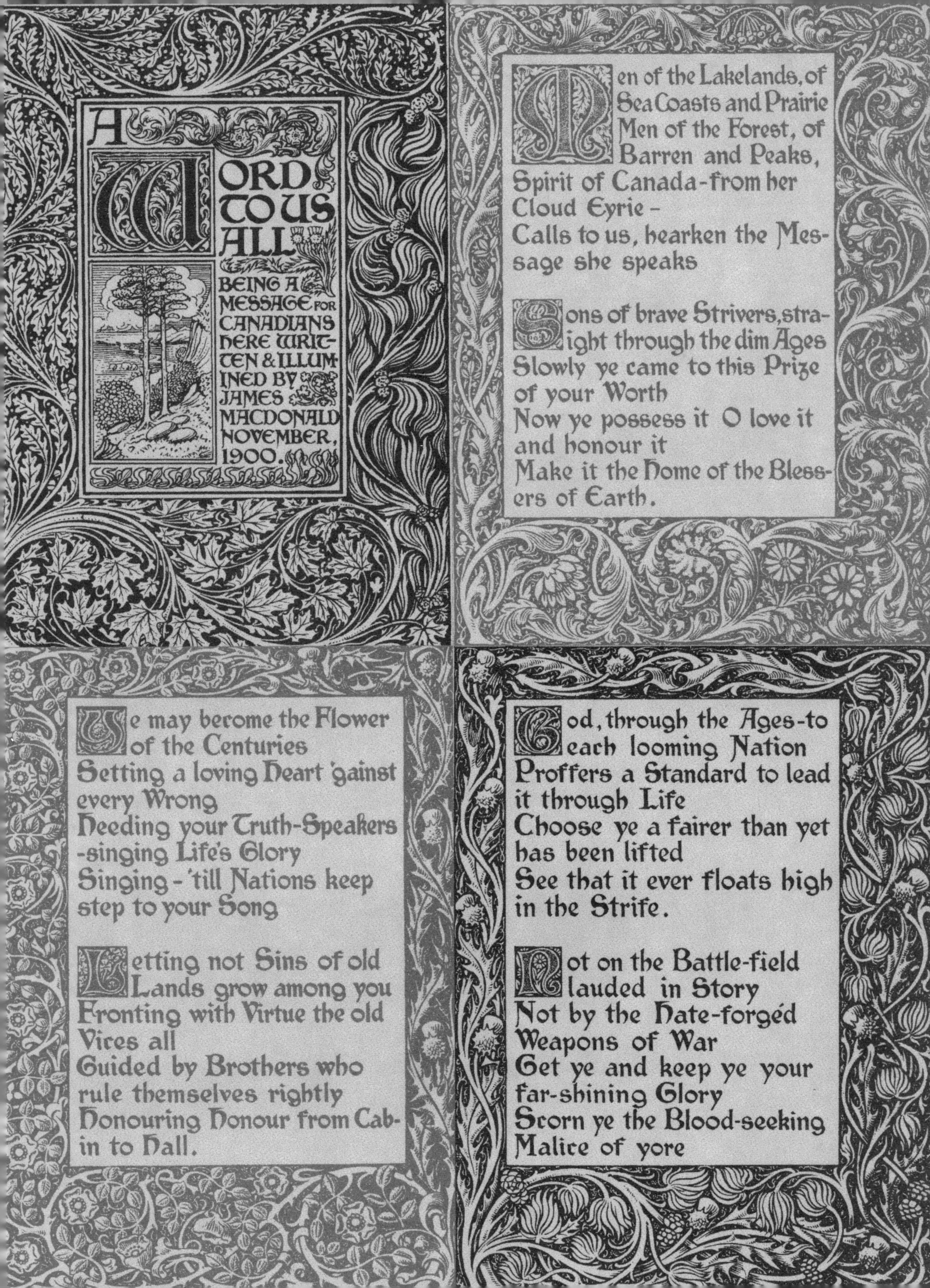

A WORD TO US ALL

BEING A MESSAGE FOR CANADIANS HERE WRITTEN & ILLUMINED BY JAMES MACDONALD NOVEMBER, 1900.

Men of the Lakelands, of
Sea Coasts and Prairie
Men of the Forest, of
Barren and Peaks,
Spirit of Canada-from her
Cloud Eyrie -
Calls to us, hearken the Message she speaks

Sons of brave Strivers, straight through the dim Ages
Slowly ye came to this Prize
of your Worth
Now ye possess it O love it
and honour it
Make it the Home of the Blessers of Earth.

Ye may become the Flower
of the Centuries
Setting a loving Heart 'gainst
every Wrong
Heeding your Truth-Speakers
-singing Life's Glory
Singing - 'till Nations keep
step to your Song

Letting not Sins of old
Lands grow among you
Fronting with Virtue the old
Vices all
Guided by Brothers who
rule themselves rightly
Honouring Honour from Cabin to Hall.

God, through the Ages-to
each looming Nation
Proffers a Standard to lead
it through Life
Choose ye a fairer than yet
has been lifted
See that it ever floats high
in the Strife.

Not on the Battle-field
lauded in Story
Not by the Hate-forgéd
Weapons of War
Get ye and keep ye your
far-shining Glory
Scorn ye the Blood-seeking
Malice of yore

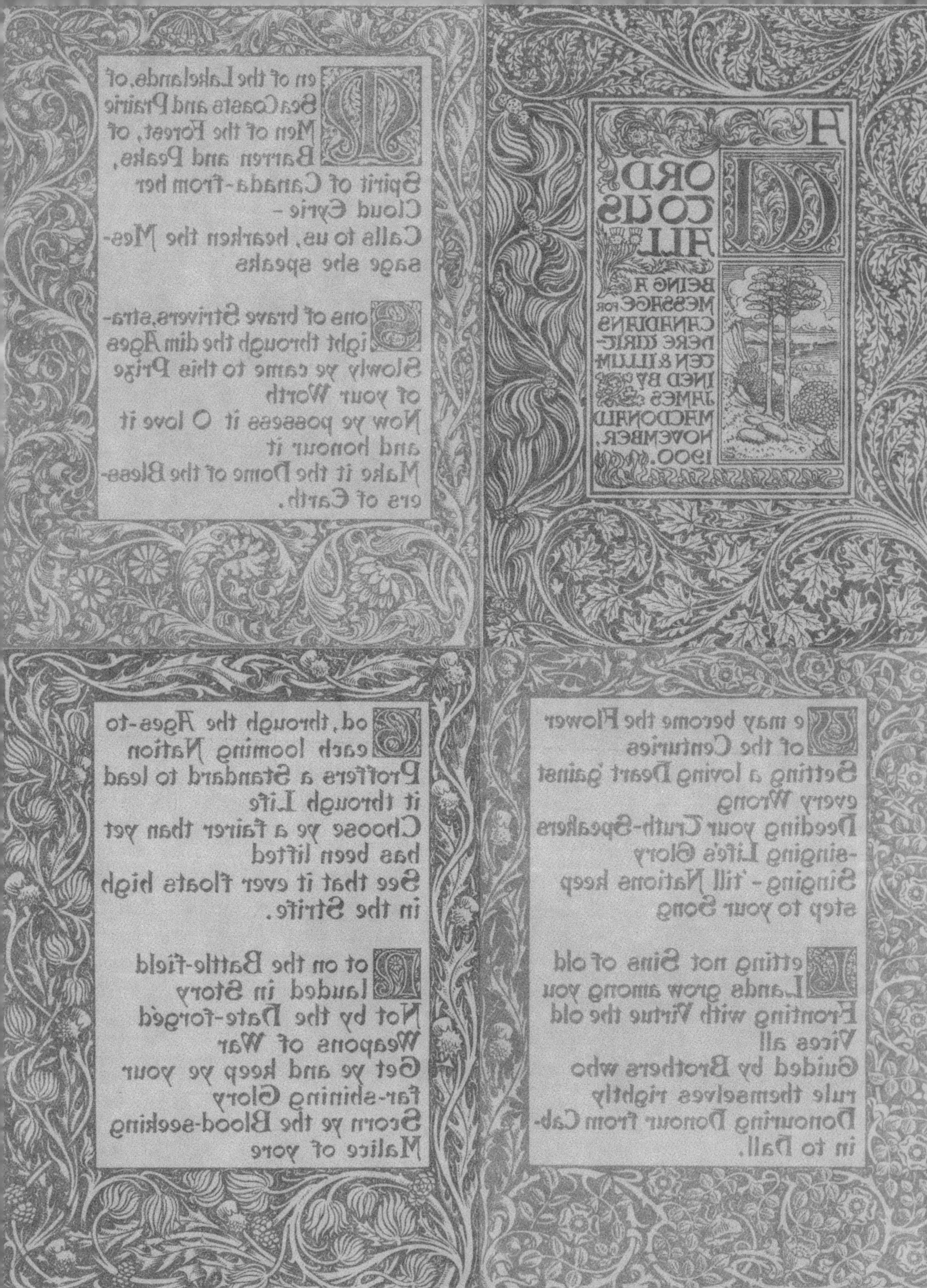
A WORD TO US ALL
BEING A MESSAGE FOR CANADIANS WRITTEN & ILLUMINED BY JAMES MACDONALD NOVEMBER, 1900.
Men of the Lakelands, of Sea Coasts and Prairie
Men of the Forest, of Barren and Peaks,
Spirit of Canada - from her Cloud Eyrie -
Calls to us, hearken the Message she speaks
Sons of brave Strivers, straight through the dim Ages
Slowly ye came to this Prize of your Worth
Now ye possess it O love it and honour it
Make it the Home of the Blessers of Earth.
God, through the Ages - to each looming Nation
Proffers a Standard to lead it through Life
Choose ye a fairer than yet has been lifted
See that it ever floats high in the Strife.
Not on the Battle-field lauded in Story
Not by the Hate-forged Weapons of War
Get ye and keep ye your far-shining Glory
Scorn ye the Blood-seeking Malice of yore
Ye may become the Flower of the Centuries
Setting a loving Heart 'gainst every Wrong
Heeding your Truth-Speakers - singing Life's Glory
Singing - 'till Nations keep step to your Song
Letting not Sins of old Lands grow among you
Fronting with Virtue the old Vices all
Guided by Brothers who rule themselves rightly
Honouring Honour from Cabin to Hall.